AF478081

CENTRAL ISSUES IN CONTEMPORARY ECONOMIC THEORY AND POLICY

General Editor: **Mario Baldassarri**, *Professor of Economics, University of Rome 'La Sapienza', Italy*

Published titles include:

Mario Baldassarri (*editor*)
HOW TO REDUCE UNEMPLOYMENT IN EUROPE

Mario Baldassarri (*editor*)
THE NEW WELFARE
Unemployment and Social Security in Europe

Mario Baldassarri, Michele Bagella and Luigi Paganetto (*editors*)
FINANCIAL MARKETS: IMPERFECT INFORMATION AND RISK MANAGEMENT

Mario Baldassarri and Bruno Chiarini (*editors*)
STUDIES IN LABOUR MARKETS AND INDUSTRIAL RELATIONS

Mario Baldassarri and Pierluigi Ciocca (*editors*)
ROOTS OF THE ITALIAN SCHOOL OF ECONOMICS AND FINANCE: FROM FERRARA (1857)
TO EINAUDI (1944) (*three volumes*)

Mario Baldassarri and Massimo Di Matteo (*editors*)
INTERNATIONAL PROBLEMS OF ECONOMIC INTERDEPENDENCE

Mario Baldassarri, Cesare Imbriani and Dominick Salvatore (*editors*)
THE INTERNATIONAL SYSTEM BETWEEN NEW INTEGRATION AND
NEO-PROTECTIONISM

Mario Baldassarri and Luca Lambertini (*editors*)
ANTITRUST, REGULATION AND COMPETITION

Mario Baldassarri, Alfredo Macchiati and Diego Piacentino (*editors*)
THE PRIVATIZATION OF PUBLIC UTILITIES: THE CASE OF ITALY

Mario Baldassarri, Luigi Paganetto and Edmund S. Phelps (*editors*)
EQUITY, EFFICIENCY AND GROWTH: THE FUTURE OF THE WELFARE STATE

Mario Baldassarri, Luigi Paganetto and Edmund S. Phelps (*editors*)
THE 1990s SLUMP: CAUSES AND CURES

Mario Baldassarri, Luigi Paganetto and Edmund S. Phelps (*editors*)
WORLD SAVING, PROSPERITY AND GROWTH

Mario Baldassarri, Luigi Paganetto and Edmund S. Phelps (*editors*)
INTERNATIONAL DIFFERENCES IN GROWTH RATES: MARKET GLOBALIZATION
AND ECONOMIC AREAS

Mario Baldassarri and Paolo Roberti (*editors*)
FISCAL PROBLEMS IN THE SINGLE-MARKET EUROPE

Mario Baldassarri and Franco Modigliani (*editors*)
THE ITALIAN ECONOMY: WHAT NEXT?

Mario Baldassarri (*editor*)
MAFFEO PANTALEONI: AT THE ORIGIN OF THE ITALIAN SCHOOL OF ECONOMICS AND
FINANCE

Mario Baldassarri, Luigi Paganetto and Edmund S. Phelps (*editors*)
INSTITUTIONS AND ECONOMIC ORGANIZATION IN THE ADVANCED ECONOMIES: THE
GOVERNANCE PERSPECTIVE

Central Issues in Contemporary Economic Theory and Policy
Series Standing Order ISBN 0–333–71464–4
(*outside North America only*)

You can receive future titles in this series as they are published by placing a standing order. Please contact your bookseller or, in case of difficulty, write to us at the address below with your name and address, the title of the series and the ISBN quoted above.

Customer Services Department, Macmillan Distribution Ltd, Houndmills, Basingstoke, Hampshire RG21 6XS, England

The New Welfare

Unemployment and Social Security in Europe

Edited by

Mario Baldassarri
Professor of Economics,
University of Rome 'La Sapienza',
Italy

in association with
Rivista di Politica Economica, SIPI, Rome

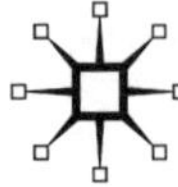

First published 2003 by
PALGRAVE MACMILLAN
Houndmills, Basingstoke, Hampshire RG21 6XS and
175 Fifth Avenue, New York, N. Y. 10010
Companies and representatives throughout the world

PALGRAVE MACMILLAN is the global academic imprint of the Palgrave Macmillan division of St. Martin's Press, LLC and of Palgrave Macmillan Ltd. Macmillan® is a registered trademark in the United States, United Kingdom and other countries. Palgrave is a registered trademark in the European Union and other countries.

ISBN 1–4039–1173–8

This book is printed on paper suitable for recycling and made from fully managed and sustained forest sources.

A catalogue record for this book is available from the British Library.

Library of Congress Cataloging-in-Publication Data
The new welfare : unemployment and social security in Europe / edited by Mario Baldassarri.
        p. cm — (Central issues in contemporary economic theory and policy)
    includes bibliographical references and index.
    ISBN 1–4039–1173–8
    1. Unemployment--Europe. 2. Social security--Europe. I. Baldassarri,
Mario, 1946- II. Series.

HD5764.A6N485 2003
331.12'042'094--dc21

                                                                2002192956

10   9   8   7   6   5   4   3   2   1
12   11   10   09   08   07   06   05   04   03

Printed and bound in Great Britain by
Antony Rowe Ltd, Chippenham and Eastbourne

Contents

---

* From International Conference chaired by Franco Modigliani: *The New Welfare: Unemployment an Social Security*, Rodengo Saiano (Brescia Province), 11-12 September 1999. [JEL Code: J18, J58, J65, J68]

I - HOW TO PROMOTE EMPLOYMENT

A Misguided Monetary Policy at the Basis of the European Unemployment

Franco Modigliani - Marialuisa Ceprini[*]

MIT, Cambridge (MASS.)

1. - Outline of European Problems

Europe is facing four main concerns. Of these, two are very serious. The first, the Financing of Public Pension System, is of a very long-term nature; the other, Unemployment, is of a short term one that we discuss in this paper since the first is considered in a separate cover. The other two concerns, Inflation and Exchange Rates, are in our opinions problems less significant, and we shall consider them implicitly.

2. - Analysis

2.1 *Unemployment: Some Basic Facts*

During the decade of the '60s, the average unemployment for Euro-15 was 2.2% and only two countries reached 5%; in the US, it was 4.7%. By 1997, the European average was 12% and only one country had just below 5%. By 1998-99, it was still 10.5%. In US, it

---

[*] A synthesis fo the analysis was presented by Franco Modigliani at the Hearing on the "Commission's Broad Guidelines of the Economic Policies of the Member States and of the Comunity" of the European Parliament on Tuesday 4 April 2000, Brussels. The authors thank Giorgio Fano, of the Chase Manhattan Bank of NY, for his devoted assistance.

was back to 4.7% and in no other developed country it is even close to 10%. Most would agree that this is an enormous waste and human tragedy. What are the reasons, and what can be done about it?

2.2 *False Explanation of Unemployment*

In an effort to deflect responsibly for this tragedy, the European establishment has come up with a large inventory of causes, supposedly beyond their control. They include: *a)* The competition of low wage countries; *b)* The high rate of technological progress; *c)* The lack of needed skills; *d)* The large share of long term unemployment; *e)* The crushing burden of taxes; *f)* The crisis of the capitalistic system; *g)* The European wages grew faster than in the US.

In the *Manifesto*[1] we have shown that these explanations are worthless: *a)*, *b)*, *c)*, and *f)*, because they are not specific to Europe; *d)* because it confuses cause and effect; *e)* because of the confusion between taxes and compulsory saving for retirement; *g)* because the faster growth of European wages, was a reflection of the faster productivity growth.

We equally reject the more sophisticated view expressed in European Parliament 1999 review that the high unemployment is the result of «adverse shocks» to presumed labor «aggregate supply and demand» curves, interacting with rigidities in the labor and product markets.

2.3 *Valid Reasons for Unemployment*

European unemployment first rose dramatically during the decade from 1973 to 1983, from 2.6% to 9.1%. But this rise can be readily accounted for by the oil crisis and the Central Banks' obligation to put an end to the wage-price spiral sparkled by a vain endeavor to recoup the lost purchasing power. In fact, up to 1983 unemployment in the US was as high or even higher than in Europe (Graph 4). But since that time the US unemployment has fallen fairly steadily, while the Eurpean one has risen substantially further.

---

[1] See «Manifesto», Banca Nazionale del Lavoro, *Quarterly Review*, September 1998.

Four motivations support our thesis is that, in view of a *(i)* the extreme rigidity of Europoean wages, one must rely on the Keynesian paradigm according to which *(ii)* unemployment is primarily due to lack of aggregate demand. This is mainly the outcome of erroneous macroeconomic policies. All member countries have shared these policies because, beginning in the '80s they have been moving to a regime of fixed exchanges. This resulted in a common monetary (interest rate) policy and hence a common Central Bank, de facto the Bundesbank. *(iii)* This bank, and lately, its successor, the ECB, have pursued policies inspired by an obsessive fear of inflation, kindled by the traumatic experience of the '20s and the spiral of the oil crisis, coupled with a benign neglect policy for unemployment. *(iv)* These attitudes in turn have resulted in systematically over tight monetary policy decisions, apparently based on an objectionable use of the so-called NAIRU approach. The contractive effects of these policies have been reinforced by common very tight fiscal policies, imposed by treaties like Maastricht. These policies had some merit, but they were inconsistent with the accompanying monetary policy. The effect of these polices has been further aggravated by labor market «rigidities» and bad government regulations.

In what follows, we intend to develop each of these four points providing supporting evidence. Anyone that is already in agreement with the thesis advanced can skip that section.

2.3.1 Wages Are Rigid Downward

As we have learned from Keynes, in a system where wages do not decline promptly in response to unemployment so as to eliminate it, employment is determined not by labor force, but by aggregate demand (as long as it does not exceed capacity). Now, the evidence shows that in every one of the member states, wages are very rigid downward. The evidence is provided by Table 1, which shows the change in wages per employee for 39 years for the Euro-15 plus the US. 624 observations. There was not a single instance of wage declines, though unemployment was mostly rising in the period, reaching distressingly high rates. Moreover, increase in wage per employee understates the relevant measure, wage per hour.

WAGE DYNAMICS PER EMPLOYEE 1960 - 1999

	B	DK	D	EL	E	F	IRL	I	L	NL	A	P	FIN	S	UK	EU-11	EU-15	US	JP
1961	3.3	12.9	10.2	4.6	12.9	10.6	8.3	8.2	2.9	7.4	10.6	5.8	7.9	8.1	6.5	9.6	8.7	3.2	13.2
1962	7.4	11.1	9.1	6.6	15.2	11.6	8.5	13.4	4.8	6.8	9.3	4.8	9.7	9.9	4.5	10.1	9.0	4.1	14.1
1963	8.1	4.6	6.1	7.7	21.1	11.4	5.2	19.7	8.0	9.3	7.9	8.1	10.8	9.4	4.9	11.6	9.6	4.0	13.2
1964	9.9	10.7	8.2	13.3	13.7	9.2	13.7	11.6	13.3	16.5	9.3	8.3	15.0	9.9	6.9	10.4	4.6	4.0	13.1
1965	9.6	13.8	9.5	12.2	15.6	6.5	5.3	8.2	4.2	11.7	9.1	11.0	9.6	8.6	6.7	9.2	8.7	3.7	11.9
1966	8.8	10.2	7.6	12.6	18.1	6.0	8.5	8.0	5.0	11.1	9.3	9.9	8.1	8.9	6.4	8.6	8.1	5.0	11.2
1967	7.5	10.9	3.3	9.5	14.7	7.0	8.0	8.3	2.8	9.3	9.5	13.7	9.7	9.2	6.2	7.1	7.1	4.3	12.1
1968	6.4	10.0	6.7	9.8	8.8	11.9	10.6	7.6	5.9	8.6	7.3	3.6	10.9	6.6	7.7	8.6	8.3	7.4	13.7
1969	8.5	11.0	16.0	8.8	9.4	10.4	16.8	15.3	15.1	12.6	8.0	22.6	9.4	7.9	12.9	13.7	12.8	7.6	16.7
1970	9.3	11.0	16.0	8.8	9.4	10.4	16.8	15.3	15.1	12.6	8.0	22.6	9.4	7.9	12.9	13.7	12.8	7.6	16.7
1961-70	7.9	10.6	8.6	9.5	14.1	9.6	9.9	10.8	6.8	10.7	8.9	9.8	9.9	8.5	7.0	9.9	8.6	5.1	13.5
1971	12.2	11.6	11.4	8.0	13.6	11.3	14.8	13.4	7.8	13.9	12.6	11.5	15.2	9.0	11.3	12.2	11.9	7.4	14.6
1972	14.2	8.0	9.6	12.6	17.7	10.1	15.8	10.6	9.7	12.9	11.0	15.8	14.6	8.5	13.0	11.3	11.5	7.3	14.2
1973	13.5	13.1	11.9	17.2	18.3	12.4	18.8	17.7	11.4	15.6	13.2	17.7	18.1	6.9	13.1	14.3	13.4	6.0	21.0
1974	18.0	18.4	11.4	19.3	21.3	17.8	18.0	22.6	22.9	15.8	13.9	35.1	24.0	12.9	18.7	17.3	17.5	8.2	25.7
1975	16.5	13.9	7.0	20.3	22.5	18.7	28.9	20.8	12.4	13.6	12.7	34.6	28.3	16.9	31.2	16.0	19.0	9.1	14.2
1976	15.8	11.7	7.7	23.2	23.4	14.8	19.6	20.9	11.1	11.0	9.2	24.6	16.5	17.9	14.8	14.8	14.9	8.2	11.1
1977	9.1	9.7	6.6	22.0	26.8	12.2	14.9	20.8	9.9	8.5	8.8	24.2	9.0	12.2	10.6	13.5	12.9	7.7	10.2
1978	7.2	9.2	5.5	23.1	24.8	12.4	15.5	16.5	5.9	7.0	14.4	18.8	6.1	10.9	13.3	12.0	12.2	7.7	7.5
1979	5.8	9.4	5.8	22.1	19.0	12.8	18.9	19.9	6.7	5.6	5.8	19.9	11.5	8.6	15.2	11.9	12.4	8.2	6
1980	10.6	10.0	6.8	15.7	17.3	15.0	21.1	21.4	9.2	5.4	6.6	25.7	13.1	10.9	19.8	13.2	14.3	10.1	6.5
1971-80	12.3	11.5	8.4	18.4	20.5	13.8	18.6	18.5	10.7	10.9	10.8	22.8	15.6	11.5	16.1	13.7	14.0	8.0	13.1

cont.

WAGE DYNAMICS PER EMPLOYEE 1960 - 1999

	B	DK	D	EL	E	F	IRL	I	L	NL	A	P	FIN	S	UK	EU-11	EU-15	US	JP
1981	6.4	9.2	4.8	21.3	15.3	14.1	18.1	22.6	8.3	3.4	8.1	21.0	14.1	9.2	14.1	12.0	12.5	9.5	6.4
1982	6.9	11.9	4.2	27.5	13.7	13.8	14.2	16.2	6.9	5.9	6.2	21.5	9.5	6.2	8.4	10.5	10.3	7.6	3.8
1983	5.8	8.2	3.6	21.6	13.8	9.9	12.8	16.0	6.9	3.1	4.7	21.8	10	7.9	58.7	9.1	9.2	5.4	2.2
1984	7.1	5.5	3.4	20.8	10.0	8.1	10.7	11.8	7.1	0.3	5.1	21.2	10.5	8.2	5.9	7.4	7.3	5.0	3.9
1985	5.0	4.7	2.9	21.0	9.6	6.4	9.2	10.1	4.3	1.3	5.3	22.5	10.3	7.5	7.6	6.5	6.8	4.6	2.9
1986	3.8	4.4	3.6	12.0	9.1	4.1	5.1	7.5	5.7	2.1	5.5	21.6	7.4	8.7	8.0	5.4	6.1	4.1	3.7
1987	2.2	7.9	3.2	11.3	6.8	3.6	5.1	8.2	4.1	1.4	4.0	14.4	7.7	7.0	7.4	4.7	5.4	4.2	3.3
1988	2.5	5.0	3.0	20.1	7.4	4.2	7.0	8.7	3.4	0.9	3.1	13.1	9.1	7.5	8.3	5.0	5.8	4.8	1.8
1989	3.4	4.2	2.9	23.2	6.9	4.3	6.5	8.7	7.7	0.7	4.5	15.2	10.4	11.3	9.3	5.1	6.2	3.2	4.8
1990	7.0	4.1	4.7	17.9	9.5	5.0	4.2	10.7	5.5	3.2	5.5	19.2	9.4	11.3	9.0	6.8	7.5	5.7	5.5
1981-90	5.0	6.5	3.6	19.7	10.2	7.4	9.3	12.1	6.0	2.2	5.2	19.2	9.9	8.5	13.7	7.3	7.7	5.4	3.8
1991	7.5	3.9	5.9	15.4	9.5	4.3	4.6	8.7	6.4	4.5	6.3	18.1	6.6	6.8	9.0	6.6	7.2	4.2	4.6
1992	5.8	4.2	10.6	11.8	10.4	4.2	7.0	5.8	5.3	4.7	5.8	16.3	2.2	3.9	5.6	7.6	7.2	5.2	1.3
1993	4.2	2.3	4.3	9.8	6.8	2.8	6.8	3.7	5.0	3.3	4.5	6.0	0.9	4.4	4.2	4.1	4.1	2.8	0.9
1994	4.7	3.5	3.6	10.9	2.8	2.2	2.4	2.9	4.1	2.8	3.4	5.6	3.1	4.8	3.4	3.1	3.3	2.3	1.8
1995	2.5	3.3	3.9	12.9	3.0	2.5	1.7	4.6	2.2	1.9	2.9	7.2	4.2	2.9	2.6	3.5	3.4	2.1	1.2
1996	1.5	2.9	2.5	11.8	3.8	2.9	3.2	6.1	1.8	1.8	1.7	6.3	2.9	6.5	3.5	3.3	3.5	2.7	0.9
1997	2.4	3.8	1.9	11.0	2.3	2.1	6.4	4.7	3.8	2.1	0.7	5.4	2.1	4.0	4.6	2.5	3.0	3.8	1.5
1998	2.5	4.3	1.5	6.3	1.8	2.0	6.8	−1.3	1.4	3.1	2.3	4.7	5.0	5.1	5.3	1.5	2.3	4.4	−4.6
1999	2.2	4.2	2.7	4.3	1.9	1.9	7.0	2.4	1.6	3.6	2.6	4.9	2.6	3.2	4.5	2.5	2.9	3.8	1.0

2.3.2 Unemployment is Due to Lack of Jobs

It must therefore be the case that Keynesian analysis applies: growing unemployment must be the result of an increasing shortage of aggregate demand and available jobs. The following three graphs, 1, 2, and 3 unequivocally support this proposition.

These graphs show for each of three countries, France Germany and UK, the path of the unemployment rate (left scale) since the sixties and the path of an estimate of the total jobs available (aggregate demand) the sum of employment and vacancies, all expressed as a percentage of the labor force (right scale, scale inverted). The two curves very nearly overlap. Thus, in the case of France, as job availability declines from 99% of the labor force in the '60s down to 88%, unemployment rises from 1% to 12%, as the unemployed cannot find jobs that are not there, the search process lengthens and so does the average duration of unemployment and the pool of unemployed.

Graphs 2 and 3 show a similar picture for Germany and UK. Everywhere unemployment has raised because of a large shrinkage in the number of positions needed to satisfy the existing de-

GRAPH. 1

GRAPH. 2

GERMANY: UNEMPLOYMENT AND JOBS AVAILABILITY
1963-1998

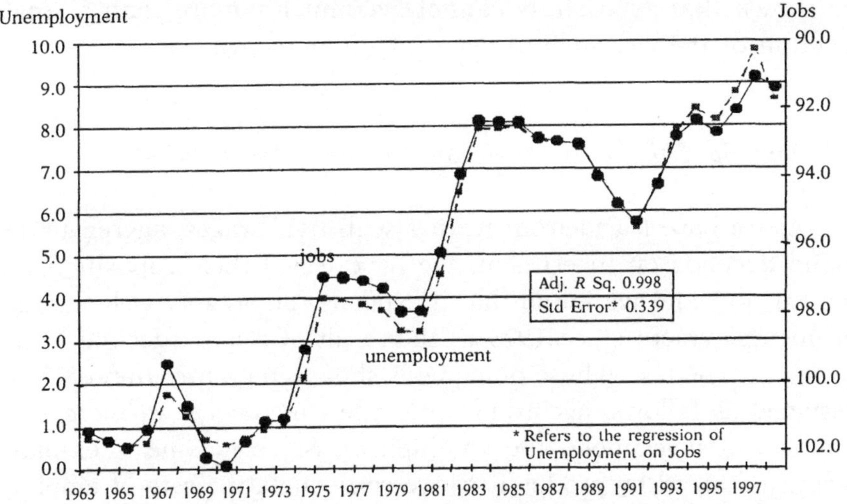

GRAPH. 3

UK: UNEMPLOYMENT AND JOBS AVAILABILITY
1963-1998

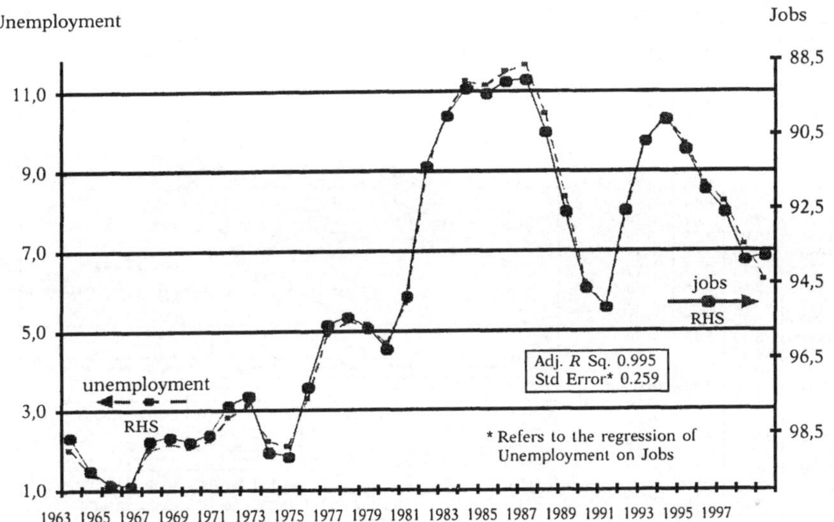

mand. (Part of the increase might result from «outward shifts» of the Beveridge curve which increase (u) for any given level of vacancies, reflecting e.g. rising unemployment benefits. But it can be shown that such shifts cannot account for more than a small fraction of the rise in European unemployment).

2.4 *Why Have the Jobs (Aggregate Demand) Declined?*

As we have learnt from Keynes with rigid wages, aggregate demand depends on investment. We have tested this proposition for the Euro-15 and we found that it explains remarkably well the rise in unemployment since 1973 as the result of a large decline in investment. The test, whose outcome is shown in graphs 4 and 5, was designed as follows: according to Keynes, income is an increasing function of investment, the «multiplier». Since income is employment multiplied by productivity, we can equate the rate of employment (net of minimum frictional unemployment) with the ratio of

GRAPH. 4

TEST OF RELATION BETWEEN u AND INVESTMENT SHORTFALL

the linear approximation: $U = 2.16 + 0.97\ SH$

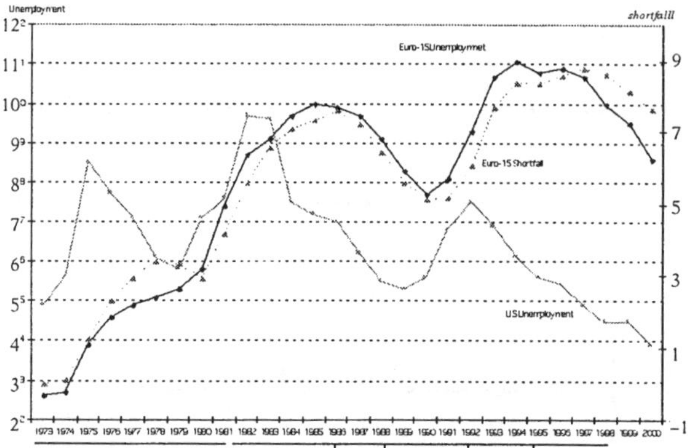

Year	Ut	SH	Lead
	(1)	(4)	(5)
1973	2.60	0.00	0.11
1974	2.70	0.11	1.15
1975	3.90	1.26	1.04
1976	4.60	2.30	0.60
1977	4.90	2.91	0.52
1978	5.10	3.42	-0.10
1979	5.30	3.32	-0.39
1980	5.80	2.93	1.26
1981	7.40	4.19	1.41
1982	8.70	5.60	0.98
1983	9.10	6.58	0.51
1984	9.70	7.09	0.24
1985	10.00	7.33	0.29
1986	9.90	7.62	-0.38
1987	9.70	7.23	-0.77
1988	9.10	6.46	-0.86
1989	8.30	5.60	-0.43
1990	7.70	5.17	0.01
1991	8.10	5.18	0.89
1992	9.30	6.07	1.62
1993	10.70	7.69	0.70
1994	11.10	8.40	-0.02
1995	10.80	8.38	0.50
1996	10.90	8.88	-0.07
1997	10.70	8.81	-0.48
1998	10.00	8.33	-0.72
1999	9.20	7.61	-0.70
2000	8.60	6.91	-0.66
2001	8.00	6.25	

Regression statistics		df	SS	MS	F
Multiple R	0,985	Regression 1	174.7531	174.75	806.2358
R Square	0,970	Residual 25	5.418795	0,2168	
Adjusted R Square	0,969	Total 26	180.1719		
Standard Error	0,466				
Observations	27		coeff.	St.error	t.Stat	P-value

	coeff.	St.error	t.Stat	P-value
Intercept	2.6132	0.208983	12.504	2.96E-12
SH	0.9749	0.034334	28.394	1.52E-20

current income to full capacity income. This means that the employment rate, (e), should be an increasing function of the ratio of investment to full capacity income, say (I/Y^*). Then, unemployment $(u = 1 - e)$ should be a declining function of the investment ratio. To make the result more understandable and striking we correlate (u) not with (I/Y^*) but instead with what we call the investment shortfall, (SH). It is defined as the extent by which (I/Y^*) in any year falls short of a «full employment investment ratio». To determine this ratio we took the historic observation of 1973, the last year of presumed full employment (24.4). It is also similar to that prevailing in earlier years of full employment. In computing the investment ratio, the full employment income (Y_t^*) was estimated using a version of Okun's law. The shortfall of course increases when the ratio falls and therefore should be correlated positively with (u). The results are striking as can be seen from graph 4 and the attached table.

The correlation between (u) and the shortfall measured by the adjusted R^2 is 0.97 an exceptionally good fit, by any standard. The remarkable quality of the fit can be appreciated by looking at graph 4, which compares the actual value of (u) with value computed from the regression equation.

A close inspection of the graph suggests that (u) might be affected not only by current investment but also by that of the next year. This hypothesis is supported by the observation that the production of capital goods typically involves a lengthy production process, which means that some of the orders, currently placed and resulting in current investment, may not be reported as investment expenditure until the next period when the finished product is delivered. This hypothesis, which is actually not novel, is strongly supported by the data: when (I/Y^*) lead one period is added, it is highly significant (a t-ratio of 4.5) and adjusted R^2 increases further to 0.983.

However, the size of the correlation could be biased upward because the Okun estimate of (Y^*) is $Y[1 - 2(u_{t-1} - u^*)]$ $(u^*$ the minimum frictional unemployment) and this could produce a spurious correlation with the right hand side variable. This problem can be avoided by non-linear estimation methods discussed in the appendix, the result is shown in graph 5: the fit is now incredibly close.

Franco Modigliani - Marialuisa Ceprini

GRAPH 5

TEST OF RELATION BETWEEN u AND INVESTMENT SHORTFALL

the linear approximation: $u = 2.18 + 1.03\ SH + 0.48\ Lead$

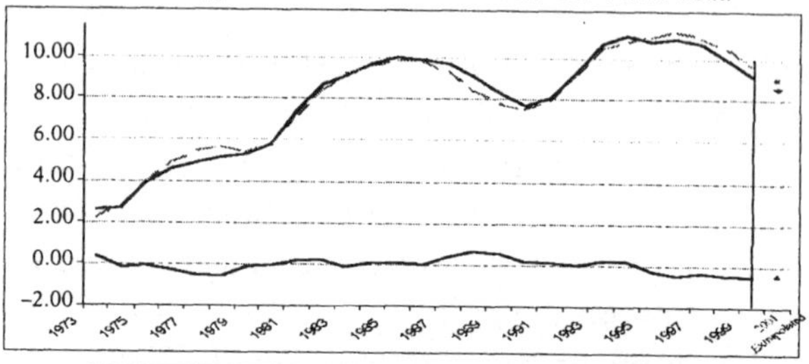

Year	Ut (1)	SH (4)	Lead (5)
1973	2.60	0.00	0.11
1974	2.70	0.11	1.15
1975	3.90	1.26	1.04
1976	4.60	2.30	0.60
1977	4.90	2.91	0.52
1978	5.10	3.42	-0.10
1979	5.30	3.32	-0.39
1980	5.80	2.93	1.26
1981	7.40	4.19	1.41
1982	8.70	5.60	0.98
1983	9.10	6.58	0.51
1984	9.70	7.09	0.24
1985	10.00	7.33	0.29
1986	9.90	7.62	-0.38
1987	9.70	7.23	-0.77
1988	9.10	6.46	-0.86
1989	8.30	5.60	-0.43
1990	7.70	5.17	0.01
1991	8.10	5.18	0.89
1992	9.30	6.07	1.62
1993	10.70	7.69	0.70
1994	11.10	8.40	-0.02
1995	10.80	8.38	0.50
1996	10.90	8.88	-0.07
1997	10.70	8.81	-0.48
1998	10.00	8.33	-0.72
1999	9.20	7.61	-0.70
2000	8.60	6.91	-0.66
2001	8.00	6.25	

Regression Statistics	
Multiple R	0.992
R Square	0.984
Adjusted R Square	0.983
Standard Error	0.347
Observations	27

	df	SS	MS	F
Regression	2	177.28	88.64	735.58
Residual	24	2.89	0,12	
Total	26	180.17		

	coeff.	St.error	t.Stat	P-value
Intercept	2.18	0.18	11.92	0.00
SH	1.03	0.03	36.26	0.00
Lead	0.48	0.11	4.58	0.00

It is worth noting that if we extrapolate our equation to the year 2000, using the *European Economy*[2] forecast of investment in 2000 and 2001, the results predict an unemployment level of 9%; which is very close to that predicted officially, of 8.6%; but our prediction is conditional on the continuing decline in the shortfall forecasted in the Outlook (graph 6).

2.5 *Why Has the Shortfall of Investment Risen so Enormously Until the Mid 90's and Fallen so Little Since?*

This is of course the crucial question we must endeavor to answer. We know from elementary economics that investments are affected by monetary policy (interest rates and credit availability). Hence, the Central Bank through this channel can control investment and thereby aggregate demand. (Graph 6). If the Central Bank chooses to claim that it has no control over aggregate demand and output (something that Central Banks are known to indulge in, when it suits them), then how can it argue that it can

---

[2] See *European Economy*, table XXIV April 1999.

EURO 15: UNEMPLOYMENT VS FINAL ESTIMATES

Year	U_t (1)	Predicted U_t (2)
1973	2.60	2.05
1974	2.70	2.72
1975	3.90	3.95
1976	4.60	4.87
1977	4.90	5.48
1978	5.10	5.72
1979	5.30	5.47
1980	5.80	5.87
1981	7.40	7.26
1982	8.70	8.49
1983	9.10	9.24
1984	9.70	9.62
1985	10.00	9.87
1986	9.90	9.85
1987	9.70	9.30
1988	9.10	8.49
1989	8.30	7.83
1990	7.70	7.60
1991	8.10	8.02
1992	9.30	9.25
1993	10.70	10.41
1994	11.10	10.76
1995	10.80	10.97
1996	10.90	11.20
1997	10.70	10.95
1998	10.00	10.39
1999	9.20	9.70
2000	8.60	9.03
2001	8.00	0.00

correlation 0,992
R square 0,984
Adjusted R Sq 0,870

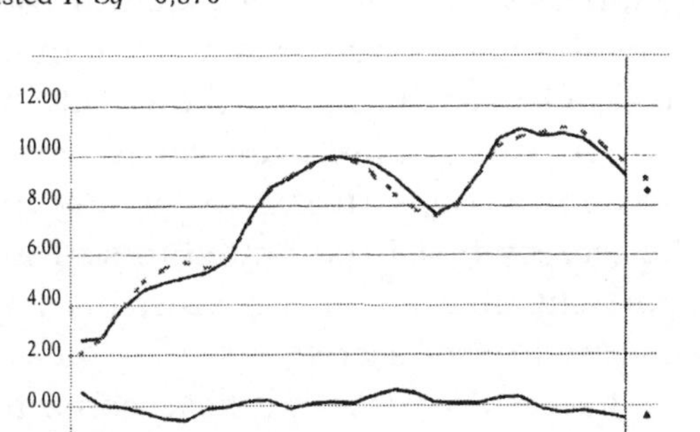

carry out its assignment of controlling inflation? Indeed, there is no economics fundamental that can lead anybody to hold the view that money can directly affect inflation up or down except trough raising or curbing aggregate demand and thus the demand for labor, wages and prices.

(One must acknowledge that, if the unwarranted view that money supply can affect «inflation» without affecting output were widely held, it could conceivably be self-validating. However, we are disinclined to believe that the public is swayed by counterfactual theories, although it maybe that some portion of European leadership has been brain washed to believe this. At any rate, it does not seem to be the prevailing case, at least in the US).

Once it is agreed that the Central Bank can control aggregate demand and unemployment through monetary policy we must conclude, however surprising and uncomfortable, that the behavior of unemployment we have observed, largely reflects the level intended by the policy of the Central Bank.

To understand the implications of this perhaps «inflammatory» statement, one must recall that since the mid '80s, European countries had *de facto* one Central Bank, being the Bundesbank. Thus to understand the sharp rise in unemployment one must understand what motivated the Bundesbank and now the ECB.

The most reliable answer to this question would come from the Central Bank (if it were willing to be explicit). Unfortunately, the secrecy that is permitted to surround its decisions, makes this short cut unavailable - at least until you might decide to abolish the privilege of secrecy.

Forced to guess, we have come to favor the guiding hypothesis stated earlier, that the Bank's behavior has been driven by an obsessive fear of inflation and «benign neglect» for unemployment (probably encouraged by the very generous treatment of the unemployed in Germany). Suppose that this mental framework, is combined with *i)* the Bank's mission of fighting inflation, disregarding totally what this policy might produce in terms of unemployment; and *ii)* with reliance on the old «theory of the Phillips curve» according to which a rise in unemployment could be counted up to reduce inflation. Then one might be able to understand some puzzling episodes of the '80s and '90s: for instance why by 1984, with German inflation down to 2% and unemployment at 7% the «real» long rate was allowed to rise over 5.5%, far higher than it had ever been during the prosperous '60s. Or turning to more recent times, how can one justify the monetary policy of the period 1994-97 when with inflation down 2.3% and unemployment already at 8% (in 1993) the real long-term rate remained consistently above 4%, with a peak (in 1995) of nearly 6.5%, raising unemployment from 8.4% to 10%? If this is the justification for the policy of high unemployment, the Central Bank should be, promptly censured. For that theory, so appealing during the '70s and once widely accepted, has long been discarded, thanks also to the contributions of Milton Friedman. Furthermore, it is solidly refused by the European evidence as can be seen from the two panels in Graphs 7 and 8.

UNEMPLOYMENT - INFLATION

country	gap	inflation	unemp
B	1.90	2.0	9.2
DK	0.05	2.2	5.5
D	1.50	1.4	10.0
EL	1.80	7.2	9.6
E	2.10	3.0	20.8
F	2.30	1.4	12.4
IRL	0.10	2.8	10.1
I	2.00	2.6	12.1
NL	0.15	1.8	5.2
A	1.10	1.5	4.4
P	1.20	3.6	6.8
FIN	0.10	1.7	15.3
S	1.50	2.4	9.6
UK	0.10	2.5	8.2
NOR	-1.40	2.5	4.0
CH	4.90	0.4	5.5
USA	-0.80	2.2	4.9

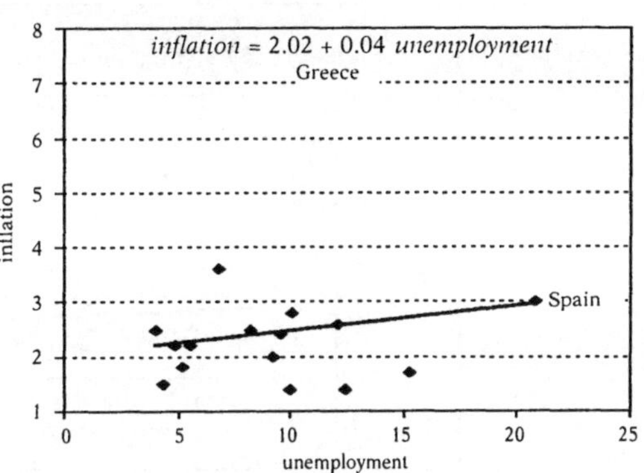

Graph 7 shows the relation between unemployment and the rate inflation for the Euro-15 countries (less Luxembourg, plus Norway, Switzerland, and the US) in a recent year, 1997. Clearly, there is no evidence that countries with lower unemployment suffer more inflation. (The regression' slope, is actually negative but not statistically significant). The OECD has developed an alternative measure of economic slack supposedly more accurate than unemployment. In the Graph 8, we have replaced unemployment with this measure called «GAP» $(Y - Y^*)$; we obtain the same result.

Could this be a «freak» accident for the year 1997? To allay this fear we have repeated the experiment using for each country the mean unemployment and the mean inflation for the years 1991-1999; the results are fundamentally unchanged.

We are therefore reluctant to believe that policy was based on a naïve «Phillips Curve» paradigm, though that view probably is widely held. We are instead inclined to the view that both banks have been relying on a paradigm that has tended to replace the traditional Phillips Curve, namely the so called «vertical Phillip curve» according to which the rate of unemployment determines not inflation but the acceleration of inflation. It implies the existence, at any point of time, of a critical level of (u), say (u^*), usually referred as NAIRU (Non-Accelerating Inflation Rate of Unemployment), such

GAP (ADJUSTED UNEMPLOYMENT) - INFLATION

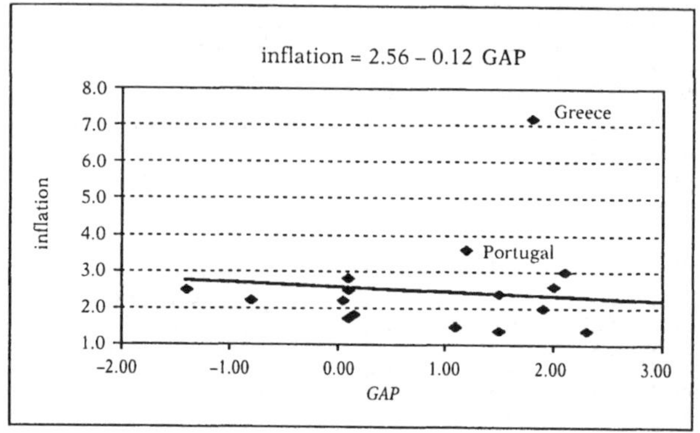

that a level of $(u < u^*)$ inflation will tend to accelerate (i.e. to grow larger and larger), at a rate which grows with the difference between (u) and (u^*); while if $(u > u^*)$ inflation will decelerate. Optimal policy would then call for aiming at unemployment smaller or equal than (u^*), to an extent depending on the target rate of deceleration.

There is nothing conceptually wrong with this paradigm. In addition, apparently there is no lack of evidence to support, the acceleration hypothesis[3]. In fact looking at European statistics during the last three decades, one can readily verify that in the '70s, with unemployment relatively low (4% average for Euro-15) inflation accelerated in a stunning fashion: from 6.6% (1970) to 12.7% (1980). Conversely, during the '80s, when unemployment grew to high levels (averaging 9.1% for Euro-15), inflation decelerated from 12.7% to 5.6% (1990).

2.6 *Pitfall Usage of the NAIRU*

Unfortunately, reliance on the NAIRU as an operational approach method runs into great problems and involves serious risks,

---

[3] See MODIGLIANI and LUCAS: «Targets for Monetary Policy». *Working Paper for Economic Activity*, 1975, pp. 141-68.

because of the enormous difficulties in estimating and tracking (u^*) trough time. These difficulties can be illustrated with reference to graph 9, which shows for each country the acceleration in the course of the decade of the '70s, '80s and of the '90s respectively.

Against the average rate of unemployment in each decade, the association is clearly negative as confirmed by regression analysis. The regression equation is:

$$\text{Acceleration} = 3.7 - 0.76u$$

The negative slope coefficient is statistically quite significant (*t*-ratio of 3.5). The equation implies a NAIRU of just below 5%

GRAF. 9

UNEMPLOYMENT AND ACCELERATION OF INFLATION

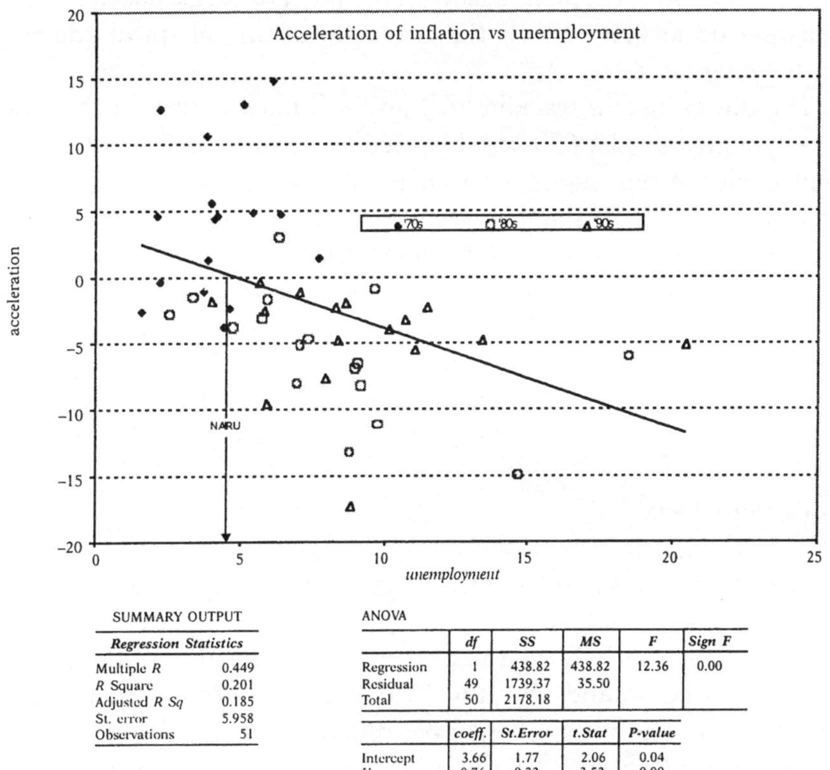

SUMMARY OUTPUT

Regression Statistics	
Multiple *R*	0.449
R Square	0.201
Adjusted *R Sq*	0.185
St. error	5.958
Observations	51

ANOVA

	df	SS	MS	F	Sign F
Regression	1	438.82	438.82	12.36	0.00
Residual	49	1739.37	35.50		
Total	50	2178.18			

	coeff.	St.Error	t.Stat	P-value
Intercept	3.66	1.77	2.06	0.04
U	-0.76	0.22	-3.52	0.00

(given by the intersection of the regression line with the horizontal line at zero. However, upon closer analysis these conclusion inferences are quite misleading. To make this point in the graph, we have evidenced the observations of each decade by a different symbol. The '70s are marked by a dark diamond. This is a period of low unemployment and high acceleration: but the high acceleration appears to reflect simply the oil crisis and the resulting inflation spiral and had little or nothing to do with excessive level of demand. There is in fact no association between the variables in this period: notice in particular that there were five countries with negative acceleration and they all had below average unemployment. Similarly looking at the most recent decade, the 90's (marked by triangles), one finds no association between acceleration and unemployment. Furthermore, acceleration is negative at all levels of (u). The '80s (circles) are the only period where there seems to be some negative association; but the large deceleration of this period largely reflects the cessation of the oil spiral and return to normality.

The difficulties in tracking (u^*) are well known even in the US, where trough the '80s (u^*) was believed to be around 5% but more recent evidence has suggested that it may be, at least temporarily closer to 4%. This has not posed a serious problem for the U.S., because the Fed has been willing to test the estimated (u^*) by pushing (u) below the supposed (u^*), even at some risk of incipient acceleration. However, clearly, the reliance on NAIRU could be, and probably has been, catastrophic in the hands of a Central Bank with the framework and mission of the Bundesbank or ECB.

3. - Conclusions

3.1. *Why Does the Unemployment Target Remain So High?*

Even with the help of the above analysis in the end, we are not able to understand why the ECB is still targeting unemployment rates of the order of 9%. We remain convinced that a rate well below that (perhaps as low as 5%), would not result in an escalation of inflation, especially if the expansion were be programmed in collaboration with the unions and the employers as part of an effort to boost investment and reduce the scourge of unemployment. Thus based on the evidence available to us, we are reluctantly led to the conclusion that the high unemployment in the European countries since the mid '80s, is largely the result of a misguided overcautious monetary policy. Perhaps one can get an idea of the magnitude of the excess unemployment from the gap between the European and the US unemployment exhibited in Graph 4. In addition, that gap probably underestimates the loss because the bulge in US unemployment in the early 90's was largely a mistake, because the European NAIRU should be lower than the American one.

3.2 *More Information from ECB*

Could we be wrong? Of course, and we can only hope that somebody can convince the reader and us of our reasoning. But we submit that the only satisfactory way of settling this issue, not so much retrospectively but especially for the future, is for the Central Bank to provide more information about the investment and employment targets (or forecasts) explicit or implicit in their policies and inflation targets; and to relate the two. Accordingly, we strongly recommend that while acknowledging that ECB's only explicit responsibility is to maintain price stability, should, with the support of the Parliament, invite (or require) to testify on the subject (at regular intervals and or special occasions, on the ground that this information is vital to the commission's functions and heavily relevant for other authorities concerned with overall economic policies.

3.3 *Supply Side Effects on Unemployment*

We have indicated at the outset that the effect of insufficient demand have been compounded by supply problems, particularly rigidities in the labor market and poor work incentive designs. We regretfully have no time here to deal with these issues whose importance we fully acknowledge. However, they have been treated extensively in the *Manifesto* and we stand fully behind the analysis and remedies suggested in that publication. In particular we want to stress the notion of complementarities between demand and supply policy; we continue to believe that pure supply policies without demand policies may succeed in reducing unemployment in some regions at the expense of others, but will not have significant effects on overall unemployment, except possibly by raising investment, (an effect which the Central Bank can easily thwart, if it targets unemployment).

3.4 *The Reform of the Financing of Public Pension Systems*

On this vital issue, we have submitted a separate paper in which we discuss our proposal «How to save the pension reforming the financing method of European Public Pension Systems. The case of Italy». The proposed solution does not mean to reduce the pension, which remains the same, but rationally to finance it by investment in capitals. Our proposal is a reform of the pensions financing and not the reform of the pension.

Employment Performance and Employment Policies in the EU

Beniamino Moro
University of Cagliari

1. - Foreword

This paper further investigates on two topics of the *Manifesto*[1] which last year were sacrificed because of the nature and the length of the document. They are: *a)* the recent employment performances of the European Union Member States, and *b)* the European strategy to improve employment after the Amsterdam Council held in June 1997, focusing on the impact that *the Manifesto* has exerted on the Council Resolutions and on the other European and Member States official documents. As far as point *b)* is concerned, it will be clear that most of the policies to tackle unemployment that were suggested in *the Manifesto* have become an integrated part of the European Strategy Policies against unemployment.

This strategy is also known as the *Luxembourg Process*, after the extraordinary European Council meeting of November 1997, which launched the process based on the implementation of a co-ordinated European employment policy. It immediately followed a Council Resolution on 15 December 1997 which approved the *1998 Employment Guidelines*, that is the reference

---

N.B., the numbers in square brackets refer to the Bibliography at the end of the paper.

[1] See MODIGLIANI *et Al.* [10].

guidelines that the Member States adopted in implementing their *National Action Plans* for employment. In the Luxembourg Summit, an *Employment Rates Report* was also requested to the Commission every three years, whose aim is to present a brief analysis of recent employment performance across the EU, and to draw conclusions about the potential contributions that individual Member States could make to achieve a significant increase in employment rates.

On the basis of the *Employment Rates Report* 1998 prepared by the European Commission and on the *National Action Plans* implemented by the Member States according to the *1998 Employment Guidelines*, a Joint Report 1998 on *Employment Policies in the EU and the Member States* was adopted by the Social Affair Council and the ECOFIN Council on the 1st of December 1998. This document represents a joint assessment of the Council and Commission on the *National Action Plans* for employment, submitted by the Member States in April 1998, describing the employment situation in the Community and examining the actions taken by the Member States in implementing their employment policy according to the 1998 guidelines.

Finally, the Vienna European Council of 11 and 12 December 1998 approved the *1999 Employment Guidelines*. In 1999, each Member State submitted to the Council and the Commission an implementation report, including the implementation of the *1998 National Action Plan*, and describing the adjustments made to it to take account of the changes introduced by the *1999 Guidelines*. On the basis of the evaluation of the Member States' implementation reports, in September 1999 the European Commission did its proposals for the *Joint Employment Report for 1999* and the revised *Employment Guidelines for the year 2000*. A third document of the *Commission Recommendations for Council Recommendations on the Implementation of Member States' Employment Policies* was also added.

In what follows we take into account all these documents and make also use of other sources of data to investigate on the two topics mentioned at the beginning of this section.

2. - The European Employment Performances in Recent Years

Employment and unemployment are often treated as two different aspects of the same phenomenon. They are considered complementary each other in the sense that attention is mainly concentrated on the latter, whereas the former is usually left without an explicit treatment. In fact, the objective of economic policies is very often specified in terms of a low unemployment rate.

Though, employment and unemployment are not complementary each other; in fact, they are two distinct phenomena which can increase or decrease together. Thus, the information we get when dealing with one of them is independent of what we learn when studying the other. The implication is that, if we focus on unemployment, we have a restricted view of the way the European labour market works, whereas a complete representation must treat separately both phenomena. This is exactly what we do in the following sections.

2.1 *Unemployment Rates*

The EU average unemployment rate was 9.2% in 1992; it rose to a maximum of 11.4% in 1996. Then it began to fall slowly, declining to 10.7% in 1997 and to 10% in 1998. Last June 1999 it was 9.4%, and expected to reach 9% by the end of the year (Table 1). Therefore, from the unemployment rate point of view, one can say that on the whole the European situation has been slightly improving in the last four years, but, as shown in the next section, the opposite is true as regards to employment rates.

Anyway, the unemployment situation is very differentiated from one country to another, and even much more across different regions of the same country. Among countries, the unemployment rate in 1998 ranged from levels of 2.3-4.6% in Luxembourg, Denmark, The Netherlands and Austria, which imply a full employment situation in these countries, up to levels of 19% in

TABLE 1

UNEMPLOYMENT RATES IN THE 'UE

Month	Euro zone	EU-15	Month	Euro zone	EU-15
1998			*1999*		
07	10.9	10.0	01	10.5	9.6
08	10.9	10.0	02	10.4	9.6
09	10.8	9.9	03	10.3	9.5
10	10.7	9.8	04	10.3	9.5
11	10.7	9.8	05	10.3	9.4
12	10.6	9.7	06	10.3	9.4

Source: EUROSTAT.

Spain. Very close to full employment is the UK, whose unemployment rate was 6.2%, while the big continental countries are in an intermediate position: Germany 9.6%, France 11.9%, and Italy 12.3%.

Usually, the unemployment phenomenon is very differentiated across regions and provinces of the same country. Since it would be rather dispersive to analyse the local situation in each country, let us take the unemployment rates of a dual developed country like Italy as an example (anyway, a similar analysis also applies to other dual developed countries like Germany or Spain). In Italy the unemployment rates in 1998 range from 2.2-5% in regions like Trentino-Alto Adige and provinces like Bolzano, Trento, Belluno, Treviso, Vicenza, Parma, and many other Northern Provinces, up to 25-27% in regions like Sicily, Calabria and Campania, and to 28-34% in provinces like Enna, Catania, Reggio Calabria, Catanzaro and Palermo. Therefore, the situation is very variegated, and confirms that the unemployment problem needs to be tackled in different ways from one region to another, even in the same country.

Furthermore, the Italian situation is not less differentiated from the gender and the age group point mof view. Male unemployment rates are below 5-6% in all Northern regions, with some exceptions for the provinces of Turin, Genova, Massa and Livorno, while exceeding 20% in many Southern provinces. On the other hand, the female unemployment rate exceeds 10% in many Northern regions and provinces and overcomes 35% in many Southern provinces, reaching 49.6% in the province of Enna in Sicily. Only in some Northern regions we find levels of the female unemployment rate under 5%, like in Bolzano, where we have a rate of 2.8%, which is much more similar to the situation of full employment countries like Luxembourg, The Netherlands, Denmark, and Austria.

From the age group point of view, the unemployment rates in Italy are usually very low for people over 30 who live in the North, whereas they are very high everywhere for youngsters, especially for women. For the group aged 15-24, for instance, the average unemployment rate at the national level is 33.4%, but it exceeds 44% in Sardinia, and is about 50% in Sicily, Basilicata and Puglia, overcoming 67% in Naples and 71% in Catanzaro and Reggio Calabria. For the female group aged 15-24, we have an unemployment rate ranging between 50-80% in all the Southern regions, while in some of the Italian provinces, like Messina and Enna, we have a rate higher than 80%.

2.2 *Employment Rates*

Much more than the unemployment rate, the employment rate is an effective measure of the performance of the labour market in the sense that it measures the attitude of an economy to provide jobs for all potential workers belonging to the active population. While the unemployment rate is the ratio of unemployed persons over the active population, the employment rate is the ratio of employed people in proportion of total population aged 15-64. In the latter, the attention is focused both on employment and on the employment potential of the non-employed, including both the economically inactive people and the unemployed.

It is worth while to stress immediately that twenty years ago the EU's employment rate was 64%, whilst that of the US was 62%. By 1997, however, the EU rate had dropped to 60.5% (61% in 1998), whilst that of the US had increased to 74%, a spread of almost 14

EMPLOYMENT RATES IN THE UNION, US AND JAPAN, 1975-1997
(% population, 15-64)

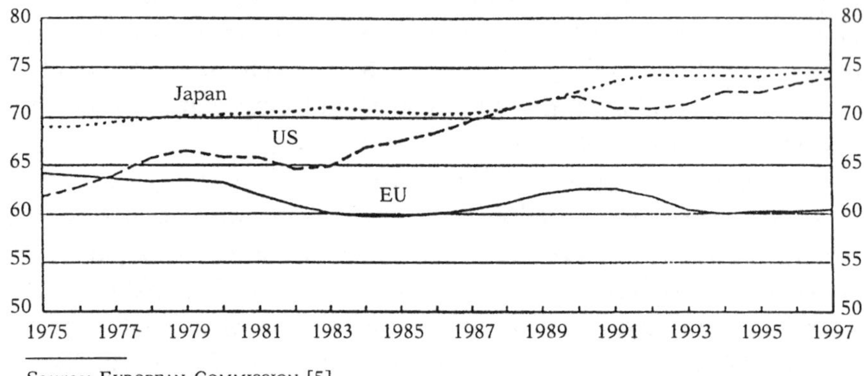

Source: EUROPEAN COMMISSION [5].

percentage points, equivalent to about 34 million jobs (Graph 1). This also means that today only slightly more than 2 of 4 persons aged 15-64 are at work in Europe, whilst in the US they are 3. This fact alone explains the greater productive potential of the US in comparison with EU. A further implication is that even if the European strategy to tackle unemployment had succeeded, and the unemployment rate had cut down to a half, so as to be equal to that of the US, nevertheless the employment rate in Europe would still only be 64%, the same level as in 1977 and well below the present levels of US and Japan. Therefore, it is not sufficient for Europe to cure unemployment, so as to catch the productive potential of these two countries, but it would be necessary to increase the European employment rates by about 14 percentage points[2].

The low employment rate in Europe means that there is a high level of unused labour stock, even beyond unemployment, and this represents an economic growth potential for the EU, which could help to significantly increase the growth process on a lasting basis. Furthermore, increasing employment rates greatly contribute to alleviate difficulties in Member States' public fi-

---

[2] Most of the data discussed in this and next sections are taken from EUROPEAN COMMISSION [5].

nance and social security systems arising from an ageing population. In fact, in 1985 life expectancy for men aged 60 was 17.5 years, and the employment rate of men aged 55-64 was 54%; ten years later, life expectancy for men aged 60 had increased to 19 years, but employment rates for the 55-64 age group has fallen to 47%.

Around the European average of 60.5%, the employment rates range from only 48.6% in Spain to 77.5% in Denmark (Table 2). Over the period 1985-1997, employment rates increased by more than the average in six Member States (The Netherlands, Ireland, Spain, Portugal, Belgium, and UK). They fell slightly in Italy, Germany and France, and sharply in Finland and Sweden.

An analysis of employment rates by gender and by age group shows where the differences between the EU and the US are. Employment rates for prime age males (25-54) vary by much less than the total, with an average of 84.5% in the Union, only slightly below the rate of 88.4% in the US. Conversely, employment rates for young people (15-24), for prime age women and for older people (50-64), especially men, are much lower in Europe than in the US and Japan.

Standard employment rates for women are lower than for men by around 21% in both the 25-54 and 55-64 age groups, although this gap is decreasing for both groups. The employment rate for prime age women in the EU is 61.9%, much lower than the 73.6% in the US, and the difference is even greater for women aged 55-64 (25.9% in the EU against 49,5% in the US). The differences of employment rates by gender in EU and in US are depicted in the Graph 2.

In the period 1985-97, employment rates of prime age women increased everywhere, except in Sweden and Finland where they were already very high in 1985 (the values of 86.5% in Sweden and 85.4% in Finland fell to 79.6% and 76.3% in 1997, respectively). Therefore, women represent a significant potential for increasing employment in the EU, and it emerges that differences are less marked in the youngest age group (15-24) and reach only 7 percentage points at the European level (39.4% for men and 32.4% for women). In The Netherlands, Sweden and UK women

TABLE 2

EMPLOYMENT RATES BY AGE, 1985 AND 1997*

1997

Age group	Belgium	Denmark	Germany	Greece	Spaia	France	Irelana	Italy	Luxembourg	The Netherlands	Austria	Portugal	Finland	Sweden	Great Britain	E-15	US	Japan
All																		
15-24	25.2	69.4	42.6	24.5	24.9	24.4	38.4	25.2	31.3	55.8	55.7	37.9	31.8	32.1	55.7	35.9	52.0	45.1
25-54	74.8	84.4	73.6	69.8	61.8	77.1	67.8	65.5	74.3	76.3	82.5	78.8	78.3	80.6	78.5	73.2	80.9	79.6
55-64	22.0	52.2	36.8	40.7	33.7	29.1	40.2	27.4	21.4	30.7	29.3	46.9	36.6	61.8	48.5	35.9	57.2	63.6
total	57.3	77.5	61.8	56.8	48.6	60.1	57.9	51.3	58.8	66.7	70.0	67.6	63.9	69.5	70.8	60.5	74.0	74.7
Men																		
15-24	28.5	73.9	45.0	30.1	29.6	27.0	41.0	30.1	37.5	58.0	59.6	43.2	34.8	32.5	57.8	39.4	53.8	45.6
25-54	86.6	90.5	82.4	90.1	80.1	86.5	82.5	83.1	92.5	89.5	93.7	88.4	80.7	81.8	85.5	84.5	88.4	95.3
55-64	32.2	62.2	45.8	59.0	50.9	33.2	59.0	41.6	31.6	42.6	42.4	58.3	38.5	64.1	58.6	46.6	65.5	80.6
total	67.6	84.0	69.8	74.9	63.5	67.7	70.5	66.3	74.3	78.2	80.5	77.3	67.0	71.3	77.7	70.6	80.8	88.5
Women																		
15-24	21.8	64.8	40.3	19.3	20.1	22.0	35.8	20.3	26.1	53.3	51.8	32.6	28.9	31.5	53.5	32.4	50.1	44.4
25-54	62.8	78.5	64.6	50.8	43.6	67.9	53.5	48.0	53.8	62.6	71.4	70.3	76.3	79.6	71.3	61.9	73.6	63.7
55-64	12.4	42.0	27.8	24.3	18.1	25.2	21.3	14.4	4.8	19.0	17.4	37.0	34.4	60.0	38.8	25.9	49.5	47.7
total	47.0	71.2	53.6	40.1	33.9	52.7	45.3	36.7	41.5	55.0	59.6	58.7	60.9	67.9	63.9	50.5	67.5	60.7

Source: EUROPEAN COMMISSION [5].

EMPLOYMENT RATES BY AGE, 1985 AND 1997*

Age group	Belgium	Denmark	Germany	Greece	Spain	France	Ireland	Italy	Luxembourg	The Netherlands	Austria	Portogallo	Finland	Svezia	Great Britain	E-15	US	Japan
1985																		
All																		
15-24	32.4	68.4	53.5	30.8	24.7	38.7	43.3	31.8	55.1	49.0	64.2	48.2	51.2	58.6	56.9	44.3	53.4	40.8
25-54	68.6	84.7	73.5	66.4	54.3	77.3	55.1	65.7	68.4	66.7	79.3	70.9	88.8	90.6	73.7	71.1	77.5	76.9
55-64	25.9	51.2	37.8	45.1	36.6	33.6	41.1	32.7	25.6	28.5	28.6	43.9	43.9	66.8	47.0	38.0	58.0	60.4
total	53.1	77.4	63.4	57.3	44.1	62.0	51.4	53.1	59.0	57.7	67.3	63.5	74.3	80.1	66.2	60.0	69.2	70.5
Men																		
15-24	35.6	72.5	55.3	39.7	29.7	43.3	45.9	38.5	55.6	52.3	67.7	57.9	50.4	56.9	60.5	48.4	56.6	40.6
25-54	88.5	90.4	89.7	90.5	78.7	91.6	79.0	90.7	94.4	89.0	98.3	88.4	91.9	94.4	86.3	88.7	89.2	94.9
55-64	43.1	63.4	55.4	65.6	56.1	42.1	65.9	52.6	40.8	45.7	47.7	62.7	48.7	75.6	62.3	54.3	71.4	78.9
total	69.1	84.8	77.2	79.0	62.7	73.9	70.2	73.7	78.2	75.4	83.1	80.1	77.3	83.7	77.3	74.8	79.6	85.5
Women																		
15-24	29.2	64.1	52.2	23.1	19.6	34.6	41.0	25.2	54.9	44.8	60.4	38.5	52.7	60.3	53.1	40.2	50.3	41.2
25-54	48.5	78.8	57.0	43.6	30.2	63.1	30.6	41.6	42.0	43.7	60.5	54.9	85.4	86.5	61.1	53.4	66.3	58.9
55-64	10.4	40.7	23.8	26.0	18.1	26.0	17.3	14.6	13.8	13.2	14.1	27.9	39.8	58.8	32.7	23.6	45.9	44.4
total	37.2	69.9	50.1	37.4	25.8	50.7	32.1	33.5	40.1	39.7	52.1	48.2	71.4	76.4	55.0	45.6	57.9	55.7

* Portugal, Greece and Austria are 1986, Netherland, Finland and Sweden are 1987. D is all Germany even in 1985, so should be comparable.

Source: EUROPEAN COMMISSION [5].

EMPLOYMENT RATES FOR MEN AND WOMEN
IN THE UNION AND US, 1997
(% population, 15-64)

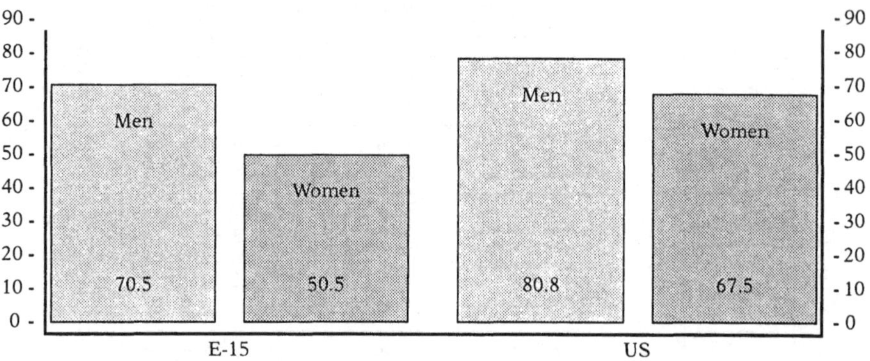

and men of the group 15-24 have basically near the same likelihood of being employed.

Employment rates of young people range from 24.4% in France to 69.4% in Denmark, with a spread of 45 percentage points. They declined by near 2% per year in the period 1985-97 and this trend was the same in all countries except in Denmark, where youth employment remained stable, and in The Netherlands, where it increased. This is not necessarily seen as a negative phenomenon, as long as it means that young people stay longer in initial education and training. The possibility of combining education or training courses with part-time jobs allows for relatively high numbers of young people over 18 to remain in education or training beyond basic schooling and for them to start working. The experience of Germany and Austria suggests that combined systems of education, training and work facilitate and encourage the integration of young people into the labour market.

The decline in employment rates for men above 55 years becomes marked in all countries. In the age group 60-64, early retirement becomes the norm. Only in Sweden, Portugal, Ireland, Greece and UK does the employment rate approach 50%. Compared with 1985, employment in this age group decreased everywhere, with an average decline of 8 percentage points across the EU to 46.6%.

If we translate real employment rates into full-time equivalent (FTE) employment rates, the differences among countries tend to be reduced, but it still remains a difference of 23 percentage points between the Member State with the highest level (Austria) and that with the lowest (Spain). These differences are depicted in table 3. FTE employment rates take account of part-time working and the usual hours worked by part-time workers relative to full-time workers. They are adjusted by calculating the ratio of average hours worked (for each age group), relative to average hours of full-time workers, which allows the conversion of the standard employment rate into a full-time equivalent. Thus, full-time equivalents measure the volume of employment, while standard employment rates measure how many people have a job.

FTE employment rates are about 2% points below the normal employment rates for men in the EU, but 8% points lower for women, reflecting the higher part-time content of female employment (Table 3). But we must stress that adjusting to full-time equivalents has comparatively little effect on the employment rate. This means that most of the countries, with the exception of Austria and Portugal, with relatively high rates of employment also have higher than average proportions of people working relatively short hours.

Anyway, it is worth stressing that availability to work part-time on a voluntary basis is one of the determinants of high employment rates for some categories of people, such as mothers, young people still in education and people nearing retirement. It is relatively limited among men and concentrated on the younger or older workers, with the result that FTE employment rates differ most in these age groups. In contrast, for women the differences are largest among the prime-age group, reaching over 20% points in The Netherlands and Denmark, and over 10% points in UK and Sweden. For young and older people, the possibility of combining work and education has a positive effect. Those countries with high youth employment rates also show great differences between standard and full-time equivalent employment

DIFFERENCES BETWEEN NORMAL AND FULL-TIME EQUIVALENT EMPLOYMENT RATES BY AGE, 1996

Age group	Belgium	Deanmark	Germany	Greece	Spain	France	Ireland	Italy	Luxembourg	Netherland	Austria	Portugal	Finland	Sweden	Great Britain	E-15	E-12
									Men								
15-19	0.7	27.1	1.0	0.6	0.8	0.5	2.5	0.2	0.2	23.5	0.4	0.6	5.7	7.9	13.2	4.0	4.0
20-24	1.7	10.8	2.3	1.4	1.7	2.6	1.9	0.7	0.3	14.7	1.6	1.1	6.7	5.4	4.7	3.0	3.0
25-29	1.4	5.3	2.8	1.2	1.7	2.0	1.5	0.8	0.6	3.9	1.8	1.0	2.8	2.9	1.7	2.0	2.0
30-39	1.0	2.1	1.4	0.7	0.8	1.4	1.5	0.7	0.2	2.9	1.2	0.2	0.9	1.9	1.2	1.2	1.2
40-49	0.7	1.4	0.9	0.5	0.7	1.1	1.5	0.4	0.3	3.3	0.9	0.6	1.1	1.9	1.5	1.1	1.0
50-54	0.8	1.1	1.0	0.6	0.5	1.3	1.5	0.6	0.2	3.7	0.9	0.7	0.9	2.2	2.1	1.2	1.2
55-59	0.9	2.0	1.2	0.8	0.9	3.1	1.4	0.7	0.2	6.1	1.5	1.5	1.6	4.1	3.5	1.9	1.8
60-64	0.7	3.8	1.5	0.7	0.8	1.1	1.2	0.6	0.1	4.4	2.9	1.7	3.3	8.6	4.8	2.0	2.0
total	1.1	5.9	1.6	1.0	1.1	1.6	1.8	0.7	0.3	6.8	1.6	1.3	2.4	4.3	3.9	2.1	2.0
									Women								
15-19	0.7	33.5	1.0	0.5	0.8	0.6	2.5	0.4	0.1	23.3	0.8	0.8	6.4	11.1	17.4	4.7	4.7
20-24	4.3	12.9	4.4	1.6	3.5	6.6	3.2	1.8	2.1	19.6	4.7	1.3	8.6	11.2	8.4	5.5	5.4
25-29	8.0	6.0	7.3	1.9	4.1	6.6	3.7	2.6	3.6	15.6	8.6	2.3	5.1	9.1	10.3	6.7	6.6
30-39	10.7	7.0	13.0	1.6	4.1	8.4	5.9	3.2	5.4	24.3	12.2	2.9	3.0	12.6	18.2	10.3	10.3
40-49	8.9	8.9	13.4	1.3	3.6	8.4	7.3	2.0	5.2	24.4	10.0	3.0	2.9	12.2	18.7	10.1	10.1
50-54	6.5	8.4	12.0	1.6	3.1	7.6	5.9	1.6	4.4	19.9	7.8	3.0	3.6	10.2	18.5	9.1	9.2
55-59	3.4	8.8	9.6	1.4	2.3	7.2	5.0	0.8	2.2	13.4	4.1	3.9	2.5	13.8	15.9	7.5	7.5
60-64	1.0	5.0	3.7	1.4	1.4	2.6	2.2	0.3	1.8	5.2	2.3	4.0	2.6	12.8	10.4	3.7	3.5
total	6.7	10.6	9.7	1.6	3.1	6.7	4.9	1.9	3.9	20.2	8.0	3.1	4.0	12.1	16.1	8.1	8.0

Source: EUROPEAN COMMISSION [5].

rates, and the same is true for countries with high levels of employment in older age groups (Ireland, Greece and Portugal have high employment in older age groups without great use of part-time because they still have a big agriculture sector, but this cannot be considered a model for other countries).

We also must stress that often part-time work is not on a voluntary basis. Simply it is the result of the difficulties that people find when looking for a job. In the EU in 1997, for instance, 20% of those working part-time say they do so because they could not find a full-time job, ranging from under 10% in The Netherlands and Austria to nearly 40% in Greece, Italy and Finland.

2.3 *Employment Rates by Broad Sector*

The sectoral analysis of the employment rates reflects the relative weight of the same sectors in the economy from the employment point of view. In 1997, employment as a share of total employment in the EU is 5% in agriculture, 29.5% in industry and 65.0% in services, compared to 2.7%, 23.9% and 73.3% respectively in the US. However, an analysis by employment rates shows that activity in agriculture and industry is roughly similar in the US and the EU (3% and 17.8% respectively in EU, 2% and 17.7% in the US). Conversely, employment in services accounts for only 39.7% of working age population in the EU, while it accounts for 54.3% in the US (Table 4 and Graph 3).

Therefore, the very difference in the employment structure of the EU and the US is not in agriculture or industry, but in the services sector. Further increase in the overall employment rate will depend on an expansion of jobs in services. Only in Denmark, Sweden, The Netherlands and UK, employment in services is near 50% or slightly more, although since 1985 employment rates in the services sector have increased in all Member States. Only in Italy, France and Germany, which together account for 50% of total EU employment, the registered increases are very small and, anyway, below the average.

If we compare the situation of the various Member States, we

EMPLOYMENT BY NACE 2-DIGIT SECTOR AS

Sector	Belgium	Denmark	Germany	Greece	[illegible]
Agriculturea, forestry, fishing	1.5	2.9	1.8	11.3	[illegible]
Mining, including oil+gas+petrol	0.2	0.1	0.4	0.4	[illegible]
Food, drink tobacco	1.4	2.5	1.5	1.6	1.4
Textile, clothing, footwear	1.0	0.5	0.7	2.0	1.3
Printing, publishing, paper	1.0	1.7	1.1	0.7	0.7
Chemicals, rubber, plastics	1.8	1.4	1.7	0.6	0.8
Iron+sleel+metal products	1.7	2.0	2.4	0.8	1.1
Machinery and computing equipment	0.9	2.3	2.3	0.4	0.7
Electrical machinery, equipment	0.7	1.1	1.2	0.2	0.4
Instrument engineering	0.2	0.4	0.5	0.1	0.1
Transport equipment	1.1	0.6	1.6	0.3	0.9
Wood, furniture, misc manufs	1.4	2.2	1.7	1.6	1.6
Total manufacturing	11.2	14.6	14.6	8.1	[illegible]
Electricity, gas and water	0.5	0.6	0.6	0.6	[illegible]
Construction	3.8	5.1	5.7	3.7	[illegible]
Sale & repair of motor vehicles	1.1	2.0	1.3	1.4	1.1
Wholesale trade	2.0	3.3	1.9	1.7	2.0
Retail trade	5.0	5.1	5.7	6.3	5.0
Distribution	8.2	10.4	8.8	9.5	[illegible]
Hotels and restaurants	1.9	2.3	2.0	3.4	[illegible]
Land transport	1.9	1.9	1.1	1.6	1.7
Water transport	0.1	0,5	0.1	0.4	0.1
Air transport	0.2	0.2	0.1	0.2	0.1
Travel agents, etc.	0.7	1.1	1.1	0.9	0.4
Post and telecomms	1.3	1.8	1.0	0.7	0.6
Transport and communications	4.3	5.5	3.3	3.6	[illegible]
Banking	1.5	1.8	1.4	1.0	0.9
Insurance	0.7	0.7	0.6	0.4	0.4
Auxiliary financial services	0.1	0.1	0.2	0.0	0.0
Finance and Insurance	2.3	2.6	2.2	1.4	[illegible]
Real estate, renting (incl car hire)	0.3	0.9	0.5	0.1	0.2
Computing and data processing	0.5	1.0	0.4	0.1	0.2
Research and development	0.1	0.3	0.3	0.1	0.1
Business activities, nes	2.8	4.1	3.0	2.1	2.5
Business services	3.7	6.2	4.3	2.4	[illegible]
Public administration	5.8	4.8	5.5	4.1	3.2
Education	5.2	5.8	3.3	3.4	2.9
Health and social work	6.2	13.0	5.7	2.5	2.7
Sanitary services	0.2	0.1	0.2	0.2	0.1
Membership organisations	0.4	1.0	0.7	0.2	0.2
Recreationgal activities	0.9	1.7	0.9	0.9	0.9
Personal+other services	0.8	0.7	1.2	0.6	0.5
Private households	0.1	0.1	0.2	0.6	1.3
Communal services	19.5	27.3	17.8	12.5	[illegible]
Total	57.3	77.5	61.8	56.7	[illegible]

Source: US Bureau of Labour Statistics (data aggregated to a NACE 2-digit bas[...] stencies between Table 4 and 5 are caused by the two different systems of classificatio[...]

TABLE 4

WORKING-AGE POPULATION IN US AND E15, 1997

France	Ireland	Italy	Luxembourg	Netherland	Austria	Portugal	Finland	Sweden	Great Britain	E-15	US	E-15 - US
2.8	6.3	3.3	1.4	2.5	4.8	9.0	5.0	2.3	1.3	3.0	2.0	1.0
0.2	0.3	0.3	0.1	0.2	0.2	0.3	0.2	0.2	0.4	0.3	0.5	−0.1
8	1.9	0.9	0.9	1.7	1.6	1.6	1.3	1.1	1.3	1.4	1.0	0.4
9	1.0	2.4	0.2	0.4	1.1	4.7	0.7	0.4	1.2	1.3	1.0	0.3
9	1.0	0.7	0.6	1.5	1.2	0.9	2.2	1.8	1.5	1.1	1.4	−0.4
4	1.3	1.1	1.8	1.3	1.2	0.8	1.0	1.1	1.7	1.3	1.3	0.1
5	0.9	1.9	2.8	1.3	2.9	1.7	1.8	1.9	1.6	1.8	1.2	0.6
9	1.6	1.4	0.6	1.0	1.5	0.5	1.6	1.9	1.6	1.5	1.5	0.0
8	0.9	0.8	0.1	0.8	0.7	0.6	1.3	1.3	1.1	0.9	1.1	−0.2
4	0.6	0.2	0.2	0.3	0.8	0.1	0.3	0.4	0.4	0.3	0.4	−0.1
3	0.3	0.7	0.1	0.6	0.7	0.7	0.6	1.7	1.4	1.1	1.3	−0.2
2	1.6	1.3	0.7	1.7	2.6	2.6	1.9	1.6	1.4	1.5	1.6	−0.1
1.1	11.0	11.4	7.8	10.5	14.3	14.1	12.7	13.3	13.2	12.2	11.8	0.5
0.6	0.5	0.5	0.4	0.4	0.8	0.6	0.7	0.6	0.5	0.5	0.7	−0.2
4.0	4.7	4.0	5.8	4.1	5.4	6.0	3.9	3.6	5.0	4.7	4.7	0.0
2	1.2	1.3	1.3	1.2	1.6	1.8	1.3	1.3	1.5	1.3	1.9	−0.6
5	2.0	1.6	2.2	3.9	2.6	1.8	2.2	3.4	2.1	2.1	2.7	−0.5
3	4.9	5.7	4.8	5.9	6.8	6.1	3.9	3.8	7.4	5.6	7.5	−1.8
8.1	8.2	8.6	8.3	11.0	11.0	9.7	7.4	8.6	11.0	9.1	12.1	−2.9
2.0	3.2	2.3	3.1	2.2	4.0	3.3	1.8	1.8	3.3	2.5	5.4	−2.9
3	1.4	1.5	2.2	1.9	2.3	1.1	2.4	1.9	1.7	1.5	1.9	−0.4
0	0.1	0.1	0.0	0.1	0.0	0.1	0.3	0.2	0.1	0.1	0.1	0.0
2	0.3	0.1	0.7	0.3	0.1	0.2	0.2	0.2	0.1	0.1	0.5	−0.3
5	0.2	0.3	0.3	0.7	0.8	0.6	0.7	0.8	1.2	0.7	0.3	0.4
3	0.8	0.8	1.1	1.1	1.2	0.6	1.2	1.4	1.5	1.1	1.2	−0.2
3.8	2.7	2.8	4.2	4.0	4.4	2.6	4.8	4.5	4.6	3.6	4.1	−0.5
1	1.3	1.2	5.3	1.3	1.8	1.4	1.1	1.1	1.7	1.3	1.3	0.0
4	0.6	0.5	0.5	0.6	0.9	0.4	0.6	0.4	0.3	0.5	1.5	−1.0
3	0.3	0.1	0.4	0.5	0.0	0.0	0.0	0.1	1.1	0.3	0.5	−0.2
1.9	2.1	1.7	6.2	2.4	2.7	1.8	1.7	1.6	3.1	2.1	3.3	−1.2
0	0.3	0.2	0.2	0.6	0.8	0.2	0.9	1.3	1.3	0.6	1.5	−0.9
5	0.5	0.4	0.2	0.8	0.3	0.2	0.7	1.0	0.8	0.5	0.9	−0.4
4	0.1	0.1	0.1	0.3	0.2	0.2	0.3	0.4	0.3	0.2	0.4	−0.1
4	2.6	2.1	3.2	5.3	3.4	2.7	3.2	4.3	4.7	3.2	5.1	−1.8
5.2	3.6	2.8	3.8	7.0	4.6	3.3	5.1	7.0	7.0	4.6	7.8	−3.2
5	3.1	3.9	8.4	5.3	4.8	4.5	3.4	3.8	4.3	4.7	3.3	1.4
5	3.8	3.9	3.9	4.3	4.1	4.6	4.5	5.1	5.3	4.1	5.7	−1.6
8	5.0	3.0	4.4	9.5	5.5	3.1	9.3	13.6	7.8	5.7	8.4	−2.7
1	0.1	0.3	0.2	0.2	0.3	0.3	0.2	0.2	0.3	0.2	0.2	0.0
8	0.5	0.3	0.3	0.6	0.7	0.3	0.8	1.1	0.6	0.6	0.5	0.0
0	1.3	0.4	0.7	1.4	1.0	0.8	1.6	1.6	1.9	1.1	1.9	−0.8
5	1.4	1.2	0.7	0.7	1.0	1.6	0.6	0.5	0.9	0.9	0.9	0.0
4	0.0	0.5	0.9	0.3	0.3	1.6	0.1	0.0	0.4	0.6	0.5	0.1
0.4	15.2	13.5	19.4	22.3	17.6	16.9	20.5	26.0	21.4	17.8	21.4	−3.4
0.1	57.8	51.3	60.6	66.7	69.9	67.5	63.9	69.5	70.8	60.5	74.0	−12.9

mmunity LFS (data converted to a benchmark employment basis). Minor inconsi-
d NACE)

EMPLOYMENT RATES BY BROAD SECTOR, 1997
(% population, 15-64)

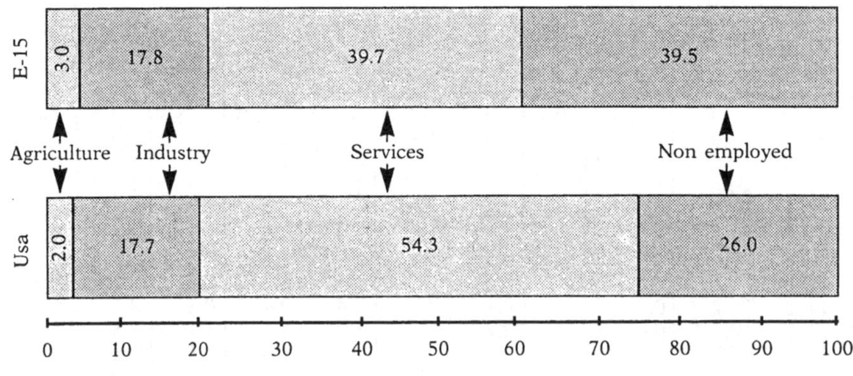

see that countries with a high level of development and a high level of employment rates also have high levels of employment in all services sectors. For example, The Netherlands and UK have a high level of employment both in distribution and in health and social work, Sweden and Denmark have a high level of employment not only in health and social work and education, but also in business services. Conversely, Germany and Italy fare relatively badly in employment in distribution, but also in business services, in education, health and social work. France performs relatively poorly in distribution and hotels and restaurants, but also in finance and insurance.

In comparison with the US, employment rates in EU are significantly lower in all services sectors, and this applies not only to low skilled jobs, but also to high skilled ones. There is a difference of around 3 percentage points for hotels and restaurants and distribution, but also for communal services and business services the differences are very high (3.4 and 3.2 percentage points, respectively in 1997). Thus, 'communal services' is the sector where there is the biggest difference between the EU and the US. It includes education, health, social services, recreational services and public administration. Within communal services, the US employ relatively less people in public administration (3.3% against 4.7% in the EU), but this is more than offset by employment in education, health and social work (14.1% against 9.8%) and even in recreational activities (1.9% against 1.1 %). In 1997, the US and the EU each had 44 million workers employed in communal services, but this represented an employment rate of 21.4% in the US and of only 17.8% in the EU (Table 4).

The implication is that in the EU there is a very large extent to improve employment in the communal and business services, especially in high skilled services. Demand for at least some of these services seems to be related to the level of female participation in the workforce, rather than to the ownership structure of these services (public or private). Higher employment of women also creates jobs to cater for activities such as child care or care for the dependants which were previously unpaid. In the same way, increasing the quantity and the quality of the labour force also requires improvements in the supply of education, which creates employment in the sector. In this way, demand and supply reinforce each other.

In 1997, the employment rates of distribution, hotels and restaurants were 17.5% in the US, but only 11.6% in the EU. Only in Austria and UK we bave figures comparable to the US's situation (15% and 14.3%, respectively). These are traditional low wage sectors; and higher employment in the US can be accounted for by greater possibilities of hiring at low wages, as well as by the more consumer-oriented nature of the US society. Employment trends in these sectors have varied between countries with increases in Austria, The Netherlands, UK, Belgium and Denmark but decreases in Germany and Italy and employment remaining stable in France. The solution could lie both in a liberalisation of product and services markets, as advocated by Community policy since the creation of the Single Market Programme, as well as in the reduction of non wage labour costs for relatively unskilled and low wage jobs.

European employment rate in financial and business services in 1997 is comparable to that of Japan (6.7%), but it is smaller than in the US (11.1%). Only in UK, The Netherlands and Denmark it is higher than in the US, and Austria is also catching up, since in all these countries employment has increased by more than 3% after 1985. Conversely, in France and Germany the increase is only 1%, so their financial and business sectors are relatively smaller than in other countries (7.1% and 6.5%, respectively). Obviously this is not the result of restrictive budgetary policies, as these services are largely in the private sector, but rather the consequence of various administrative and legislative obstacles to the creation of new enterprises, and rigidities in the services and products market. This services are not only creators of employment in their own right, but also create value-added as inputs into industry and other services. This generates more economic activity and in turn creates new employment opportunities.

2.4 *Benchmarking Labour Market Performance*

The labour market performance in the EU and in the single Member States can be benchmarked by the use of the 'radar chart approach', which is one of a number of special analytical tools that have been developed in connection with benchmarking in the private and public sectors. The institutional context for this exercise in benchmarking is the new annual process of formulation of employment guidelines, monitoring and reporting on Member State' labour market performance, which has been institutionalised at the European level by Art. 4 (Employment Title) of the *Treaty of Amsterdam*[3].

The name 'radar chart' comes from its resemblance to a radar screen although other names are also sometimes used (measure matrix, net chart, etc.). Radar charts have four or more axes integrated in a single radial figure on which data for one or more countries (cases) can be presented simultaneously. They are particularly useful for comparing performance on multiple dimensions or for comparing cases with multiple performance dimensions. In the case of four axes, when four dimensions (benchmarks) are taken into account, we also speak of 'diamond charts'.

---

[3] The techniques of benchmarking presented in this section are taken from MOSLEY H. - MAYER A. [11].

The radial axes of the radar chart quantify performance in terms of the degree of attainment of the benchmarking goals. In order to present several indicators of labour market performance in the same radar chart, the original data are standardised to a common interval scale with values between 0 and 1. On the basis of a mathematical formula, a value of 1 is assigned to the best performer benchmark and a value of 0 is assigned to the worst performer. Other countries are assigned values between 0 and 1 according to their relative performance on each indicator, i.e. a value of 0.5 indicates performance at the middle point of the scale half way between the lowest and the highest case. In the radar charts on labour market performance presented here, higher values represent best performance.

The radar chart approach makes two important contributions: first, it provides a simplified presentation of multiple performance indicators, which is highly intuitive even to non experts; and, second, the polygon formed by the four axes of the radar chart provides not only a visual representation of performance, but its surface area can also be used as a composite performance indicator. This is indicated as the «surface measure of overall performance» (SMOP), which is calculated simply on the basis of the mathematical formula for the area of the polygon. The SMOP yields an interval index measure of overall performance that can be used, for example, to rank performance of countries, or to measure changes in performance over time. The maximum value of the SMOP indicator depends on the number of sides, assuming that the maximum benchmark value of 1 is achieved on all performance dimensions. Thus, a radar chart of four axes has a maximum SMOP of 2^4.

Two sets of labour market performance goals, one for ernployment and the other for unemployment, have been selected for separated representation and analysis. For benchmarking the em-

---

[4] The following standard mathematical formula is used for the *SMOP* calculation:

$$SMOP = [(P_1 * P_2) + (P_2 * P_3) + (P_3 * P_4) + (P_4 * P_1)] * \sin 90°/2,$$

where P_1, P_2, P_3, P_4 are the four data points on the axis of the radar chart. If $P_1 = P_2 = P_3 = P_4 = 1$, which happens when all four performance indicators assume the maximun value of 1, we have a *SMOP*=2.

ployment performance, the four dimensions (benchmarks) used are: *employment growth* (defined as the average annual growth rate in occupied population, in the previous 5 years), *employment rate* (defined as the employed population 15-64 years as percentage proportion of total in the same age bracket), *employment gender gap* (defined as the ratio of female to male employment rate), and *employment rate 50-64* (defined as the employed persons 50-64 as percentage proportion of total in the same age bracket).

For benchmarking the unemployment performance, the four

TABLE 5

EU LABOUR MARKET PERFORMANCE: GOALS, INDICATORS, AND BENCHMARKS

Performance dimension	Performance goal	Indicators of performance	Definition of performance indicators	Source
Employment				
Employment growth	High employment growth	Employment growth 1993-1997	Average annual growth in occupied population, previous 5 years, %	EUROSTAT, *Employment Benchmark Series*
Employment level	High employment level	Total employment rate	Employed population (15-64 years) as proportion of total in the same age bracket, %	EUROSTAT, *Employment Benchmark Series & LFS*. USA, Japan, Austria, Finland Sweden for 1992, national LFS
Equal opportunity	Gender equality in employment	Female/male employment ratio	Ratio of female to male employment rate	EUROSTAT, LFS. Usa, Japan, Austria, Finland, Sweden for 1992, national LFS
Integration of older workers	High employment level, equity	Employment rate 50-64	Employed persons 50-64 as proportion of total in the same age bracket, %	EUROSTAT, LFS. Usa, Japan, Austria, Finland, Sweden for 1992, national LFS

TABLE 5 *continued*

EU LABOUR MARKET PERFORMANCE:
GOALS, INDICATORS, AND BENCHMARKS

Performance dimension	Performance goal	Indicators of performance	Definition of performance indicators	Source
		Unemployment		
Combating unemployment	Reducing unemployment	Total unemployment rate	Unemployed as proportion of total active population, %	EUROSTAT, *Harmonized unemployment rates*
Equal opportunity	Gender equality in labour market	male/female unemployment ratio	Ratio of male to female unemployment rate	EUROSTAT, LFS; Usa & Japan, OECD
Integration of youth into labour market	Reducing youth unemployment	Youth unemployment ratio	Unemployed youth (15-24 years) as proportion of total in the same age bracket, %	EUROSTAT, LFS; Usa & Japan, OECD
Integration of problem groups	Reducing long-term unemployment	Long-term unemployment share	Long-erm unemployed (>12 m) as proportion of total unemployment, %	EUROSTAT, LFS; Usa & Japan, OECD

dimensions (benchmarks) used are: *unemployment rate* (defined as the unemployed as percentage proportion of total active population), *long-term unemployment* (defined as the long-term unemployed, more than 12 months, as percentage proportion of total unemployment), *youth unemployment ratio* (defined as unemployed youth, 15-24 years, as percentage proportion of total in same age brackets), and *unemployment gender gap* (defined as the ratio of male to female unemployment rate). In table 5, the EU labour market performances (goals, indicators, and benchmarks) are summarised.

Benchmarking national labour market performances requires the choice of appropriate goals or targets in terms of which performance is to be assessed. In this benchmark exercise, performance standards have been defined in terms of 'best performance' in 1997, i.e. the country with the best score on the chosen indicator among EU Members States, the US and Japan. This procedure yields the following best performance benchmarks on the basis of the indicators reported in table 6. For benchmarking the employment performance, the best performance benchmarks are Ireland (employment growth), Denmark (employment rate), Sweden (employment gender gap, and employment 50-64); whereas for benchmarking the unemployment performance, the best performance benchmarks are: Luxembourg (unemployment rate, and youth unemployment), Japan (unemployment gender gap), and US (long-term unemployment).

TABLE 6

ORIGINAL DATA SERIES: EMPLOYMENT AND UNEMPLOYMENT
PERFORMANCE INDICATORS, 1997 AND 1992

	1997	*1992*	*1997*	*1992*	*1997*	*1992*	*1997/92*	*1992/87*
	Employment rate		*Employment ratio 50-64*		*Employment gender gap*		*Employment growth*	
B	57.28	56.82	35.30	32.67	0.70	0.65	0.36	1.71
DK	77.49	75.75	63.97	62.25	0.85	0.86	0.71	-0.70
D	61.75	65.89	46.26	50.33	0.77	0.73	-1.09	1.20
GR	56.74	55.42	47.08	45.64	0.54	0.50	0.92	0.46
E	48.57	48.42	41.31	40.55	0.53	0.48	0.64	1.75
F	60.08	61.39	45.63	43.21	0.78	0.74	-0.03	0.53
IRL	57.79	52.43	46.50	43.52	0.64	0.55	3.63	1.20
I	51.30	53.72	36.51	39.56	0.55	0.53	-1.36	0.28
L	60.58	61.96	33.85	36.92	0.62	0.61	1.86	3.69
NL	66.70	63.55	44.71	39.90	0.70	0.65	1.47	2.28
A	69.92	70.72	43.88	48.11	0.74	0.71	0.95	1.50
P	67.54	68.72	55.13	54.29	0.76	0.70	0.00	1.52
FIN	63.86	66.18	51.00	50.43	0.91	0.96	0.06	-2.07
S	69.47	77.24	71.25	74.91	0.95	0.97	-1.40	-0.49
UK	70.83	69.43	58.74	56.90	0.82	0.81	0.65	0.77
EU	60.50	61.79	46.80	47.16	0.72	0.68	-0.15	0.70
JP	74.58	74.22	63.60	64.50	0.69	0.69	0.38	1.78
USA	73.99	70.88	65.70	61.10	0.84	0.81	1.87	1.08
min	48.57	48.42	33.85	32.67	0.53	0.48	-1.40	-2.07
max	77.49	77.24	71.25	74.91	0.95	0.97	3.63	3.69
average	63.83	64.14	49.85	49.55	0.73	0.70	0.53	0.95

TABLE 6 *continued*

ORIGINAL DATA SERIES: EMPLOYMENT AND UNEMPLOYMENT PERFORMANCE INDICATORS, 1997 AND 1992

	1997	*1992*	*1997*	*1992*	*1997*	*1992*	*1997/92*	*1992/87*
	Employment rate		*Employment ratio 50-64*		*Employment gender gap*		*Employment growth*	
B	9.20	7.30	6.81	4.80	0.61	0.52	58.70	54.79
DK	5.50	9.20	6.01	8.90	0.70	0.82	27.27	26.09
D	10.00	6.60	5.30	3.50	0.86	0.61	49.00	31.82
GR	9.60	7.90	11.01	9.50	0.42	0.38	55.21	49.37
E	20.80	18.50	15.93	14.70	0.57	0.57	51.92	42.16
F	12.40	10.40	9.91	8.60	0.74	0.64	40.32	33.65
IRL	10.10	15.40	7.25	10.50	0.97	0.94	56.44	56.49
I	12.10	9.98	12.78	11.80	0.56	0.49	66.94	59.02
L	2.60	2.10	2.72	1.90	0.47	0.61	34.62	19.05
NL	5.20	5.60	6.15	5.00	0.57	0.51	48.08	42.86
A	4.40	3.60	4.42	12.42	0.68	0.57	34.09	16.10
P	6.80	4.20	6.24	4.90	0.77	0.72	51.47	28.57
FIN	13.10	12.30	17.16	14.70	0.92	0.61	33.59	30.60
S	9.90	5.60	8.98	9.59	0.93	0.50	35.35	8.30
UK	7.00	10.10	8.75	10.60	0.70	0.47	38.57	34.65
EU	10.70	9.20	9.76	9.00	0.75	0.73	48.60	41.30
JP	3.50	2.20	6.60	2.41	0.97	0.95	21.80	25.30
USA	4.90	7.40	11.30	8.79	0.96	0.63	8.70	11.20
min	2.60	2.10	2.72	1.90	0.42	0.38	8.70	8.30
max	20.80	18.50	17.16	14.70	0.97	0.95	66.94	59.02
average	8.77	8.20	8.73	8.42	0.73	0.63	42.26	33.96

Sources: In general data are from Eurostat except for Usa and Japan and 1992 data for Austria, Finland, and Sweden, which are drawn from OECD or national sources. The Eurostat data used are identical with the data in the *1998 Joint Employment Report*. See table 5 for sources and definitions of indicators. *Employment rates*: total occupied population (15-64) from Eurostat benchmark employment series as proportion of total population in the same age bracket; data on structure of employment from Eurostat LFS or comparable national sources for non Member States. Japanese data for employment rate 50-64 = 55-64 and 1996 not 1997. *Employment gender gap* = ratio of female to male employment rates. *Employment growth* = average annual change for period. Eurostat benchmark employment series but A & L 1992-1996. Employment growth 1987-1992: Germany and Italy from OECD, *Economic Outlook* 1998 because of break in EU series. *Unemployment*: Eurostat harmonized unemployment rates. *Youth unemployment ratio*: USA, Japan, A, Fin, S = 1993 data from *Employment Outlook*, 1996 (OECD, 1996). *Unemployment gender gap*: 1-absolute value of 1-F/M, where F is the female and M the male unemployment rate. *Long-term unemployment* (share>12 months) for 1997 & 1992 from Eurostat and OECD (Japan and USA). 1992 data for Sweden from OECD. *Employment Outlook*, 1995; A interpolated on the basis of national data reported in *Trends* No. 30, Summer 1998, p. 70, Fin = 1993.

The benchmarks are those countries that in table 7 take the best score of 1 on the chosen indicator. To obtain the transformed data contained in this table, which are used to depict the radar charts, we start from the original data series reported in Table 6. The original data were transformed in order to make them suitable for use in radar charts, whose axes depict performance in relationship to benchmarks and whose surface area can be used as a composite indicator of overall performance. In each case, the underlying labour market indicators for the year 1997 and 1992 are transformed into index values with a common scale in which the benchmark (best performance) value in 1997 is equal to 1, and the lowest value (worst performance) in 1997 or 1992 is equal to 0. The benchmark performance values for the other countries reflect their relative position in the range between best and worst performance.

In table 8, the results of the benchmarking exercise on the basis of a composite indicator or surface measure of overall performance (SMOP) for 1997 are reported. Among EU Member States, the best overall performers were Denmark, Sweden, UK and Austria in that order, all of which received total SMOP benchmarking scores of 1.5 or greater in 1997 out of a theoretical maximum of 4. Japan and US attained the highest overall performance scores. By contrast, three countries (Spain, Italy and Greece) were clearly worst performers, with total SMOP benchmarking scores of less than 0.40. The remaining EU Member States (Portugal, Ireland, The Netherlands, Germany, Luxembourg, Finland, France and Belgium) constitute a distinct group of intermediate level countries with mixed performance profiles.

If we analyse the changes in overall labour market performance in the period 1992-97, we see that, on the basis of the composite indicator, whereas eight Member States show a decline in performance on the indicators observed (Italy, Spain, Luxembourg, Germany, Portugal, Sweden, Belgium and France, in the order of worst performance), six show improvement (Ireland, UK, Finland, Denmark, Austria, and The Netherlands, in the order of best performance), while Greece showed virtually no change over the period 1992-1997. For the EU as a whole, this mixed pattern

TABLE 7

STANDARD DATA SERIES: EMPLOYMENT AND UNEMPLOYMENT PERFORMANCE INDICATORS, 1997 AND 1992

Countries	1997	1992	1997	1992	1997	1992	1997/92	1992/87
	employment rate		*employment ratio 50-64*		*employment gender gap*		*employment growth*	
A	0.74	0.77	0.29	0.40	0.55	0.49	0.53	0.63
B	0.30	0.29	0.07	0	0.46	0.36	0.43	0.66
DK	1.00	0.94	0.81	0.77	0.78	0.81	0.49	0.24
E	0.01	0	0.22	0.20	0.11	0	0.48	0.67
EU	0.42	0.46	0.37	0.38	0.50	0.43	0.34	0.49
F	0.40	0.45	0.34	0.27	0.63	0.55	0.36	0.46
FIN	0.53	0.61	0.48	0.46	0.91	1.01	0.37	0
GER	0.46	0.60	0.35	0.46	0.61	0.52	0.17	0.57
GR	0.29	0.24	0.37	0.34	0.12	0.03	0.52	0.44
I	0.10	0.18	0.10	0.18	0.15	0.09	0.12	0.41
IRL	0.32	0.14	0.36	0.28	0.35	0.16	1.00	0.57
JP	0.90	0.89	0.80	0.83	0.43	0.44	0.43	0.67
L	0.42	0.47	0.03	0.11	0.28	0.27	0.69	1.01
NL	0.63	0.52	0.31	0.19	0.47	0.37	0.62	0.76
P	0.66	0.70	0.58	0.56	0.59	0.46	0.36	0.63
S	0.72	0.99	1.00	1.09	1.00	1.05	0.12	0.28
UK	0.77	0.72	0.68	0.63	0.72	0.69	0.48	0.50
USA	0.88	0.77	0.86	0.74	0.75	0.70	0.69	0.55
Stand Deviation	0.28	0.29	0.28	0.29	0.26	0.30	0.22	0.22
Mean	0.53	0.54	0.45	0.44	0.52	0.47	0.46	0.53
Median	0.49	0.56	0.36	0.39	0.52	0.45	0.45	0.56
	employment rate		*employment ratio 50-64*		*employment gender gap*		*employment growth*	
A	0.90	0.95	0.88	0.33	0.50	0.32	0.56	0.87
B	0.64	0.74	0.72	0.86	0.38	0.23	0.14	0.21
DK	0.84	0.64	0.77	0.57	0.53	0.74	0.68	0.70
E	0	0.13	0.09	0.17	0.31	0.31	0.26	0.43
EU	0.55	0.64	0.51	0.57	0.62	0.59	0.31	0.44
F	0.46	0.57	0.50	0.59	0.61	0.43	0.46	0.57
FIN	0.42	0.47	0	0.17	0.91	0.38	0.57	0.62
GER	0.59	0.78	0.82	0.95	0.81	0.39	0.31	0.60
GR	0.62	0.71	0.43	0.53	0.05	0	0.20	0.30
I	0.48	0.59	0.30	0.37	0.30	0.18	0	0.14
IRL	0.59	0.30	0.69	0.46	1.00	0.95	0.18	0.18
JP	0.95	1.02	0.73	1.02	1.00	0.97	0.78	0.72
L	1.00	1.03	1.00	1.06	0.15	0.38	0.56	0.82
NL	0.86	0.84	0.76	0.84	0.31	0.22	0.32	0.41
P	0.77	0.91	0.76	0.85	0.65	0.57	0.27	0.66
S	0.60	0.84	0.57	0.52	0.92	0.20	0.54	1.01
UK	0.76	0.59	0.58	0.45	0.54	0.15	0.49	0.55
USA	0.87	0.74	0.41	0.58	0.98	0.41	1.00	0.96
Stand Deviation	0.24	0.24	0.27	0.27	0.30	0.26	0.25	0.26
Mean	0.66	0.69	0.58	0.61	0.59	0.41	0.42	0.57
Median	0.63	0.72	0.63	0.57	0.57	0.38	0.39	0.59

Source: original data series from Table 6. Benchmark (1.00) = top performing country on indicator in year 1997; lowest performoer in 1992 or 1997 = «0». No minimum value.

in the individual Member States resulted in an overall negative trend. It is primarily the result, as we bave seen in the previous sections, of the decline in employment growth and increase in unemployment during the period.

Whereas the overall performance ranking slightly decreased from 1 to 0.82 in the period 1992-1997, anyway there were a number of shifts in the Member Countries. Two countries with high performance scores in 1997 (Austria and UK, with 1.53 and 1.56, respectively) had only intermediate scores in 1992 (1.35 and 1.17, respectively), whereas two other countries with only intermediate scores in 1997 (Luxembourg and Portugal, with 1.05 and 1.31, respectively) belonged to the group of top performers in 1992 (1.65 and 1.79, respectively). The German SMOP index value, that was only slightly below the 1.5 level in 1992, decreased to 1.07 in 1997

TABLE 8

COMPOSITE INDICATORS OF PERFORMANCE (SMOP), TOTAL, EMPLOYMENT, AND UNEMPLOYMENT, 1997 AND 1992

Countries	1997	1992	1997	1992	1997	1992
	employment		*unemployment*		*total*	
B	0.18	0.18	0.40	0.46	0.58	0.64
DK	1.16	0.90	0.99	0.88	2.15	1.78
D	0.30	0.58	0.77	0.89	1.07	1.47
GR	0.20	0.12	0.18	0.25	0.38	0.37
E	0.06	0.05	0.04	0.12	0.11	0.17
F	0.36	0.36	0.51	0.58	0.88	0.95
IRL	0.46	0.14	0.69	0.39	1.15	0.53
I	0.03	0.08	0.13	0.18	0.15	0.27
L	0.22	0.35	0.83	1.30	1.05	1.65
NL	0.51	0.39	0.59	0.62	1.10	1.01
A	0.54	0.64	0.99	0.70	1.53	1.35
P	0.59	0.68	0.72	1.11	1.31	1.79
FIN	0.63	0.45	0.38	0.32	1.01	0.77
S	0.92	1.38	0.85	0.76	1.77	2.14
UK	0.87	0.80	0.69	0.36	1.56	1.17
EU	0.32	0.38	0.49	0.62	0.82	1.00
JP	0.79	0.98	1.49	1.72	2.28	2.71
USA	1.26	0.95	1.29	0.88	2.55	1.82

Source: employment and unemployment composite indicators (SMOPs) based on area of polygon formed by data points of radar charts (averaging).

(Table 8). As yet said, Denmark and Sweden are the two top ranking EU Member States, with a total SMOP in 1997 of 2.15 and
1.77, respectively.

Although individual European countries score better than the
US and Japan on most dimensions, a comparison of the composite
results for the EU, the US and Japan for the year 1997 show that
the latter two countries achieve markedly higher overall performance ratings on the total composite indicator and on its separate employment and unemployment components. For the four
unemployment indicators examined, the performance of the EU
surpasses that of the US only in youth unemployment and that of

GRAPH 4

EU LABOUR MARKET PERFORMANCE, 1997 AND 1992

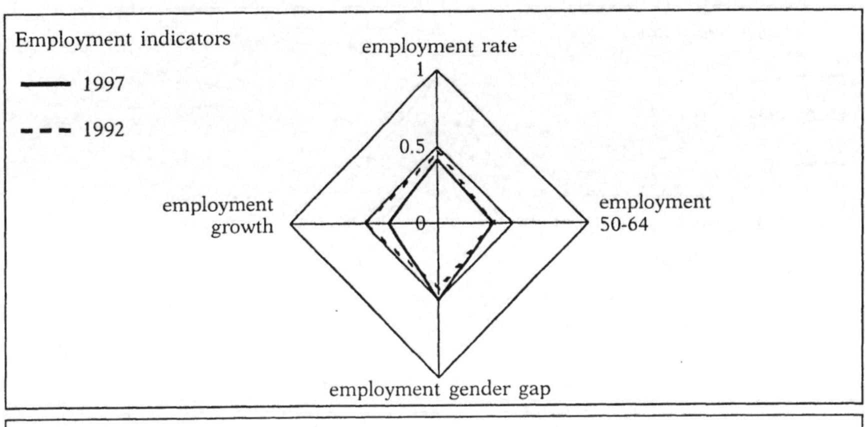

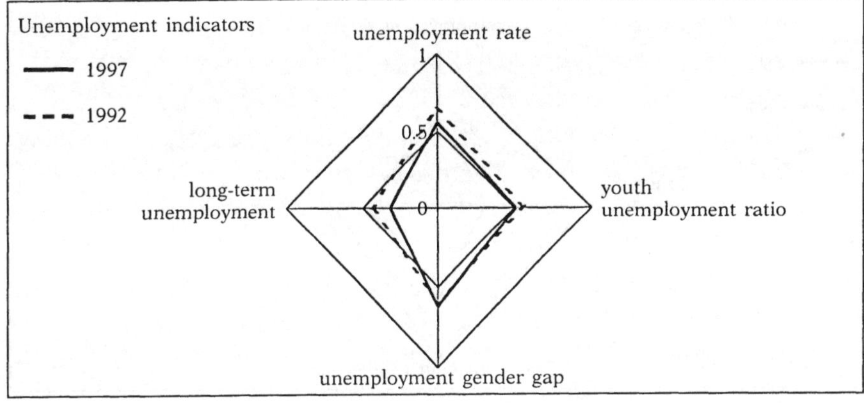

Japan in no case. In the other dimensions of unemployment examined (unemployment rate, long-term unemployment, unemployment gender gap) there is a wide performance gap between EU and both US and Japan. For the four employment indicators, the comparison is more favourable for the EU. Although there is a large gap in the employment rates, the performance of the EU surpasses that of Japan on the gender gap in employment and shows only slightly lower rates of employment growth during the past 5 years. By contrast, there is a marked gap to the US on all dimensions of relative performance (Table 8 and Graphs 4 and 5).

GRAPH 5

LABOUR MARKET PERFORMANCE
IN THE EUROPEAN UNION, USA AND JAPAN, 1997

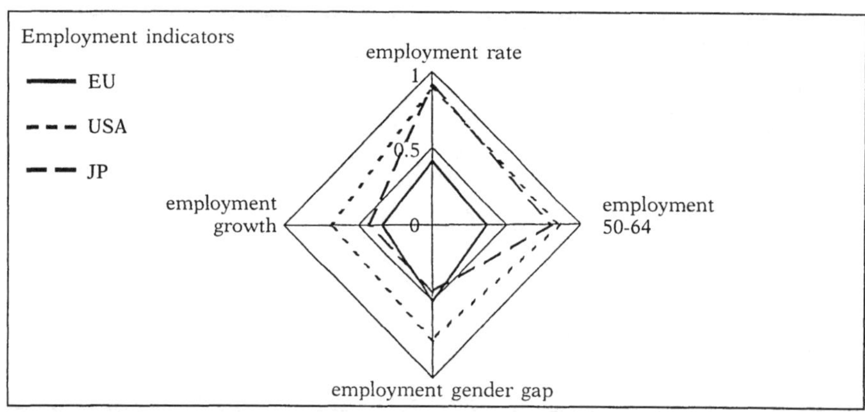

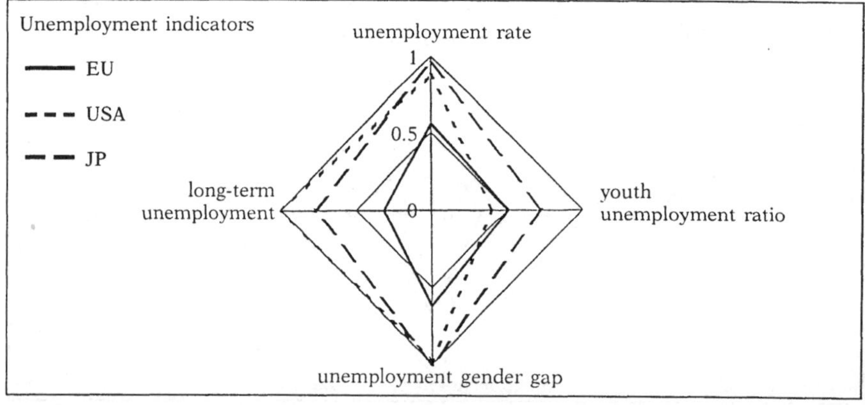

Table 8 also reports the component employment and unemployment indicators separately. While Spain, Italy, and Greece form a distinct group of worst performers (SMOP 0.25) on both sets of performance indicators in 1997, only Sweden and Denmark, among the group of four best EU-performers, are also among the top performers in both categories in 1997, together with US and Japan.

3. - The European Strategy to Improve Employment

As we said in the foreword, on the basis of the *Employment Rates Report 1988* prepared by the European Commission and the *National Action Plans* implemented by the Member States according to the *1998 Empoyment Guidelines*, a «Joint Report 1998» on *Employment Policies in the EU and the Member States* was adopted by the Social Affair Council and the ECOFIN Council on the 1st of December 1998. This document together with the *1999 Employment Guidelines* are to be analysed in the following sections. In doing so, we must keep in mind that during this year, each Member State has submitted to the Council and to the Commission one implementation report, comprising the implementation of the 1998 National Action Plan, and describing the adjustments made to it to take into account the changes introduced by the 1999 Guidelines. On the basis of its evaluation of the Member States' implementation reports, the European Commission has made its proposals for the *Joint Employment Report 1999* and the revised *Employment Guidelines for the Year 2000*, where many of the suggestions contained in *the Manifesto* have been taken into account.

3.1 *The «Joint Report» and the «Employment Guidelines»*

The *Joint Report* (both for 1998 and 1999) is a progress report that presents a first assessment of how Member States have implemented into action the *Employment Guidelines* and their *Na-*

tional Action Plans (*NAPs*). As it was stressed in *the Manifesto*, it is recognised that employment creation is strongly related to GDP growth. Over the last 20 years, and 3 economic cycles, there has been a very close relationship between the rate of GDP growth and the change in employment. According to this long-term trend, GDP growth of 2% (or over) a year is needed for job creation. This very stable 2% trend at the Union level does not reflect differences between Member States, and high or low employment rates cannot easily be related to the level of per capita income of a country. In fact, three of the countries with low employment rates (Spain, Ireland and Greece) are among the countries with below average per capita GDP in the Union. On the other hand, Belgium has a low employment rate and is among the most prosperous Member States, while three of the five countries with the highest employment rates (Portugal, UK and Sweden) have levels of income per head below or around the EU average. In any case, the Commission stresses that economic policies, both macro-economic and structural measures on the demand side, encourage economic activity.

Since 1996, the EU economy is growing faster than in the past and a small net job creation has allowed some catching-up on the job losses of the period 1985-1995. Yet, many challenges remain. Job creation is insufficient and the employment rate is low, unemployment is falling slowly and long-term unemployment is high. Little progress has been made in combating youth unemployment. As we have seen in the preceding sections, compared with US and Japan, the EU shows a markedly worse labour market performance.

Anyway, after the *Luxembourg Process* began in 1998, the transparency and political profile of the debate on employment policy has risen in many Member States and at EU level. It is our opinion that the *Manifesto* greatly contributed to the success of this strategy in this last year. In the Member States, employment policy co-ordination is improving and new inter-departmental structures, in some cases at a regional level, have been set up. Social patterns as well as local and regional authorities are keen to participate and contribute to the formulation and monitoring of the *National Action Plans* (NAPs), and this has led to new joint initiatives involving the social patterns. This includes making the strategy more concrete in budgetary terms. From this point of view, Member States should restructure public expenditure to make spending on employment measures more effective and targeted than in the past, as the situation now varies greatly among Member States. For instance, France (1.4% of GDP) and Spain (1.2% of GDP) provide an overall and detailed estimate of funding their NAPs, whereas Belgium, The Netherlands and Luxembourg report on additional public spending required (0.7%, 0.55% and 0.35% of GDP, respectively). Ireland has also provided a preliminary estimate of expenditure amounting to 2% of GDP, while other Member States specify the funding only for some measures and initiatives, but give no overall estimate.

The Luxembourg process to combat unemployment and promote employment policies, as has been implemented by the *Employment Guidelines*, is based on four pillars: I) improving employability, II) developing entrepreneurship, III) encouraging adaptability of businesses and their employees, and IV) strengthening the policies for equal opportunities, between women and men. Thus, in drawing up their NAPs, Member States must take into account these four pillars, so as to fully exploit the new possibilities opened up by information and communication technologies for job creation, employability, more flexible and adaptable forms of work organisation and progress on equal opportunities. In the following sections, we discuss these four pillars as regards to 1998, as well as to 1999, and their implementation made by NAPs up to now.

3.2 *Pillar I: Improving Employability*

According to the EU *Employment Guidelines*, in order to influence the trend in youth and long term-unemployed, the Member States must intensify their efforts to develop preventive and employability-oriented strategies. Within a maximum period of four years, Member States should ensure that every unemployed young person is offered a new start before reaching six months of unemployment, in the form of training, retraining, work practice, a job or other employability measure; in the same way, unemployed adults are also offered a fresh start before reaching twelve months of unemployment by one of the aforementioned means or, more generally, by accompanying individual vocational guidance. These preventive and employability measures, should be combined with measures to promote the re-employment of the long-term unemployed.

Anyway, as suggested in the *Manifesto*, a transition from passive measures to active measures of intervention is necessary. To this regard, benefit, tax and training systems, if necessary, must be reviewed and adapted to ensure that they actively support employability. To pursue this aim, each Member State will endeavour to increase significantly the number of persons benefiting from active measures to improve their employability. In order to increase the number of unemployed who are offered training or any similar measure, it will in particular fix a target, in the light of its starting situation, of gradually achieving the average of the most successful Members States, and at least 20%.

To these regards, while Denmark, Spain, France, Luxembourg, Portugal, Finland and Sweden have fully addressed the preventive targets defined in the *Guidelines*, others have interpreted them more flexibly (Belgium, Ireland, The Netherlands and UK). More focused efforts are needed in countries where the dual training system has been the main instrument for prevention (Germany, Austria). Finally, in Italy and Greece, where policy is mainly focused on the social re-insertion of people after long spells of unemployment, there is now a strong pofitical commitment to switch to a more preventive approach.

As regards to the activation of 20% of the unemployed, six countries (Denmark, Germany, Sweden, Finland, Ireland and UK) claim to have already met the objective; Belgium and The Netherlands set no clear targets, while the other countries (Portugal, Spain, Luxembourg, France, Austria, Italy and Greece) have set a target in line with or above 20% on the basis of their own estimates.

In addition to these measures, in the context of a policy for active ageing, it is important to develop measures such as maintaining working capacity, lifelong learning and other flexible working arrangement, so that older workers are also able to participate actively in working life. The social partners are also urged to conclude as soon as possible agreements with a view to increasing the possibilities for training, work experience, traineeships or other measures like to promote employability, such as lifelong learning, particularly in the fields of information and communications technologies, and improving the quality of their school system. In this context, a special attention must be reserved to the needs of the disabled, ethnic minorities, immigrants and other groups of individuals who may be disadvantaged.

As regards to these policies, all Member States have addressed the need to reduce the proportion of young people leaving the basic education and training without a minimum level of qualification, mainly through relative comprehensive reforms of their basic education systems. In any case, the Commission underlines the need for efforts to be pursued in the direction of a real switch of labour market policies from passive to active measures and from curative to preventative approach in all Member States, in the same way as it is suggested in *the Manifesto*. In this respect, a first success may be achieved in cutting the rate of inflow into long-term unemployed.

3.3 *Pillar II: Developing Entrepreneurship*

The development of new enterprises, and the growth of small and medium-sized enterprises (SMEs), especially in the less developed areas, as it was pointed out in *the Manifesto*, is essential for job creation and for the expansion of training opportunities for young people. This process must be promoted by encouraging greater entrepreneurial awareness across society, by providing a clear, stable and predictable set of rules and improving the conditions for the development of risk capital markets. The Member States should reduce and simplify the administrative and tax burdens on SMEs, giving particular attention to reduce significantly the overhead costs and administrative burdens for businesses, especially when an enterprise is being set up and when hiring additional workers; accordingly, they should reform tax and social security regimes in order to encourage self-employment and the setting up of small businesses as well as promoting training for entrepreneurship and targeted support services for entrepreneurs.

In other words, according to the suggestions of *the Manifesto*, the taxation system must be made more employment friendly, reversing the long-term trend towards higher taxes and charges on labour, which have increased from 35% in 1980 to more than 42% in 1995. To this regard, each Member State should set a target for gradually reducing the overall tax burden and, where appropriate, a target for gradually reducing the fiscal pressure on labour and non-wage labour costs, in particular on unskilled and low-paid labour, without jeopardising the recovery of public finances or the financial equilibrium of social security schemes, and examine the advisability of reducing the rate of VAT on labour-intensive services not exposed to cross-border competition.

According to the *Guidelines*, the Member States should also promote measures to fully exploit the possibilities offered by job creation at local level, in the social economy, in the area of environmental technologies and in new activities linked to needs not yet satisfied by the market, and reduce any obstacle in the way of such measures.

The key role played by SMEs is recognised by Member States; many initiatives have addressed their specific problems by simplifying administrative procedures for business, promoting business start-ups, enhancing job creation in new services, and facilitating access to capital or innovative projects. One promising course of action is the creation of «one-stop shops» for business start-ups when dealing with the State (Italy, Portugal, Luxembourg, France), support to business start-ups and self-employment (Austria, Belgium, The Netherlands, Sweden and Germany), and financial support for hiring the first employee (France, Spain). Several countries (Finland, Italy, and UK) have developed partnerships between local authorities and entrepreneurs in exploiting business opportunities and the social economy. Some progress has been made towards reducing social security charges and, more generally, the overall tax burden on labour. Major reforms were announced or have started to be implemented in Denmark, Spain, The Netherlands, Finland, Belgium, Italy, France and Ireland. But, the approach is somewhat gradual and there is a need to give a new political impulse to restructuring taxation systems. As regards to the suggested VAT reduction on labour-intensive services, this has not yet found any support among the majority of the Member States.

3.4 *Pillar III. Encouraging Adaptability of Businesses and Their Employees*

In order to promote the modernisation of work organisation and the diversification of various forms of work, the EU documents suggest to develop a strong partnership at all appropriate levels (European, national, sectoral, local and enterprise levels). In this regard, the *Employment Guidelines* stress the need for the social partners to negotiate agreements to modernise the organisation of work, including flexible working arrangements, with the aim of making undertakings productive and competitive and, as it was stressed in *the Manifesto*, achieving the required balance between flexibility and security. Such agreements may cover the expression of working time as an annual figure, the reduction of working hours, the reduction of overtime, the development of part-time working, life-long training and career breaks. It is also stressed, like in the *Manifesto*, that each Member State should examine the possibility of incorporating in its law more adaptable types of contract, taking into account the fact that forms of employment are increasingly diverse.

Furthermore, in order to renew skill levels within enterprises, Member States should remove the obstacles, in particular tax obstacles, to investment in human resources and possibly provide for tax or other incentives for the development of in-house train-

ing; they will also examine new regulations and review the existing regulatory framework to make sure they will contribute to reducing barriers to employment and helping the labour market
adapt to structural change in the economy.

The implementation of this pillar by Member States has promoted a process of reforms and policy initiatives that have been
signposted in the *National Action Plans* (NAPs), in order to bring
about a higher degree of flexibility in productive systems and
working relations in a changing environment. Human resources
development for the updating of skills and the promotion of new
competences is receiving particular attention in all Member States.
In some countries (Germany, Spain, and Italy), the NAPs have encouraged social partners to be more active and to adopt a more
comprehensive approach to modernising work organisation, even
in the course of often difficult and lengthy negotiations.

Partly as a result of the Luxembourg process, attention has
now been focused on new rounds of negotiations covering key issues such as a more encouraging framework for in-house training (France, Luxembourg, Portugal, Spain, Sweden, Finland, Italy
Greece and The Netherlands), the reduction and reorganisation of
working time (France, Luxembourg), and, as it was suggested in
the Manifesto, the adaptation of labour legislation to more flexible forms of contracts (Portugal, Finland, Spain, Italy, Luxembourg, Greece). The need to reconcile flexibility and security has
been the object of specific reforms in The Netherlands and Spain.

3.5 *Pillar IV: Strengthening Equal Opportunities Policies for Women and Men*

As we have seen in the preceding sections when discussing
on the EU employment rates, women still have some problems in
gaining access to the employment market, in career advancement,
in earnings and reconciling professional and family life. It is therefore important to ensure that active labour market policies are
made available for women in proportion to their share of unemployment, to reduce tax-benefit disincentives, because of their neg-

ative effect on the female labour supply, to give particular attention to obstacles which hinder women who wish to set up new business or become self-employed, and to ensure that women are able to benefit positively from flexible forms of work organisation.

Therefore, the Member States are invited to adopt a gender-mainstreaming approach in implementing the guidelines of all four pillars, and translate their desire to promote equality of opportunity into increased employment rates for women. They should also pay attention to the imbalance in the representation of women or men in certain economic sectors and occupations, as well as to the improvement of female career opportunities; they will initiate positive steps to promote equal pay for equal work or work of equal value and to diminish differentials in income between women and men.

In order to reconcile work with family life, policies on career breaks, parental leave and part-time work, as well as flexible working arrangements which serve the interests of both the employers and the employees, are of particular importance. Implementation of the various directives and social-partners agreements in this area should be accelerated and monitored regularly. There must be an adequate provision of good quality care for children and other dependents in order to support women's and men's entry and continued participation in the labour market.

Finally, an equal sharing of family responsibilities is crucial in this respect. In order to strengthen equal opportunities, Member States and social partners should also design, implement and promote family-friendly policies, including affordable, accessible and high quality care services for children and other dependents, as well as parental and other leave schemes.

To these regards, preparing and implementing the NAPs has raised awareness of the importance of equal opportunities policies for women and men, as well as policies addressing the particular needs of people with disabilities. The labour market is highly segregated, even in Member States where employment rates are similar between genders (Sweden, Finland). Both women and men find it difficult to re-enter the labour market after a period of absence, as they may have problems of reduced employability due to outmoded skills. The employment rate of the disabled is 20-30% below the average and persons disabled represent a disproportionate share of the long-term unemployed.

4. - Final Remarks

Except for Spain, Portugal, Sweden and Austria, in general this fourth pillar has not yet received a large implementation by the Member States. Most initiatives address problems of childcare, with fewer measures aiming at supporting for female entrepreneurs. In some countries (Spain, UK, Italy, the Netherlands and Portugal), tax subsides and benefits help to make the costs of childcare affordable, whereas Austria, The Netherlands, UK and Luxembourg have set concrete targets for the provision of nursery and childcare facilities. Assistance to the elderly and other family dependents receives hardly any attention, which is in clear contradiction to the ageing of the EU's population.

Finally, a more decisive action by Member States is required for policies designed to reconcile work and family life, and for policies addressing the particular needs of disabled people. Some progress in this direction is envisaged in Spain, France, Austria, Portugal, Sweden and UK. Similarly, the Member States should adopt specific measures to guarantee equal opportunities for immigrant population.

BIBLIOGRAPHY

[1] COUNCIL OF THE UE, *The 1998 Employment Guidelines*, Luxembourg, Office for Official Publications of the European Communities, 1998.

[2] — - —, *The 1999 Employment Guidelines*, Luxembourg, Office for Official Publications of the European Communities, 1999.

[3] EUROPEAN COMMISSION, *Employment Policies in the EU and in the Member States: Joint Report 1998*, Luxembourg, Office for Official Publications of the European Communities, 1999.

[4] — - —, *Joint Employment Report 1999*, Luxembourg, Office for Official Publications of the European Communities, 9 September 1999.

[5] — - —, *Employment Rates Report 1998: Employment Performance in the Member States*, Luxembourg, Office for Official Publications of the European Communities, 1998.

[6] — - —, *Modernising Public Employment Services to support the European Employment Strategy*, Luxembourg, Office for Official Publications of the European Communities, 1998.

[7] — - —, *Proposal for Guidelines for Member States' Employment Policies 2000*, Luxembourg, Office for Official Publications of the European Communities, 9 September 1999.

[8] — - —, *Recommendation for Council Recommendations on the Implementation of Member States' Employment Policies*, Luxembourg, Office for Official Publications of the European Communities, 9 September 1999.

[9] EUROPEAN UNION, *1999 National Action Plan for Employment*, Luxembourg, Office for Official Publications of the European Communities, 1999, Various Member States.

[10] MODIGLIANI F. - FITOUSSI J.P. - MORO B. - SNOWER D. - SOLOW R. - STEINHERR A. - SYLOS LABINI P., *An Economists' Manifesto on Unemployment in the European Union*, «Banca Nazionale del Lavoro Quarterly Review», vol. 206, September 1998.

[11] MOSLEY H. - MAYER A., *Benchmarking National Labour Market Performance: A Radar Chart Approach, Final Report*, Report prepared for European Commission, December 1998.

Productivity and Job Creation in US and Europe

Robert M. Solow
MIT, Cambridge (Mass)

The main topic previously dealed in the *Rivista di Politica Economica* was the contrast between a decade or more of high unemployment in Europe and a somewhat shorter period of low, even falling, unemployment in the US. In the course of my talk then I referred in passing to a group of studies of comparative economic performance in Europe and the US, recently carried out by the McKinsey Global Institute with the participation of some European and American economists. I mentioned those studies in one rather special context.

In comparing economic performance, industry by industry, across major economies, one sees immediately that job creation in the 1990s was very weak in France, Germany and the UK but very strong in the US. From both a scientific and a policy-oriented standpoint, it is vital to understand the causes of this difference. It is fair to say that in Europe the dominant opinion is that it is nothing but a symptom of greater labor-market rigidity in Europe. The only way to deal with the problem, therefore, is to make labor markets more flexible, and that is all that is needed. I was arguing against that position, and claiming that rigidity and over-regulation of the labor market was only a part of the problem, so that achieving labor-market flexibility could be only part of the solution.

Among other things, some of which I plan to discuss in a moment, the McKinsey studies asked experienced expert consultants and industry participants what they perceived to be the underlying causes of poor industrial performance. With almost no exceptions, they judged labor-market problems and deficient skills to be at most a minor factor. Since these were not people one would normally expect to adopt trade-union or social-democratic or similar views as a matter of habit. I proposed this finding as one piece of evidence that the conventional European analysis is inadequate. But then what does appear to be the main underlying cause of weak industrial productivity performance in Europe? That is the subject of this talk.

The main vehicle of the McKinsey studies was a group of cross country case studies of selected industries. In each case the focus was on recent performance as measured by productivity and job creation. We were very careful to include some service-sector industries, as you will see, and not to make the mistake of confining the comparisons to traditional manufacturing. Unfortunately for our purposes here, I will have to talk mainly about comparisons among the US, France and Germany, and occasionally Japan. The group has also studied Korea and Brazil, and is now working on Russia, but it has never extended its analysis to Italy. Maybe it should.

The fact that our coverage of industries and countries is far from complete does not matter so much, because our interest is not primarily in just observing, documenting and measuring differences in productivity and job creation, but rather in trying to understand the deeper causes of those differences. The lessons learned from these case studies undoubtedly carry over to a much broader context.

I will not go into detail about the methods the team has used in its work, except to remind you that they appeal both to careful collection and analysis of the usual statistical data and to the expert judgment of McKinsey consultants experienced in each industry and of their associates in the industry itself. The series of original reports is available; and Martin Baily (who began as an academic advisor like me, then joined the McKinsey Global Institute for several years, and has just become the Chairman of the

Council of Economic Advisers in Washington) and I are currently preparing an article which will describe the approach much more fully.

I will begin with some more conventional comparisons of aggregate productivity. The aggregate concept we use is the "market sector", meaning what is left of GDP after government employment and output is excluded along with a few sectors like health care and education that are usually not conducted like ordinary industries. For international comparisons market-sector output and value added have to be deflated; for this purpose we use the appropriate sectoral purchasing-power-parity exchange rates.

The first graph (Graph 1) contains few surprises. Output per hour worked in the market sector of countries like France, Germany and the Netherlands was just a bit lower than in the US in the mid-1990s. The UK and Japan come in much lower, a good 30% less than in the US. The figure for Japan may be surprising at first, but the reasons for it will become clear as we go along. It would be interesting, to know where Italy fits into this picture, but the work has not been done. Brazil and Korea are less than half as productive as the US, and the scope of the Russian disaster is obvious.

The bottom half of the graph makes similar comparisons for total factor productivity, where possible. "Total factor productivity" comes closer to measuring level of technology in each country, because it accounts separately for those differences in labor productivity that can be traced to differences in capital intensity. So we can say that France, Germany and Japan look a little worse in terms of total factor productivity than in labor productivity; the interpretation is that those countries make up for part of their deficiency in general efficiency by operating their industries in a more capital-intensive way than the US. Korea, on the other hand, looks better in terms of total factor productivity, because it gets along with less capital per worker than the US. Again, one can only speculate about Italy.

The second graph (Graph 2) gives some productivity comparisons for manufacturing industries. There is nothing very sur-

AGGREGATE PRODUCTIVITY COMPARISONS
indexed to US = 100

Labor productivity

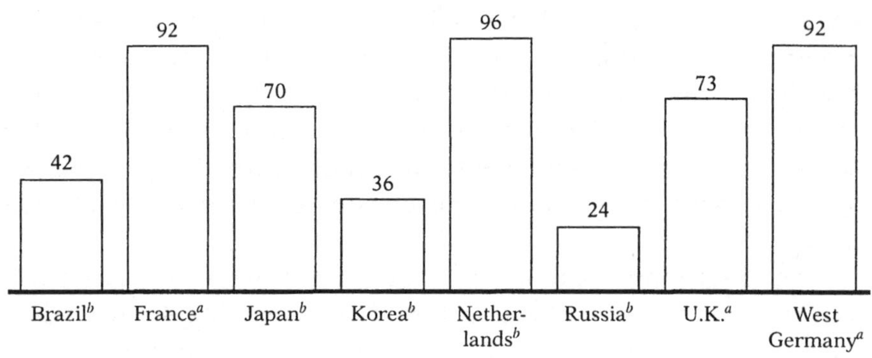

Total factor productivity

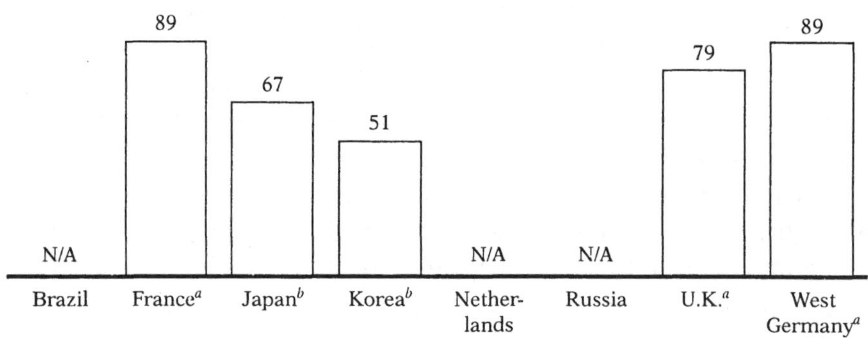

[a] Market sector, average 1994-1996 (1993-1995 for the Netherlands).
[b] Total economy, average 1993-1995 (1995 Brasil, 1997 Russia).
N/A: not available.
Source: MCKINSEGY GLOBAL INSTITUTE (1997a, 1997b, 1998b, 1998a).

prising here, but one extremely important point emerges. You will notice that Japanese labor productivity exceeds that in the US in such high-profile industries as automobiles, steel, consumer electronics and metalworking, usually by about 20%. In food processing, however, output per hour in Japan is only about one third

MANUFACTURING PRODUCTIVITY RELATIVE TO THE US BY COUNTRY

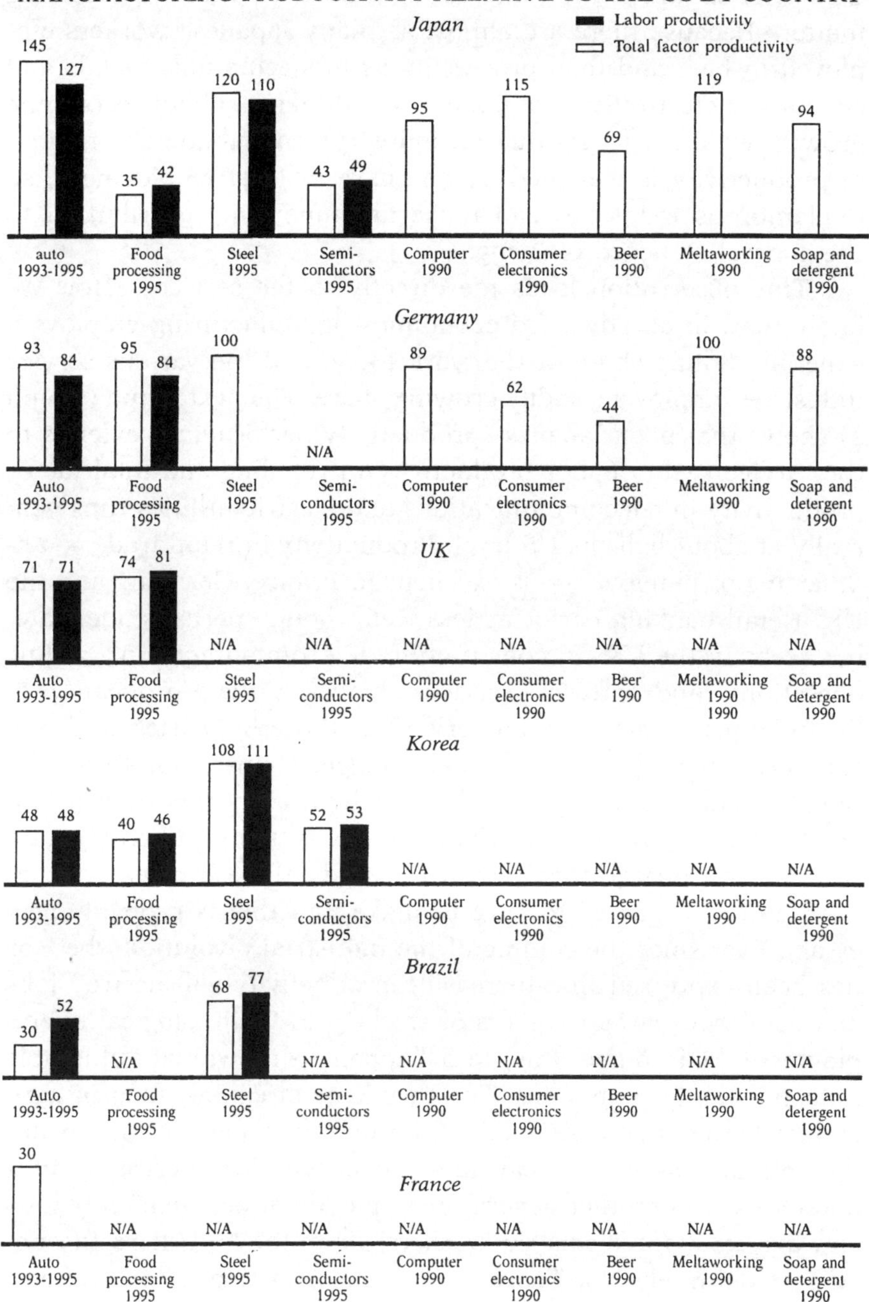

of the level achieved in the US (In Beer Japan is at 70% of the US). Why should such uninteresting industries of food processing matter? Because there are almost as many Japanese workers employed in beer and food processing as in steel, autos, metals and consumer electronics combined. In thinking about economic growth, we often forget that an industry's contribution to national productivity is weighted by its share of total employment, so unglamorous industries can make an important contribution to the general standard of living.

This observation leads me directly to the service sector. We know that, in all advanced economies, manufacturing employs a generally falling share of the work force, and the various service industries employ a steadily growing share. The next graph (Graph 3) shows that poor Japanese productivity performance extends to the service sector. Labor productivity in retailing and total factor productivity in telecommunications and electric utilities runs generally at about half the US level. Productivity in retail trade — another major employer — is excellent in France, Germany and the UK. Retail banking performs less well, though perhaps adequately, except in the UK. In construction, telecommunications, airline operations, and software services, however, the European productivity performance is not very good; those industries, and presumably some others, could make a bigger contribution to the national standard of living, and that is why it is so important to understand what are the underlying causes of the productivity gap.

Before I turn to that part of the study, there is a remark that I am almost ashamed to have to make, but that is probably necessary. Ever since the coming of the industrial revolution, the fear has been expressed that increasing productivity will destroy jobs and condermn large numbers of workers to "technological unemployment". Of course, this does happen to individual vulnerable industries and occupations. The shrinkage of employment in agriculture is the great historically important example. But that is not the relevant issue: the real question is whether increasing productivity creates either general unemployment or a markedly lower wage level for displaced workers, or both. And there the answer is definitely No. There is no sign of lasting adverse effects

SERVICE SECTOR AND CONSTRUCTION PRODUCTIVITY RELATIVE TO THE US BY COUNTRY

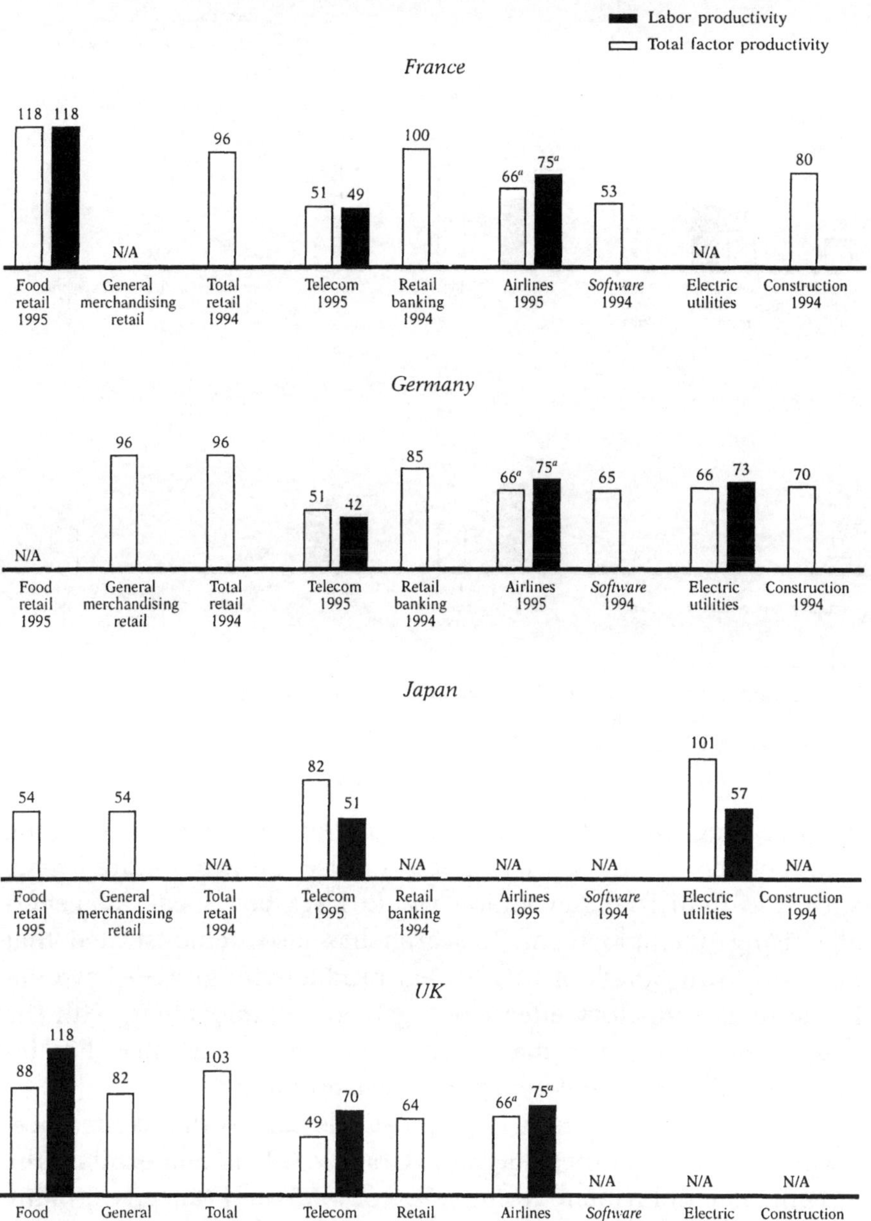

GRAPH 3 *continued*

SERVICE SECTOR AND CONSTRUCTION PRODUCTIVITY
RELATIVE TO THE US BY COUNTRY

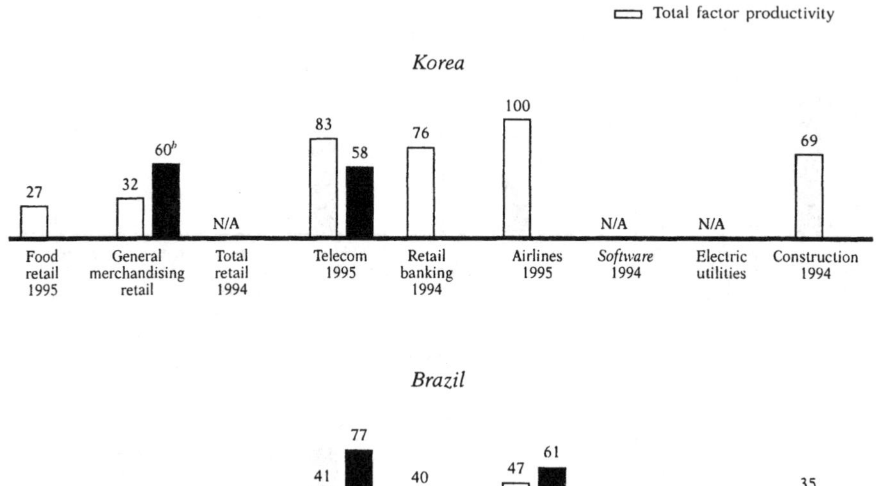

[a] Estimated fot he major European carriers as a group.
[b] Routh estimate only.
Source: MGI analysis.

of increasing productivity on aggregate employment. In the long run, there could not be such effects, or else the two hundred years since the Industrial Revolution would have been years of generally rising unemployment. Research has also demonstrated that even shortrun bursts of accelerated productivity growth have only the most transitory effects on aggregate employment, with the effect wearing off in a matter of a year on two at most. For individuals, displacement remains a real problem.

To put this point in a form most relevant to this conference, I will show you another diagram (Graph 4). This one exhibits the growth of employment from 1970 to 1995 in France, Germany and the US. Business-cycle fluctuations are clearly visible, but they

GRAPH 4

NET JOB CREATION BY SECTOR 1970-1995
CUMULATIVE JOBS CREATED PER 100 OF WORKING AGE POPULATION*

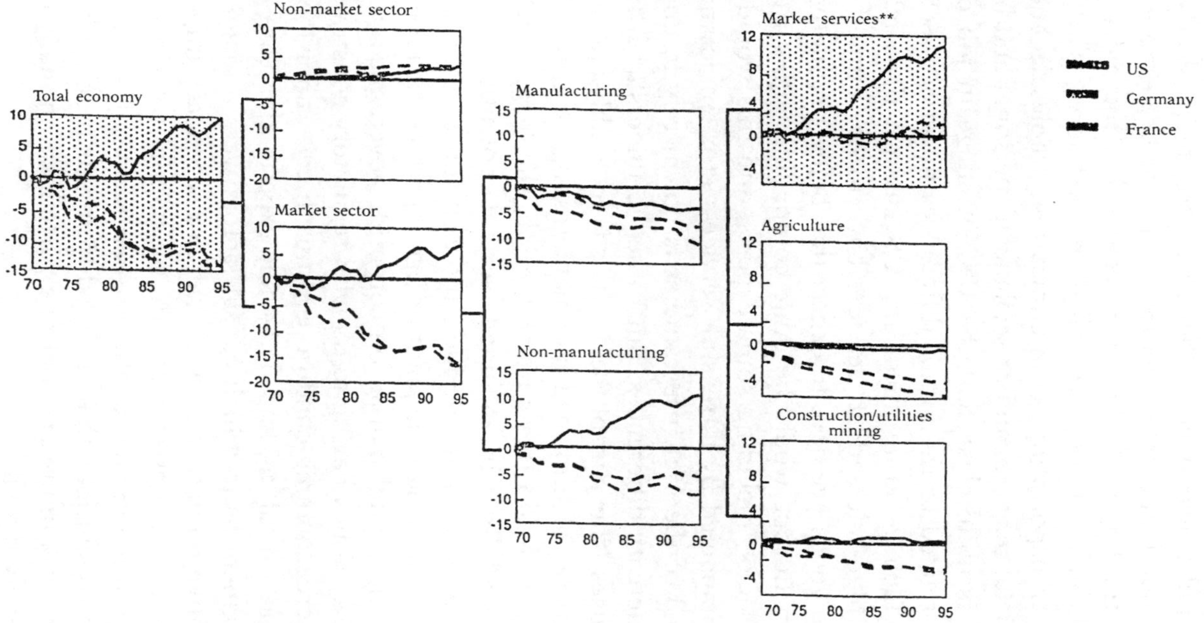

* Adjusted for hours worked and *part-time* and growth of working age population.
** Market services include transportation, communications, wholesale and retail trade, finance, insurance, real estate, and services.

Source: ISDB, OECD, *National Accounts*, OECD, *Employment Outlook*, national statistics, McKinsey.

are not the main part of the story. One sees that the US experience differs from that of France and Germany primarily in the market sector, and within the market sector primarily in the non-manufacturing part of the economy. (Employment in manufacturing has fallen everywhere, though a little more slowly in the US). In the non-manufacturing area, there has been more net job creation in the US in all three sub-sectors, but the most striking difference is in what we have called "market services" including things like transportation, communication, wholesale and retail trade, financial services, and miscellaneous personal and business services. It is quite clear that the US advantage in job creation can not be related to the minor differences in service-sector productivity, which generally favor the US anyway. Especially now that many high-value-added services have to be counted among the tradable goods, we have to expect that better productivity performance in Europe would be quite compatible with an expanded service sector, including some exports, and this would probably be accompanied by intreasing service-sector employment.

The goal of the McKinsey studies is not merely to document these productivity differences, but rather to understand their immediate causes. This part of the analysis is inevitably partially subjective, a matter of informed judgment resting on many detailed facts. In trying to do this part of the job, the team developed a standard check-list. It included several potential plant-level sources of differences in productivity, went on to characteristics of the markets in which the plant or firm operates, including pressures from the capital market on corporate governance, and then to higlier-level issues having to do with regulatory constraints and general macroeconomic conditions. In each case, after looking at the facts and consulting knowledgeable experts, the team tried to form a judgment as to which causal factors were a major source of comparative differences, which were of secondary importance, and which seemed not to play any substantial role in observed productivity differences. It is obvious that I can not try to describe the detailed conclusions that emerged from this process; but I can report the overall impressions of one participant in many of these studies, namely myself.

One important conclusion has already been mentioned. On the whole, characteristics of the relevant labor markets played a distinctly minor role in accounting for the observed productivity gaps and the consequent differences in job creation. This result was too general to be just a quirk of our particular choice of industries to be studied. It does not mean that labor-market reform is unimportant, only that it can not be the main agenda for economic policy.

A second broad conclusion from our analysis of causality is that the important causal factors at the plant level are matters of management. It does not appear to be the case that deficiencies in productivity can be traced to deficiencies in technological knowledge. Firms in advanced economies have access, as economists say, to the same "production function" as the "best-practice" firms in their industry. Nor is it the case that European and Japanese firms suffer generally from low capital-intensity; their labor is not unproductive because not equipped with enough in the way of machinery. In fact, as we saw earlier, in some cases European and Japanese firms make up for some of their lower total factor productivity by operating more capital-intensively than their counterparts in the US.

Then what is important? In most cases, the team traced plant-level productivity gaps to a factor that they called "organization of functions and tasks". The concrete meaning of this factor differs from case to case, of course; sometimes it may refer to plant layout, sometimes to production scheduling, sometimes to choice of product mix or to the proliferation of products, sometimes to the interplay between marketing functions and production, sometimes to the organization of decision-making within the firm in other ways. What all these have in common is that they refer to the things that managers do.

(A dozen years ago I was part of a faculty group at MIT that made an analogous study of American manufacturing, at a time when Japanese superiority in some export industries set off a good deal of self-examination; we wrote up our results in a book called *Made in America* that was widely read, and led to parallel studies elsewhere. In that book we came to the same kind of conclusion that I just reported from the McKinsey studies: deficiencies in management practice, though not the same deficiencies we find in Europe, were the key factor in underperformance. American manufacturers seem to have improved a lot since then. Presumably Europeans can do the same.)

A different sort of issue, at a somewhat "higher" level, surfaced in our study of the telecommunications industry, especially telephone service. We found that the productivity advantage of US telephone systems traced to a significantly higher volume of calls, and thus a fuller utilization of network and switching capacity. In an industry with essentially zero marginal cost, utilization is naturally very important. We wondered if this could be just a matter of scale, or maybe a greater propensity of American teenagers and adults to chatter aimlessly. In the end we concluded that the ultimate cause might be a difference in pricing practices.

In most US regional or statewide systems, the price of an additional local call is essentially zero, matching the marginal cost. The system requires revenue, however, and much of this comes from a fixed charge for being connected to the system. This scheme certainly encourages use of the telephone, once it is connected to the network. The danger is that poor families may be cut off entirely because they can not afford the fixed charge. This danger can be met, and in many places is met, by regulations that require the company or the community to subsidize connection for those with low income. In Europe, the fixed connection charge is kept low, and revenue is provided by setting a price for each call appreciably higher than marginal cost. The predictable consequence is a lower volume of calling (and, of course, a weaker habit of using the telephone). This is a case where relatively low productivity is the consequence of decisions at the level of the market.

Another interesting chain of causality arises in the case of residential construction, where the Netherlands and the US are the productivity leaders. In dealing with the homebuilding industry, we have tried our best to make allowance for national differences both in consumer tastes and in standards of quality. It is hard to be precise in such matters, but there is no particular reason to expect that we have introduced a bias.

Construction is a case where scale matters, not so much the scale of the building enterprise as the scale of the building project. Scale economies arise when developers and construction companies can plan and build fairly large numbers of similar, not necessarily identical, houses at the same time. Therefore land-use policies are an important determinant of productivity in house-building. If good-sized plots of land are made available for building, the resulting economies of scale tend to raise productivity. In some European urban areas, land-use regulations limit availability to small tracts, suitable for only one or two buildings. This limitation may reflect true local preferences — though that would be more convincing if both options were actually available to consumers — but the lesson for productivity remains.

Since construction employs several categories of skilled workers, one might suspect that this might be a case where the labor market plays a decisive role. Our conclusion was rather different, however. Many manual skills appear to be learned on the job, even in the most productive-cases. There are two qualifications to this, however. Large construction projects require management and co-ordination skills which may not be available; and certain skilled specialized trades can best be managed if the organization of the industry allows such workers to be brought into a site just when their skills are needed, after which they move to another job. Both of these exceptions, however, seem to us to come under the heading of scale economies and management advantages, not to be achieved by anything one would describe as "labor-market flexibility".

Finally I come to an important conclusion that emerged first in our studies of manufacturing industries. We believe, however, that the same will apply to those modern service sectors that are already playing, or will soon play, a role in international trade.

It seems to be a good generalization that exposure to active competition, especially exposure to direct competition from firms that embody current best practice and highest productivity, is the surest way to force domestic firms to achieve high productivity on their own. Conversely, a domestic industry that is protected from competition, either by regulations that limit the options of domestic rivals or by tariffs, quotas or other devices that limit import competition, is very likely to fall behind the highest standards of productivity and product design.

At any moment in a given industry, even in an economy as large as the us best-practice producer is likely to be a foreign company. Exposure to competition with the world leader is an excellent incentive to improve domestic practices. This incentive can take the form of the need to protect market-share against imports, or to preserve sales in third markets against rivals, or to meet the competition of transplanted branch plants of the best-practice firm. In many ways, the need to fight off transplants sends the sharpest message to the domestic industry. That is probably because the exposure to best-practice is most direct, higher-productivity methods can be observed at first hand, and the excuse that foreign workers can do things that our own people can not do is visibly contradicted. The prize example of this process comes from the US automobile industry. General Motors, Ford and Chrysler were able to convince themselves that the Toyota manufacturing system could not be operated with American workers until transplanted Japanese factories showed that they could achieve near-Japanese levels of productivity in assembly using local labor.

I mentioned that this conclusion about causality emerged in a study of some manufacturing industries in Germany, Japan and the US. But something very similar can happen in the rapidly growing area of traded services. And even in non-tradable services, like retailing, the point about competition from foreign transplants retains its validity. In the case of retailing a very large employer, by the way-big advances in productivity often come from the adoption of new formats, new types of stores, new methods of adapting product design to market tastes, etc. Transplants are an effective way to spread these major innovations.

I have taken the time to outline some fairly general and persistent conclusions that have come out of the McKinsey studies. The full collection of studies includes very many cases with a great variety of detailed results about comparative facts and their likely causes. They do not lend themselves to summary in a short talk. But the underlying studies are available, and I hope many people will be moved to consult them. I will use my last few minutes to remind you of the main broad themes that emerge from these studies.

1) Inspection of conventional data and intensive case studies tell us that there are substantial productivity differences, industry by industry, between advanced economies, and of course between advanced economies and those just emerging into the world of modern industry. These productivity gaps need not be permanent; they arise from causes that can be changed.

2) These productivity differences are not confined to highly visible or high-tech industries. They are equally apparent in sectors like retailing and food processing. These sectors absorb a large fraction of the labor force in countries at every stage of development. Low productivity in these sectors, which is very common, can have major consequences for the overall standard of living on a national scale, precisely because employment in them is so large.

3) Service-sector productivity is important for the same reason, because their share of total employment is already large and still growing. It is possible to make progress with the measurement and analysis of productivity in the service sector. In general it appears to obey the same broad patterns as in goods-producing industries.

4) A large part of observed productivity gaps can be traced to deficiency in management practices, more so than deficiencies in labor skills or technology. In particular, the "organization of functions and tasks"» is often at fault.

5) If one tries to go one layer deeper, one finds that the incentives favoring state-of-the-art management practices are often weak, and sometimes obstructed by policy. This can happen because, the capital market does not adequately impose discipline on corporate governance, or because the side-effects of ill-judged regulations create obstacles to best-practice, or because competition is stifled in one way or another, by restrictions on land use, on foreign direct investment, or on untraditional products and services.

6) The last point is of a different kind. My academic colleagues

and I have found it difficult to get the macroeconomic perspective correctly represented in the McKinsey studies. This is because our McKinsey colleagues are very micro-oriented, only to be expected in a team oriented to management consulting. So at the very end I want to connect up with last year's Iseo conference, and remind you that actions aimed at improving productivity performance are almost always supply-side policies. They will be wasted, in whole or in part, unless fiscal and monetary policy do their share, and see to it that aggregate demand is strong enough to translate gains in productive potential into actual sales and production.

Working Hours and Employment

Riccardo Paternò
Università «Federico II», Napoli

Introduction

Although industry has been losing workers to the service sector in recent years, in manufacturing, the introduction of more and more complex technologies has in the meantime made the human capital «embodied» in each and every employee an increasingly important element, so that it becomes harder to replace such workers with others. On top of this, the pressing need to ensure full plant utilisation has altered the concept of full-time, which now no longer applies to just a daily or weekly basis but a monthly or yearly unit. It would be naïve to imagine, therefore, that a shorter working week for everyone would have major effects on employment. Those effects will actually differ quite considerably depending on the technology and organisational models firms adopt, on the type of workers concerned, and on the macroeconomic repercussions.

The problem, then, is not to decide «whether» there is a trade-off between working hours and employment, but to know in «what circumstances» it occurs, «how big» it is, «what» effect it produces at microeconomic and macroeconomic levels, and what connections exist between those two levels. We would be taking too narrow a view if we were not to look beyond analyses of the ini-

---

N.B. the number in square brackets refer to the *Bibliography* at the end of the paper.

tial microeconomic trade-offs, as the medium- to long-term macroeconomic repercussions might cancel or overcompensate any early, positive, short-term effect.

We will assume here a shortening of the working week, partly because it is the most widely discussed option and partly because it the solution expected, in theory, to produce the largest
impact on employment. So, if it is demonstrated that this type of
reduction has a very minor impact on employment, then any other form of reduction will at best have an identical if not a worse
effect.

1. - Microeconomic Analysis

An analysis of the trade-off between shorter working hours
and employment in a microeconomic context and with exogenous
aggregate demand involves closely related technical and econom-
ic/financial aspects.

1.1 *The «Technical» Aspects*

1.1.1 Contractual Working Hours and Actual Working Hours

We will start with a fairly marginal question. We all know that
one thing is «the number of — hours paid, — [and another is]
the number of hours actually worked, meaning the hours when
the worker is applied to the stock of capital»[1].

The first are the contractual working hours; the second, the
actual working hours, which are greater than the first when overtime is worked, and less than the first when hours are paid but
not worked, such as those lost through bank holidays, holiday
leave, sickness, strikes, unjustified absences (though not recorded
as such), breaks, labour hoarding, participation in trade union activities, and so on.

---

[1] See CASSONE A. [17].

While some types of absence exist irrespective of contractual working hours because they are connected with the economic cycle, general labour market conditions, existing labour law and so on[2], there is also a whole set of absences (various types of leave, sickness, some forms of typically female absenteeism, etc.) and other elements relating to work organisation (rest times and meal breaks, breaks at the start and end of work, labour hoarding[3], etc.) which probably depends on the amount of contractual working hours, in the sense that they increase the longer those working hours are, and vice versa.

If contractual working hours are not very long, not only will workers probably not need to «make use» of similar absences, that reduce actual working hours, but there should also gradually be a more than proportionate reduction in the various types of break that effectively represent «losses» in any form of work organisation[4].

So, if contractual working hours are not very long at the outset, reducing them might produce a much less than proportionate drop in actual working hours[5]. However, since production is linked to actual working hours, it is clear that if a reduction of contractual working hours leads to an insignificant decrease in actual working hours, all things being equal, there will be practically no scope for new job creation.

---

[2] For example, in Italy, from 1982/1983 it was possible to observe a sharp drop in the number of absences even though contractual working hours were largely unchanged. Briefly, a decrease in this type of absence is absolutely unrelated to any reduction of contractual working hours.

[3] This phenomenon occurs during cyclical downswings and is attributable to the fact that during such periods it may be to a firm's advantage to pay for work that is not performed rather than lay-off specially qualified staff that would be very costly to re-select, re-train and re-recruit during cyclical upswings. Of course, this only holds when it would not actually be even more advantageous to make them work all the same for stock-building purposes.

[4] Briefly, the elasticity of contractual working hours to actual working hours varies point by point, i.e. it decreases with a drop in actual working hours.

[5] In 1979, when annual contractual working hours were around 2,000, the rate of absence out of total workable hours was approximately 11%. In 1984, with approximately 1800 annual contractual working hours, the rate of absence dropped to around 7.7% and, according to a survey made in 1996 by the Unione Industriale of Turin, in 1995 out of a total of 1,661 theoretical annual working hours in the metal engineering sector, actual working hours were 1,587 and absences were down even further to 7.4%.

1.1.2 Technological Discontinuity and Overtime

The matter does not end here. We should not forget that whatever decrease in actual working hours occurs as a result of a reduction of contractual working hours, it can be offset sufficiently to keep total production at the same level (irrespective of any increases in productivity) either by recruiting new workers or by making greater use of overtime. Often, technological and institutional discontinuity can dissuade firms from taking on new workers or even make it impossible for them to do so.

As we know, in many firms[6] «given the same work organisation, shorter working hours (all other things being equal) reduce the length of time that equipment is used by the same percentage and hence also the firm's productive capacity. In some industries, (in fact) jobs are organised so that each machine has a corresponding, technically fixed number of workers. A system like this does not allow a reduction of working hours to be offset by increasing the number of people working simultaneously at the same machine»[7].

As a consequence, in cases like this firms can only react either by reorganising work so as to produce in fewer hours what was previously produced in more hours (for instance, by making work less «porous») or, if existing technology makes that impossible, then by using overtime[8] until the technology can be changed

---

[6] See OUDIZ G. - RAOUL E. - STERDYNIAK H. [44], p. 405.

[7] This means that if working hours are reduced by one a day (or by five hours all on the same day) what will happen is simply that - apart from what has already been said regarding contractual and actual working hours and what will be said further on concerning the change in productivity - the reduction cannot be offset by any increase in employment because if a production line requires, say, eight men working eight hours a day, one hour less on the part of each of these eight men cannot be made up by a new employee working the missing eight hours a day but should instead be made up by eight new employees working only one hour, the hour that was reduced. This, of course, is impossible (if the reduction is concentrated within a single day the terms of the problem do not change in any way).

[8] In Great Britain, for example, successive reductions of contractual working hours have been systematically offset by using overtime and this does not rule out the possibility that in the future what happened in that country may happen in other European Union countries. See DELL'ARINGA C. [25].

for one that that will allow habitual production levels to be maintained without changing employment by altering the capital/labour ratio[9].

1.1.3 *Working Hours, Productivity and Employment*

Having clarified this point, let us suppose, contrary to the conclusions just reached, that a reduction of contractual working hours can be transformed into an increase in employment of much the same magnitude because it is matched by an equivalent decrease in actual working hours without any problem of technological discontinuity and/or any increase in overtime.

What we must ask ourselves is whether this theoretical increase in employment would be compatible with the other economic variables considered so far, and if so under what conditions. To do so we must first recall that the level of production in real terms basically depends on the level of employment, on working hours per employee and on hourly productivity.

Therefore, if we imagine for the moment that production remains constant, clearly it can only increase by a similar amount to

---

[9] A number of field surveys have tried to work out how entrepreneurs would be most likely to behave in the face of a reduction of working hours. The results of the surveys are very much in line with our theoretical conclusions. For example, in England, in 1979, the London Policy Studies Institute received unequivocal answers. Almost all the interviewees answered that in the case of a reduction of working hours the best options would be reorganising work and using overtime. They also said that in the case of a 5% reduction of working hours, employment would only increase by 1.8% among production workers, and by barely 0.3% among administrative workers, who are evidently expected to increase their productivity more. Finally, in 1978, the journal Usine Nouvelle interviewed 526 firms to ask how they would react to a 2.5% reduction of working hours if monthly wages remained the same despite it (later we will see how the wage variable plays an important part in this). 46% of them replied that neither production nor employment would change and only 17% said they would recruit new permanent employees (the study does not give any figures on the possibility of new jobs, however). Lastly, Lucchetti and Staffolani (LUCCHETTI R. - STAFFOLANI S. [37]) have very recently demonstrated in the case of Italy that firms adapt immediately to shocks they have already envisaged and therefore taken into account. It would also seem that when permanent and unexpected shocks occur, as would be the case with a reduction of working hours, it takes large firms approximately four years to adjust the number of actual workers to the desired level.

the reduction of working hours if hourly productivity remains constant and consequently daily productivity per worker decreases.

In terms of causal links, however, labour productivity is quite obviously also a function of capital stock utilisation, which in turn depends on the type of work organisation, which in turn also depends on the way working hours are used[10]. So, a change in working hours can have any type of effect whatever on productivity, even that of decreasing it, if a reduction of working hours happens to be regarded as an imposition and may therefore cause a lack of attention and dedication to work. Naturally, this too is possible, in theory, although the effect is normally held to be the opposite.

To begin with, a reduction of working hours tends to make work less «porous», as it is termed. It eliminates or reduces the need for certain breaks; it helps to make better use of slack periods; it reduces physical effort and so removes the cause of potential accidents; last, it helps to increase certain work rhythms.

Secondly, there is the phenomenon of labour hoarding. Every firm has a certain stock of hours of work that have been paid but not always fully used, so that a reduction of working hours brings back into play part of this stock that was under-utilised and therefore had low productivity.

Of course, the longer initial working hours are, the more productivity should increase once they are reduced, and according to some experts, shortening working hours by a whole day per week would increase productivity less than would a reduction of daily working hours[11].

Moreover, if the reduction were to take place all at once, the increase in hourly productivity might be less than would perhaps occur if the reduction were programmed to be very slow and gradual. In the first case, the impact of the reduction of working hours

---

[10] Cassone offers a very instructive example in regard. «If (on a Saturday, and hence at a time when the supply of working hours is rigid) a firm can carry out plant maintenance without interfering with the normal cycle of production, capital stock utilisation increases and hence also labour productivity.» CASSONE A. [17], p. 101.

[11] See LEVESON I.F. [38].

would be absorbed by reorganising work and productivity would increase «for a given technology». In the second case, there would be enough time to restructure and reorganise production and it would be possible to introduce new plants, with obvious effects on labour productivity.

Finally, it is obvious that a reduction of working hours might have a different impact on productivity depending on the type of product, on how capital intensive the production function is, on the type of manpower used, on the degree of plant utilisation, and on the type of work organisation.

In any case, there can be no doubt that the variety of arguments in favour of the theory that a reduction of working hours increases average hourly productivity is so great as to have prompted several economists[12] to state that a reduction of working hours generates increases in labour productivity of the same magnitude as capital accumulation, technical progress or aggregate demand.

On the other hand, according to many empirical studies, for every 1% reduction of working hours there is a corresponding increase in hourly productivity ranging from 0.30% to 0.50%[13].

It follows, therefore, that if, in a perfect identity, we can always say that «if working hours decrease, employment can only increase proportionately if hourly productivity remains constant». In terms of causal links, this is impossible because if working hours decrease productivity, almost always increases, sometimes even quite considerably.

We can draw our first conclusions, then, by stating that there are many de-multipliers between a reduction of contractual working hours and any increase in employment. The first occurs in the passage from contractual working hours to actual working hours; then there is the problem of technological discontinuity and hence of overtime; finally, the increase in productivity.

---

[12] See, for example, MALINVAUD E. [39].

[13] For example, see DENISON E.F. [26]; OWEN J. [45]; OUDIZ G., RAOUL E., STERDYNIAK H. [44]; EUROPEAN STATISTICS INSTITUTE, VAN DEN BERGH R.C. - WITTELSBURGER H. [62]; ALLEN R. [3]. See also VAN GINNEKEN W. [63], and the *Henize Model* for Germany and *Treasury Model* for Great Britain.

None of this takes into account the nature of the labour market, because no one can guarantee that a possible increase in labour demand for a certain job, and a certain place, will match up with an appropriate supply[14].

So it is obvious that once again a generalised reduction of working hours dictated by law is the opposite of what the market would want.

1.2 *«Financial» and «Economic» Aspects*

1.2.1 Working Hours, Productivity, Wages and Employment

While technological discontinuity and productivity increases as such represent technical limitations on new employment, the situation is further aggravated by an economic/financial element as well.

There are three factors to be taken into account: the interplay between costs of recruiting and laying-off; the trend of unit labour costs and, lastly, the cost of overtime.

Let us begin with the first. In general, every firm has its own curve for recruitment costs (selection, supervision of a larger number of employees, administrative cost of formalities for a larger number of workers, special research and training activities for highly qualified staff, and so on) and for lay-offs. The higher those costs, the more reluctant firms will be to abolish jobs during cyclical downswings and create new ones during upswings because of

---

[14] So far, in fact, we have always implicitly imagined that labour supply is infinitely elastic and refers to a homogenous and divisible factor, so that when working hours are reduced the resulting increase in labour demand, however great or small, never comes up against any bottlenecks on the supply side. In reality, this is not so. An increase in labour demand associated with a reduction of working hours may be directed towards types of labour that are not available on the market (because what is demanded is qualified labour and unemployment affects poorly qualified labour); alternatively, it may occur in areas where unemployment rates are already very low. In such cases as these, poor territorial and sectoral labour mobility, powerful social buffers to make unemployment less painful, psychological reluctance on the part of workers to offer labour that does not adequately match their aspirations, all help considerably to create the strange combination of a large number of unemployed workers and large number of unfilled jobs.

these sunk costs (i.e. never recovered). Since to create a new job the expected marginal profit must be greater than the cost of recruitment, and since to abolish that job the marginal gain from doing so must be greater than the cost of the lay-off (payment of months without work, possible penalties, etc.), there is obviously an interval within which the firm will not be elastic to any event and will not take any decision to either recruit or lay-off. This interval changes from one firm to another and will be larger the higher the costs and the more the future cycle is uncertain. Obviously, then, in the event of a reduction of contractual working hours and hypothetical need to recruit new staff, a firm will first have to evaluate those factors, combining them with two additional elements before reaching a final decision on whether to recruit or to use overtime. These two additional elements are, of course, unit labour costs and the cost of overtime.

As far as unit labour costs are concerned, when we talk of reduced working hours we also include the resulting wage levels, i.e. whether or not the one completely compensates for the other.

Given that the only situation in which unit labour costs do not change with full wage compensation[15] is when this is combined with the unrealistic condition of a productivity increase equal to 100% of the reduction of working hours[16], it is clear that with full compensation, unit labour costs normally increase. So, if, in such a case, we wanted to keep the level of production unchanged by recruiting new workers, we would have to meet the sunk costs mentioned, as well as the increased unit labour cost.

In every case this will reduce profits, either because unit profit margins decrease (for the same selling prices) or because a rise in prices causes sales to fall.

Therefore, we would be right to expect that before a firm takes the option of recruiting new staff it will evaluate the possibility of solving the situation by using overtime. In fact, at least in the short term and before labour-saving investments can restore tech-

---

[15] This only occurs if the increase in hourly wages completely compensates for the reduction of working hours so that total wages remain unchanged.

[16] As when working hours decrease by 10% and productivity increases by 10%.

nical and financial equilibrium, overtime may ensure normal production levels at what might be a lower cost[17].

In other words, new workers will only be recruited if the sum of sunk costs and increased unit labour costs is less than the overtime bonus, which depends on current relative legislation and on the attitude of the trade unions.

Laws and attitudes that are not always clear in their contents might instead produce undesirable results if their aim were to make overtime increasingly costly and difficult as a means of boosting employment. Even if the most balanced procedure were chosen — i.e. raising the cost of overtime while reducing social security contributions on ordinary work so as to weigh the balance in favour of more employment without changing the total cost of labour — this would obviously not eliminate the entry costs of new workers nor even the implicit fixed costs, and so unit labour costs would increase anyway and the consequent micro and macro repercussions might in the end be more than compensatory. If this argument is applied to Italy it becomes even more forceful, even bearing in mind that unit labour costs in manufacturing rose 11.1% between 1996 and 1999 compared with –1.7% in the euro area. It is equivalent to saying that whatever

---

[17] This equation «reduction of working hours equals increase of overtime» can only be avoided if the firm is already organised in three shifts for market reasons or productive requirements (24-hour production cycle) and if the reduction of working hours is such that, assuming it is impossible or undesirable to reduce production, a full fourth shift can be created. This is possible in theory but unlikely. Since the elasticity of labour demand (on the external market) to the reduction of working hours is small but not entirely absent, and is generally (for exclusively technical business reasons) proportionately greater as the reduction of working hours becomes larger, a fourth shift would only be feasible if the reduction of working hours was indeed very large, sufficiently so to «trigger» that elasticity and allow little scope for using overtime or for reorganising the firm. In theory, of course, this is possible, but it should be pointed out that with very large reductions of working hours the costs of adjustment might be exceedingly high and in the long term offset almost all the initial advantages because the larger the reduction of working hours, the more serious (as we will see later) are the problems concerning wage compensation and labour supply and hence the unemployment rate.

In other words, employment might initially increase, but would then fall back again and the unemployment rate would not drop at all. (This question should be considered from a macroeconomic point of view, and we refer to that section). Moreover, since a reduction of working hours increases productivity, the effects of a large reduction need to be properly taken into account.

Italy may need it is certainly not new measures to reduce even further the country's competitiveness, which anyway seems to be diminishing constantly. During that same period, Italy' exports increased by 6% while those of the euro area rose 19.3%[18].

It should never be forgotten, moreover, that if competitiveness were to seriously deteriorate for these reasons, the first thing a firm would do would be to redesign its production function with a new capital/labour ratio. This would increase the apparent productivity of labour and the firm would be able to recover profit margins and retain its previous level of production without recruiting new workers. And, besides this, it is clear that in highly globalised and integrated markets, there is a tangible risk that over-rigidity will lead to widespread international dislocation, and that instead of new recruitment, such measures could lead to de-industrialisation and a national loss of productive capacity.

To conclude, we think there are good grounds for stating that the trade-off between working hours and employment is extremely tenuous and that, anyway, it is mainly empirical because everything depends on the cost structure of the individual firm, its technical and organisational structure, trade union behaviour, how viscous the labour market is and so on. So it would be very strange to imagine bureaucratic and State-managed regulations that are equal for all.

2. - Macroeconomic Analysis

So far we have analysed the relationship that exists within individual firms between a reduction of contractual working hours and external labour demand[19]. As we will see, these very uninspiring conclusions are further confirmed by macroeconomic analysis.

---

[18] IMF estimates processed by CSC.

[19] To use the words of CASSONE A. [17] the theories that state that this relationship is quantitatively significant «are very restrictive because in one respect they are not easy to justify in theoretical terms and in another they are not confirmed by sufficient empirical evidence».

2.1 *Working Hours, Productivity, Wages and Employment*

Since a reduction of working hours affects productivity and
is reflected in wage levels, the macroeconomic effects are evident
in prices, the balance of payments and aggregate demand. In turn,
these effects have repercussions on the cycle and hence on employment. So, obviously, to try to analyse the macroeconomic effects of a reduction of working hours, we have to establish be-
forehand a frame of reference for the amount of wage compensation, performance of productivity, level of production and so on.
And since many of these variables themselves interact, it will only be possible to draw a few useful indications with an econometric model.

A number of tests have been undertaken which will be described further on, but we think it would still be useful, even in
theory and using the initial hypotheses, to examine what possible
chains of macroeconomic effects would be triggered by a reduction of working hours.

Let us imagine a first hypothetical scenario in which a reduction of working hours is accompanied by a partial increase in
productivity and full wage compensation. This will cause unit
labour costs to increase (the more, the less the supposed increase
in productivity) and therefore also affect the cycle.

Since investment is generally a function of expected demand
and of the profit level firms achieve and expect, either one of the
following two things will occur. If wage compensation is reflected on end prices, unit profits expected by firms will not change
but there will be internal demand and balance of payments difficulties (due to weaker competitiveness), requiring tight economic
policies[20]. The cycle and employment are bound to be effected.

If, on the other hand, wage compensation is not transferred
onto prices, or cannot be (assuming a highly competitive market),
the balance of payments will not be affected but the rate of unit

---

[20] In fact, demand for domestic goods by residents and non-residents will decrease but imports will increase. Hence policies to promote external equilibrium,
despite the domestic demand deficit.

profits will decrease and with it investment and employment should similarly decline.

Hence, a reduction of working hours that takes place under these assumptions should, in the medium to long term, generate a set of adverse effects that are all of a macroeconomic nature.

In a second and more virtuous scenario we can suppose that there is no such compensation. In that case, the macroeconomic effects will be ambiguous because investment might equally increase or decrease since consumption demand drops if there is no compensation but profits might rise and/or so may non-resident demand if competitiveness improves. In such a case, therefore, the adverse macroeconomic repercussion on employment will be equally ambiguous and certainly not be as strong as when there is wage compensation because the depressive effects analysed before will probably not be as strong.

Finally, if, in a third scenario, a reduction of working hours, with or without wage compensation, were to cause a decrease in production, clearly all the effects on employment would be smaller than if productive capacity were to remain unchanged.

In sum, the conclusions reached in theory do not appear optimistic about the medium- to long-term trade-off between working hours and employment.

Unfortunately, these theoretical findings have been generally borne out by all the simulation models that have attempted to tackle the problem.

Indeed, according to some models[21], in the most likely case of a 5% reduction of working hours, full wage compensation and a small increase in productivity (equal to only a third of the decrease in working hours) in the manufacturing sector, the increase in employment in manufacturing after a year compared with a situation in which there had been no reduction of working hours would be 1.1% and in the sixth year only +0.3%.

In other words, the «added value» of the reduction of working hours in terms of increased employment would only be equal to a fifth of that reduction in the first year and, in the sixth, about

---

[21] See Bodo G. [10].

one seventeenth because of macroeconomic repercussions. If we consider the economic sector as a whole, employment would actually decrease by 0.2%[22].

These disappointing effects would apparently be the result of

---

[22] According to Bodo's theory (using the Banca d'Italia model), wages, productivity and productive capacity (which is fixed) are endogenous variables. Even monetary policy and exchange rate policy are assumed to be endogenous. It is also assumed that the exchange rate reacts to external imbalances and adjusts to price differentials. Nominal interest rates are assumed to adjust to the expected rate of inflation. Thus, monetary and exchange rate policy are established by the model. It is assumed that productivity increases, if there are any, equal one third of the reduction of working hours. Bodo also assumes that actual working hours adjust fairly quickly to contractual hours. This also means that use of overtime cannot be institutionalised but may be the economy's first reaction to shorter working hours. Finally, the period tested runs from 1980 to 1986 and the simulations are compared with a basic simulation so that their results are in effect changes with respect to that.

These assumptions generally favour a trade-off between shorter working hours and employment because the rapid adjustment of actual to contractual working hours, the small increase in productivity and the possible exchange rate change all point in this direction. Bodo simulates four scenarios, two with wage compensation and two without; since Bodo always distinguishes between employment in manufacturing (where it is supposed the reduction of working hours takes place) and total employment, figures on the latter will always be less favourable that those for the manufacturing sector alone.

Having said this, in his first two scenarios Bodo establishes a number of common elements and dissimilarities. The points in common are that a 5% reduction of working hours introduced in two stages (2.5% each time) 3 months apart in manufacturing alone gives rise to full wage compensation. The dissimilarities are that there may or may not be an increase in productivity and, if there is, it equals only a third of the reduction of working hours (1.67%). The results are as follows. In the first year, with full wage compensation, employment in manufacturing increases by 1.1% or by 2.6% depending on whether or not productivity increases; between the first and second year, there is another small increase but then the macroeconomic repercussions cause it to decrease constantly from the third year on, to reach values of +0.3% and +1.6% respectively in the sixth year.

In the two other scenarios Bodo removes wage compensation and leaves only the two secondary assumptions as to the existence or lack of productivity increases.

As in the theoretical assumption, the impact on employment, short- and long-term, is stronger in the two earlier scenarios. In the best case for increased employment, although it is also the most unlikely (no wage compensation and no productivity gains), the impact (in manufacturing) in the first year would be +3.0% and in the sixth year +3.2%. In the favourable case again of no wage compensation but at least some increase in productivity, these same figures drop to 1.5% and 1.9% respectively. In these two scenarios, if we turn from employment in the manufacturing sector to total employment the figures are naturally again very different. In the scenario with no productivity gains the increases would be +0.8% and +0.5% respectively in the first and sixth year, and in the scenario with them they would be +0.4% and +0.2%.

a negative impact on prices[23] and on the cycle, which would show a downturn (-1%) compared, of course, with the basic model. Thus there would be stagflation and non-quantifiable adjustment costs for industry.

Although other models[24] start with a more favourable assumption[25], i.e. that the reduction of actual working hours is as-

---

[23] Specifically, again in the sixth year, the consumption deflator increases respectively by 8.6% without productivity gains and by 6.9% with.

[24] There are two of them: *DMS* and *METRIC*. The first, *Dynamique Multi Sectorielle* (multi-sectoral dynamics) is used by the INSEE. See FOUQUET D. - CHARFIN J.M. - GUILLAUME H. - MUET P.A. - VALLET D. [30]. The second, *Modèle Économétrique Trimestriel de la Conjoncture (Quarterly Econometric Model of the Economic Cycle)»* is used by the Direction de la Prévision (Forecasting Department). See ARTUS P. - MORIN P. - NASSE P. - STERDYNIAK H. [5].

[25] The general assumptions underlying these models are the following. To begin with, they assume a decrease in actual working hours and not in contractual hours, so that the de-multiplier between the two is eliminated. In our opinion, this is as misleading as Bodo's equivalent assumption that actual working hours adjust fairly quickly to contractual hours, leading him to reason in terms of effective working hours. In fact, according to this hypothesis, the medium/long-term adjustment should not imply any increase in overtime and, irrespective of the effect of reorganisation, the whole situation would be forcibly solved by recruiting new workers. Second, in the *DMS* and *METRIC* simulation models, productivity gains are nil in the short term (except in a situation involving the service sector and assuming a 100% productivity increase). It follows that the impact on employment, already magnified by the assumption that the decrease directly concerns actual working hours, is magnified a second time. Third, since these models basically refer to the short-term (they only test a three-year period), the medium/long-term effects are not examined, although they are considerable and very evident in Bodo's simulations. This is borne out by the fact that *DMS* and *METRIC* simulations involving a sometimes considerable external imbalance never show that it produces repercussions on internal equilibrium and so on production and employment. Thus, on the one hand, microeconomic de-multipliers are eliminated or de-activated using very special hypotheses and, on the other, the macroeconomic feed-back is not taken into consideration.

Fourth, in these models the more realistic assumption of wage compensation is combined (in *METRIC* only) with a revival of investment because this is assumed to be a function of expected demand (accelerator effect). Whatever the case, there are five scenarios. Whereas in Bodo's models the difference lies between wage compensation and productivity, in these models productivity is regarded as constant and compensation and productive capacity interplay.

Here again, the following figures are the difference with respect to a basic simulation model (which Oudiz, Raoul and Sterdyniak call «the reference account or basic account), in which the performance of the economy (French in this case) from 1979 to 1981 does not take account of the reduction of working hours or of the other accompanying assumptions. Consequently, the figures for the four scenarios summarised below are obtained by inserting into this basic account the various assumptions regarding shorter working hours, changes in productive capacity, and so on. In other words, they should be interpreted as deviations from trend values.

sumed to be equal to that of contractual hours, and do not en-
visage the negative, medium/long-term macroeconomic repercussions, they still reach the conclusion that the elasticity of employment to shorter actual working hours is poor on average, even
though it increases as the starting hypotheses become less and
less realistic. Thus, the elasticity would be 0.2, assuming an in-

---

The first and second versions share the assumption that actual working hours decrease by 2.5% and that there is no wage compensation. They differ as regards to productive capacity, which either decreases (by 2.5% to be precise) or remains constant.

The results obtained by these simulations are as follows.

In the two scenarios without wage compensation and with unchanged productivity, the impact on employment in the first year is +0.85% and +1.0%, and in the third
year +1.3% and +1.8% depending on whether productive capacity decreases or not.

In the third scenario there is again no wage compensation, productive capacity
remains unchanged, but it is assumed that productivity increases by 100% in the
service sector. In one respect, this is a realistic scenario, in another, less so because the productivity increase is too great and limited to only one sector, while
it seems frankly unrealistic to assume the absence of wage compensation, with a
100% productivity increase. Whatever the case, the result of this simulation is that
if actual working hours are reduced by the usual 2.5%, after three years employment will increase by +0.5%. Hence, as soon as the more likely hypothesis of increased productivity is included, even if there is still no wage compensation, the
trade-off between working hours and employment immediately becomes less
marked. The impact of these simulations on employment would therefore seem to
err on the excessive side for two reasons. There are no microeconomic de-multipliers (and this magnifies the initial impact) and the macroeconomic return is not
taken into account (which would appear only in the medium term). The last two
scenarios, instead, contemplate full wage compensation and no loss of productive
capacity. Their distinguishing feature is that investment can increase or decrease.

In the first case (increased investment), the usual 2.5% reduction of actual working hours produces an impact on employment in the first year of +1.0% and at the
end of the three years of around +2%. Irrespective of the very positive result, this is
a little surprising because the simulation itself maintains that at the end of the three
years, production is only slightly higher than in the reference account. But since the
purchasing power of wages more than offsets the reduction of working hours, inflation increases (moving well away from the base account figure) and foreign accounts
deteriorate considerably. All this should give rise to macroeconomic repercussions
that will probably be incompatible with a roughly 2.0% increase in employment, i.e.
80% of the reduction of working hours. The caution we use when handling these figures is additionally justified by the last simulation, in which investment decreases
instead of increasing because it is a function of profits. On the one hand, this simulation shows that in the third year production drops off (at the end of the three-year
period, it is 0.7 points down on the base account), inflation is even stronger because
firms have tried to restore their profit margins by raising prices, and the balance on
foreign account has deteriorated because of inflation and tensions on productive capacity; on the other it also indicates that employment increases by around +1.6% at
the end of the three years. This would appear to be the conclusion of an analysis that
takes no account of the repercussions that simulation reveals on the side of prices,
balance of payments and production.

crease in productivity (in the service sector alone) but without wage compensation. Instead, it would be 0.32 if, despite there being no wage compensation, productive capacity decreased somewhat but productivity did not increase.

Finally, when it is assumed that there is not only no wage compensation, not only no productivity gain, but not even a decline in productive capacity, the elasticity rises to 0.4 in the first year and 0.6 in the third[26]. Except for this last case, totally unrealistic in both fact and theory, we believe that if these models had started from a reduction of contractual working hours and had analysed the macroeconomic repercussions, the results would have been even smaller than those described[27].

It is no surprise that when other models begin to reason in terms of medium/long-term macroeconomic effects we see that these elasticity values literally plummet: 0.048 with wage compensation and 0.28 without[28].

---

[26] Only in the extremely favourable assumption of an acceleration effect do, these models obtain an elasticity of 0.593. According to some Authors, if we start by assuming an acceleration effect, i.e. that investment is a function of demand expectations, because full wage compensation ensures that demand stays at a higher level than without, it may exert a greater effect on employment than would the absence of wage compensation. Briefly, the result just described would be overturned. The reason would be that wage compensation would prompt firms to invest and recruit and the increase in production would offset the downward pressures on profits of wage increases. This result is correct in theory and has been adopted by one of the simulations, but it must be pointed out that this assumption, too, has an effect on prices and competitiveness, which could have repercussions on employment just as in models that do not include an «accelerator»-type function. So, although this hypothesis cannot be discarded, and is by far the most likely one, both theoretically and in terms of empirical results, wage compensation will, in the long term, diminish employment. See also VAN GINNEKEN W. [63].

[27] It should not be forgotten that the most difficult and important test a model has to overcome is comparing the result obtained with the economic situation studied by the model. In France, in 1982, the working week was reduced by one hour (2.5%, that is) with full wage compensation. Since the DMS model mentioned earlier had made precisely these assumptions for the French economy, the estimates of the model were compared with the results actually obtained after that reduction of working hours. Approximately nine months after the reduction, the French authorities stated that employment had increased by between 0.1% and roughly 0.15%, compared with 1.0% in the *DMS* simulation. We will never know whether this difference of 7-10 times between reality and simulation would have increased even more in the medium/long term.

[28] The Treasury model for the British economy has calculated that, with

Finally, other models even obtain negative results[29] in absolute terms. According to those simulations, a reduction of working hours, with wage compensation and lower productive capacity, might produce a -1.6% change in employment in the first year of simulation and -2.3% in the last year, whereas, still with wage compensation but without lower productive capacity, the change in employment would be respectively -1% and -2.1%, i.e. always a negative elasticity.

These simulation models also suggest that only in the very optimistic, and we think unrealistic, assumption of no wage compensation and unchanged productive capacity, would employment increase, although by very little. The shorter working hours-new jobs elasticity would then be between 0.11 in the first year and 0.19 in the last.

Finally, there is an interesting model[30] that not only entirely confirms these very poor results for the elasticity of employment to shorter working hours (0.04) but also looks at the elasticity of the use of overtime, which is instead fairly marked (1.3%).

This would apparently confirm that, when working hours are reduced, firms do not recruit in the short term but compensate by using more overtime and in the long term make up for the reduction with the results of labour-saving investments made in the meantime.

2.2 *Working Hours, Labour Supply and Employment*

Naturally, the impact of a reduction of working hours is not the same for the employment rate and the unemployment rate[31].

---

a 2 hour reduction in the working, week (approximately 5%), the impact on employment would range from 0.2% to 1.4% depending, respectively, on whether there was wage compensation or not. Naturally, with respect to the trend.

[29] The *Vintaf Model* for the Netherlands was based on a 2.5% yearly reduction of working hours (1979-1983) and found generally negative effects on employment.

[30] See KONIG - POHLMEIER [00].

[31] This is not the place to establish whether an increase in employment, even without any decrease or even with an increase in the unemployment rate,

Labour supply is a function of two variables: wages and working time. If a reduction of working hours causes an increase in real hourly wages because of some degree of wage compensation or Phillips-type effects, the labour supply will increase by definition, in terms of numbers and hours. On the other hand, if we also consider that shorter working hours raise the activity rate (of women or whoever does not welcome the additional leisure time because they want to earn more), then again the labour supply increases. These two reasons may give us a rising rate of unemployment despite any small increase in jobs.

Returning to some of the earlier simulations, this phenomenon can be seen in all its force.

In all the models, in fact, at best the unemployment rate improves by 0.1%[32] and 0.3%[33], but more often it worsens by 0.1%[34], reaching a maximum of 1.1-1.2%[35]. In short, generally the number of unemployed increases!

---

is still a positive effect. There can be no doubt that the present high rate of unemployment is basically due to the fact that labour supply has increased much faster than demand and that if we were to content ourselves with just the increase in jobs, modern economies would have nothing to either worry or complain about. However, it is equally true that an increase in employment is essential for growth and wealth and must as such be welcomed as highly positive in itself.

This does not change the fact that our earlier analyses are incomplete if they do not take this phenomenon into account.

[32] In Bodo's simulations, without wage compensation and productivity increase.

[33] *DMS* and *METRIC* models. In these simulations, if no wage compensation and no loss of productive capacity are assumed, in the third year employment rises by 1.8% from the reference account.

Continuing to assume no wage compensation but assuming a loss of productive capacity, after the third year employment rises by a smaller amount: approximately 1.3%. If we now look at the unemployment rate, these same simulations give us a completely different value, respectively a decrease of only 0.7% and 0.5%.

Finally, if we turn to the case of the service sector, for which a 100% productivity increase is assumed, given the same hypotheses of no compensation and constant productive capacity, at the end of the three years employment rises by 0.5%. In this scenario, the unemployment rate instead decreases by only 0.3%.

[34] In Bodo's simulations, with wage compensation and productivity increase.

[35] In *Vintaf's Model*, depending on the initial assumptions.

3. - Two More Questions

3.1 *Reduction of Working Hours, Employment and Productivity: Where Do we Start?*

In the preceding pages we have tried to show that, for micro and macro reasons, as a result of a change in working hours employment increases by an uncertain amount, and in any case less that proportionate to the reduction of hours; the unemployment rate stays practically the same or increases very little; and industry faces heavy adjustment costs, the amount and effects of which are difficult to assess.

Vice versa, if a reduction of working hours follows, rather than precedes, a productivity increase, the results will obviously not be the same because there will be no technological or institutional discontinuity to prevent a reduction of working hours proportionately equal to the productivity gain already obtained, and no economic or financial reason why total wage compensation is inadvisable, since in this case, by definition, it would not raise unit labour costs.

On the contrary, the reduction of working hours will, in any case, give way to another productivity increase specifically associated with it and we can therefore also assume that, since it is hard to imagine an additional compensatory increase in wages, unit labour costs will actually tend to decrease. And that is not all. In this virtuous scenario of a reduction of working hours following a productivity increase, it is highly likely that new jobs will be created.

If we assume, in fact, that part of the productivity increases depend on gross investments made autonomously by firms to beat competition, it follows that employment might also increase somewhat because the growth rate of aggregate demand, and hence of income, is affected by that increase in autonomous investment[36].

-----

[36] In such cases there may, of course, be some negative effects, not in any way because of the reduction of working hours but due to tensions affecting the cycle. Even if there is no wage compensation (which is equivalent to the case in which

In this virtuous scenario, moreover, small increases in employment may also occur and, at the same time, workers may be able to re-position their wage/leisure time indifference curve and choose a point on it where more leisure time may even be combined with a small wage rise that will not produce macroeconomic repercussions. This, in fact, is neither more nor less than what has happened over the years.

However, the reasoning above is very different from the one discussed so far, which instead points to the reduction of working hours as prime mover and produces all the negative repercussions examined at length2[37].

3.2 *Another Problem: Shorter Working Hours and Fewer Lay-offs*

Given all the above – apart from recent French and Italian measures that still elicit criticism and in France, at least, where they are at a more advanced stage, seem to have created so many problems that the Ministry of Labour has had to postpone applying the law on shorter working hours by a year and combine it with various forms of support for firms[38] – what has in fact

---

total compensation equals the productivity increase) there may be repercussions caused by the Phillips curve. It is a well-known fact that the relationship between unemployment rate and wage trend is not generally linear, in the sense that low unemployment rates have inflationary effects on wages, while high unemployment rates diminish wage pressures very little. It follows that any decrease in employment will affect wages and trigger price-competitiveness spirals that in turn have repercussions on income and employment.

[37] For example, full wage compensation will, in any case, raise unit labour costs because the productivity increase will certainly be less than proportionate to the reduction of working hours that caused it.

[38] For instance, the additional cost of overtime has been limited to 10% (from 35 to 39 hours) in the transitional period and set at 25% after that, with a ceiling of 130 hours when fully operational. In addition, the Minister Mrs. Aubry has acknowledged all agreements stipulated by firms and trade unions. Finally, the additional cost to firms not introducing the 35-hour week on the first deadline will be just 0.7% of their total wage bill, rising to 2.6% the following year. Firms will anyway have the faculty not to reduce working hours, in which case they will be obliged to grant a sixth week of paid holiday.

In addition, aid is offered to firms (21,500 FF per annum per employee on minimum wage and 4,000 FF for employees on 1.8 times the minimum wage, soon to be increased by 11.4% under the law owing to total wage compensation) for a

been gradually happening internationally in recent years is that specific firms have reduced working hours, not to increase employment but to avoid staff cuts.

This variation on a theme is of by no means secondary importance, for not only is this sort of reduction of working hours only possible in an easier technical context, it is also less difficult to impose certain financial conditions, which are apparently harder to obtain when working hours are reduced to create new jobs. It is wise not to underestimate these aspects, or otherwise the economic policy debate loses touch with reality.

Let us suppose, as a first example, that a firm wants to reduce working hours instead of making staff cuts because a market crisis has forced it to decrease production. The firm's choice in this case will be between stopping one or more production lines and laying-off the workers or reducing the time of use of all its production lines. To do the second, you only need to reduce working hours.

In the other case that working hours are reduced maintaining equal productive capacity to create new jobs, the technical discontinuity and other elements examined so far may make it advisable to increase overtime and/or redesign the production function rather than create employment.

Moreover, whereas in the case of shorter working hours and equal production, bargaining will begin to obtain full wage compensation (implying very adverse macroeconomic repercussions), if an industry reduces working hours to avoid lay-offs it is extremely likely that total wages will be reduced proportionately, in that any compensation will at most apply to the productivity increase caused by that reduction of working hours. However, since fewer hours will be worked by each employee, the total wage bill should decrease. And sometimes this is an essential joint condition for the success of the operation.

---

total of 65 billion FF (approximately 20,000 billion lire) to be subsequently recovered through taxes on profits and a special eco-tax (one giving, the other taking away). Briefly, it would seem that the government has understood the problems associated with such a measure but is not sure how to square things.

Another example could well be that of a firm faced not with a market crisis that forces it to reduce production, but labour-saving innovations combined with a further need to reduce total labour costs because they have somehow become incompatible with a balanced financial position. Here again, the reduction of working hours can avoid lay-offs because, on one hand, the firm will presumably try to reduce working hours by as much as is needed, with the new technologies, to avoid increasing production, and on the other will try to agree to a level of wage compensation that will anyway, in the interplay between productivity increases and shorter working hours, reduce unit labour costs. This is what some firms can generally hope for to rebalance their profit and loss accounts and satisfy the two requirements of modernising technology and more or less preserving jobs.

This is the line followed by the two Volkswagen agreements[39].

---

[39] Regarding the first agreement, the Company initially declared that its objective was to reduce labour costs by 20% by reducing working hours 20% without any compensation. According to the company, the intention was that this should also generally help to avoid the lay-off of excess workers.

In actual fact, the agreement (which ran from 1 january 1994 to 31 december 1995) was concluded on a slightly different basis because the working week was reduced from 36 hours to 28.8 (28 hours and 48 minutes) but the economic part envisaged a 10% cut in monthly wages and further 3% cut in annual wages by reducing the holiday and Christmas bonuses. In compensation, however, the agreement also incorporated the pay rises already acknowledged for the future under earlier agreements.

Thus, when the agreement was signed there was an imbalance between the reduction of labour costs and reduction of working hours because, for an immediate decrease in labour costs of 13% (10% + 3%), working hours were instantly reduced by 20%. Only in the following two years, when the agreed pay rises were incorporated, was a balance achieved between the two reductions. This means that during the adjustment period, unit labour costs increased irrespective of technological elements.

Nevertheless, the agreement prevented around 30,000 lay-offs and saved the Bundesanstalt approximately 700 million DM of disbursements for unemployment benefits (January 1994).

On the basis of this first element, we must point out that the result was only possible because the productivity gains obtained by the company (through technological development) prior to the reduction of working hours, as well as those obtained afterwards (and as a direct consequence of the reduction) were used to recover financial equilibrium and restore the accumulation rate. In other words, despite the sum of autonomous or derived productivity gains, the total wages of Volkswagen workers decreased by 20% and so, although their leisure time increased by the same amount, their purchasing power decreased by 20%. This side effect may be well known but is nonetheless worth recalling.

Conslusions

In our analysis we have shown clearly how the reduction of working hours is a tool of economic policy that can operate in two different ways to achieve two different objectives.

It can be used: 1) *ex ante*, i.e. before any changes in productivity take place; 2) *ex post*, after those changes have taken place.

And its objectives may be: *a)* to increase employment; *b)* to reduce possible lay-offs.

As far as the first method of operation is concerned, we have

---

Between 11 and 12 September 1995 Volkswagen negotiated a second agreement for six of its factories in west Germany involving 98,700 workers.

Briefly, the positions at the outset were as follows.

On one side, the trade unions were basically asking for three things: *a)* a 5% pay rise; *b)* the working week to remain at 28.8 hours; *c)* unlimited job guarantee (i.e. no lay-off).

On the company's side, although the workforce was still extremely large and something had to be done to improve competitiveness (notably by reducing vehicle delivery times), the point of departure was the following: 1) a 3% pay rise, on condition it was combined with broader measures for flexibility; 2) the working week to stay at 28.8 hours but with the possibility of extending it to between 32 and 48 hours, including Saturday, which would be regarded as part of normal working hours and so not paid at a 50% higher rate (the motto was: «Saturday cars should not be any more expensive than others»); 3) job guarantee for a maximum of two years.

Starting from these positions, an agreement (running from 1 january 1996 to 31 december 1997) was finally reached on the following main points: *a)* the company undertook to make no lay-offs for the following two years only (until 31 December 1997) and only if the reasons were associated with the company's own market. However, the company also announced that over the next two years it would nevertheless reduce the workforce by around 6,000, using the system of early retirement; *b)* the working week stayed at 28.8 hours, but it was agreed that this would be calculated on an annual basis. However, working hours, spread over four or five days a week, could be raised to a maximum of 38.8 without any pay rises or, consequently, cost to the company; *c)* the duration of paid hourly breaks was halved from 5 minutes to 2.5 minutes. Compared with the earlier agreement this produced a gain of 1.2 hours per week that was in fact unpaid; and is equivalent to a 4% approximate recovery of costs per year; *d)* it was decided that Saturday would not become part of the normal working week, but for 12 Saturdays a year the company would be able to request attendance at work simply by notifying the Works Council. Instead of the wage bonus that had been set at 50% in the earlier agreement, Saturday would be paid at an additional rate of 30%; *e)* as of 1/1/1996 wages would increase by 4%. Finally, an equal lump sum bonus of 1000 DM was granted to everyone for the months August-December 1995. The holiday bonus was also increased by 836 DM for 1996 and 1997 and the Christmas bonus by 150 DM.

The figures need no comment.

come to the conclusion that a generalised, ex ante reduction of working hours will have little effect on employment and unemployment rates because there are several de-multiplier effects that minimise the trade-off between working hours and employment.

A reduction of contractual working hours gives rise to a less than proportionate reduction of actual working hours. It is possible to make use of overtime, especially in the short term, and this may become unavoidable with technological and institutional discontinuity; labour productivity tends to increase; unit labour costs may rise if any wage compensation that occurs is larger than a possible productivity increase; finally, the firm's reaction to shorter working hours may be to reorganise work, make better use of productive capacity, and undertake capital-intensive investment, rather than create new jobs.

In a long-term macroeconomic analysis, and still assuming an *ex ante* reduction of working hours, the de-multiplier that reduces the impact on employment is the potential rise in labour costs caused either by the interplay between wage compensation and productivity gains or by Phillips-type effects. A vicious circle is thus triggered between inflation, external imbalances and slack demand, ending with a drop in employment which may even more than offset any initial increase. Finally, still at macroeconomic level, it has also been observed that unemployment rates may rise.

Naturally, if working hours are reduced without wage compensation, and the productivity of the system increases only slightly and in sectors not exposed to competition, the long-term employment effects may be slightly better[40].

---

[40] It is important to emphasise in this regard that even the resolution passed by the European Parliament inviting a reduction of working hours to 32 per week apparently takes account of the constraints described here. Economic, financial and technological compatibility aside and irrespective of whether it is capable of achieving its objective — something we strongly doubt — this resolution also recommends substantially cutting the social security charges and tax burdens of firms that reduce their working hours. As things stand, it is not clear what the balance would be between shorter working hours and higher unit labour costs if total wages remained unchanged as advocated in the resolution, but clearly the European Parliament implicitly acknowledges that if we want to follow this course the only way to achieve some degree of success is to reduce working hours dramatically (a 20% reduction is proposed); that an attempt must be made to neutralise

To conclude, an ex ante reduction of working hours would seem to be a costly option for firms, as well as for the economy in general, and its effects on employment (or on a decrease in the unemployment rate) are far milder than usually thought.

Vice versa, a reduction of working hours after a period of major innovations and consequent productivity gains has nothing in common with the same measure taken as the prime mover of a policy to boost employment. In fact, when working hours are reduced *ex post*, the additional benefits already obtained are spread between real wages, leisure time and increased employment[41].

Last, working hours can be reduced either to increase employment or to reduce lay-offs.

In this case, whether working hours are reduced because production cuts are necessary or because labour-saving innovations have been introduced, or again because the aggregate cost of labour has somehow become incompatible with the firm's financial soundness, the effects of that action would seem to be greater in terms of reducing lay-offs than if the aim is to increase employment.

So, if we want to summarise everything examined so far in a long list, we could say that if aggregate production increases; if technical and institutional discontinuity does not interfere too much; if actual working hours adjust quickly and closely to contractual hours; if it somehow becomes more difficult to use overtime; if labour productivity does not increase too much after the introduction of shorter working hours; if the interplay between wages, working hours and productivity gains does not cause an

---

the macroeconomic repercussions (there is a suggestion to reduce social security charges and hence unit labour costs); that the industrial system should receive strong support, since it must meet the adjustment costs such a measure will inevitably involve (to be done through tax facilities). Briefly, the resolution of the European Parliament acknowledges that a provision to reduce working hours has costs that in the end are also borne by the community and must be taken into account.

[41] Naturally, a number of micro and macro de-multipliers are at work in this case too, but their effect can be neutralised or more than offset either by the earlier technological development and productivity increase, or by the possible rate of increase of aggregate demand (whether or not autonomous gross investment increases).

increase in unit labour costs; if the macroeconomic repercussions are not too great as a result; if exchange rates can move to rectify any external imbalances; if labour supply does not increase too much; if trade union agreements help to reduce (or maintain) wages in exchange for more leisure time; if an international agreement is reached to bring all countries into line with any decision to reduce working hours; if that reduction takes place in sectors unaffected by international competition: if, then, all this were to happen, an ex ante reduction of working hours might have a small effect on employment. However, since we have seen that this is not so, and is not often likely to be so, then working hours should be reduced either ex post or to reduce lay-offs in certain firms.

BIBLIOGRAPHY

[1] ABBATE A. - PIACENTINI P. - POTESTIO P., «Una nuova ricostruzione degli orari di lavoro nell'industria italiana e un confronto con le fonti prevalentemente utilizzate», *Rivista di Politica Economica*, June 1994.

[2] ADDIS E., «Orari più corti: un'occasione di pari opportunità», *Politica ed Economia*, vol. 25, n. 1, 1994.

[3] ALLEN R., «Gli effetti economici di una riduzione degli orari di lavoro», *Rivista Internazionale di Scienze Sociali*, n. 3, 1981.

[4] AMENDOLA A., (ed.), *Disoccupazione: analisi macroeconomica e mercato del lavoro*, Napoli, ESI, 1995.

[5] ARTUS P. - MORIN P. - NASSE P. - STERDYNIAK H., «Gli insegnamenti del METRIC sull'analisi di breve termine» *Economie et statistique*, n. 101, 1978.

[6] BATTINELLI A., «Variable Working Hours in a Simple Model of Macroeconomic Equilibrium with Rationing», *Economia e Lavoro*, n. 1, 1986.

[7] BERTOLA G., «Vincoli istituzionali ai licenziamenti e domanda di lavoro» in PADOA SCHIOPPA KASTORIS F. (ed.), *Squilibri e rigidità del mercato del lavoro italiano: rilevanza quantitativa e proposte correttive*, Milano, F. Angeli, 1993.

[8] BODO G. - GIANNINI C., «La relazione fra orari di fatto e ore contrattuali nell'industria italiana», in BANCA D'ITALIA, *Contributi all'analisi economica*, March 1985.

[9] — - —, «Average Working Time and Influence of Contractual Hours: An Empirical Investigation for the Italian Industry», *Oxford Bulletin of Economics and Statistics*, n. 2, 1985.

[10] BODO G., «Ore contrattuali, orari di fatto e occupazione nella recente esperienza italiana», in VALLI V. (ed.), *Tempo di lavoro ed occupazione*, Roma, NIS, 1988.

[11] BOOTH A. - SCHIANTARELLI F., «The Employment Effects of a Shorter Working Work», *Economica*, vol. 54, 1987.

[12] BRUNELLO G., «The Employment Effects of a Shorter Working Hours: an Application to Japanese Data», *Economica*, vol. 56, November 1989.

[13] BRUNETTA R., «L'obiettivo della riduzione dell'orario di lavoro: una sintesi critica tra conflittualismo e compatibilità», *Economia e Lavoro*, n. 3, 1979.

[14] BRUNI M. - DE LUCA L., *Flessibilità e disoccupazione: il caso Italia*, Roma, Ediesse, 1994.

[15] CALMFORS L., «Job Sharing, Employment and Wages», *European Economic Review*, vol. 27, n. 3, 1985.

[16] CALMFORS L. - DRIFFIL J., «Bargaining Structure Corporatism and Macroeconomic Performance», *Economic Policy*, n. 6, 1988.

[17] CASSONE A., «Il dibattito sul tempo di lavoro nella teoria economica», in VALLI R. (ed.), *Tempo di lavoro ed occupazione*, Roma, NIS, 1988.

[18] CHURAQUI J. - DRISCOL M. - STRAUS-KAHN M., «The Effect of Monetary Policy and Real Sector: and Overview of Empirical Evidence for Selected OECD Counties», in OECD *Working Papers*, n. 51, April 1988.

[19] CHIES I. - TROMBETTA F., «Riduzione dell'orario di lavoro e disoccupazione: il dibattito tedesco», Università degli Studi di Ancona, *Quaderni di Ricerca* n. 71, March 1992.

[20] CUCCHIARELLI A., «Le conseguenze di una riduzione dell'orario di lavoro: l'analisi della letteratura», in TRONTI I. - CUCCHIARELLI A. (eds), *La flessibilizzazione del tempo di lavoro*, 1992.

[21] D'ASCENZIO D., «La riduzione dell'orario di lavoro: costi e compatibilità», *Industria e Sindacato*, n. 2, January 1983.

[22] DE CAPRARIS G., «Riduzione del tempo di lavoro e occupazione», *Rassegna di Statistiche del Lavoro*, n. 4, 1983.

[23] DE GRAUWE P., *Economia dell'integrazione monetaria*, Bologna, il Mulino, 1993.

[24] DEL BOCA A., *Appunti di economia del lavoro*, Torino, Giappichelli, 1998.

[25] DELL'ARINGA C., «La crisi e le ore di lavoro: introduzione», *Rivista Internazionale di Scienze Sociali*, n. 3, 1981.

[26] DENISON E.F., «The Sources of Economic Growth and the Alternative before U.S.», New York, *Committee for Economic Development, Supplementary Papers*, n. 13, 1962.

[27] DI TOMMASO M.L., «Effetto della riduzione dell'orario standard di lavoro sull'occupazione: il caso italiano», *Economia e Lavoro*, n. 3-4, 1995.

[28] FELIZIANI D., «Organizzazione e regolamentazione degli orari di lavoro nei paesi industriali», Università degli Studi di Ancona, *Quaderni di Ricerca*, n. 46, 1994.

[29] FRANCO D. - SESTIO P., «Il sistema di protezione sociale dei disoccupati: alcune riflessioni su una possibile riforma», *Politica Economica*, n. 3, 1995.

[30] FOUQUET D. - CHARFIN J.H. - GUILLAUME H. - MUET P.A. - VALLET D., «DMS, Modello di previsione a medio termine», *Economia et Statistique*, n. 79, 1976.

[31] GUGLIELMETTI P., «Orario di lavoro e disoccupazione in Italia», *Rivista Economica del Mezzogiorno*, n. 4, 1993.

[32] HOEL H. - VALE B., «Effects of Unemployment of Reduced Working Time in an Economy where Firms Set Wages», *European Economic Review*, n. 5, 1986.

[33] JOSSA B., «C'è rimedio alla disoccupazione?», *Il Ponte*, n. 9, 1994.

[34] — —, «La riduzione della durata del lavoro come rimedio alla disoccupazione», *Note Economiche*, n. 1, 1995.

[35] — —, «Sulla proposta di una riduzione continuativa dell'orario di lavoro», *Politica ed Economia*, January-April 1995.

[36] KIRMAN A., «The Intrinsic Limits of Modern Economic Theory: The Emperor has no Clothes», *The Economic Journal*, vol. 99, 1989.

[37] LUCCHETTI R. - STAFFOLANI S., «Orari di lavoro ed occupazione: un approccio teorico con un'applicazione alla grande industria italiana», Università degli Studi di Ancona, *Quaderni di Ricerca*, n. 52, 1994.

[38] LEVESON I.F., «Riduzione dell'orario come fonte per un incremento di produttività», *Rivista Internazionale di Scienze sociali*, n. 3, 1981.

[39] MALINVAUD E., «Una spiegazione della evoluzione della produttività oraria del lavoro», *Rivista Internazionale di Scienze Sociali*, n. 3, 1981.

[40] MARCHETTI A., «Orario, flessibilità, formazione: per una ricomposizione del dibattito sul tempo di lavoro», *Economia e Lavoro*, n. 1, 1989.

[41] MESA J.M., «Short-Time Working or lay-offs? Experience from Canada and California», *International Labour Review*, vol. 123, n. 1, 1984.

[42] MODIGLIANI F., «La crisi della disoccupazione in Europa: un approccio monetarista-Keynesiano e le sue implicazioni», *Rivista di Politica Economica*, n. 6, 1995.

[43] OLINI G., «Anni ottanta: lavorando meno solo sulla carta», *Politica ed Economia*, vol. 25, n. 1, 1994.

[44] OUDIZ G. - RAOUL E. - STERDYNLAK H., «Ridurre l'orario di lavoro: quali conseguenze?», *Rivista Internazionale di Scienze Sociali*, n. 3, 1981.

[45] OWEN J.D., *Working Hours*, Lexington (Mass), Lexington Books, 1959.

[46] PADOA SCHIOPPA KOSTORIS F., (ed.), *Squilibri e rigidità del mercato del lavoro italiano: rilevanza quantitativa e proposte correttive*, Milano, F. Angeli, 1993.

[47] PATERNÒ R. - PROSPERETTI L., *Orario di lavoro ed occupazione*, Venezia, Marsilio, 1997.

[48] PHELPS E.S., «Phillips Curve, Expectation of Inflation, and Optimal Unemployment over Times», *Economica*, n. 2, 1967.

[49] — —, «Le determinanti della disoccupazione in Italia nel dopoguerra: un confronto fra fattori interni e fattori internazionali», *Rivista di Politica Economica*, n. 6, 1995.

[50] PHILIPS A.W., «The Relation between Unemployment and the Rate of Change of Money Wages in United Kingdom, 1861-1957», *Economia*, November 1958.

[51] POTESTIO P., «Orari di lavoro ed andamento dell'occupazione, le esperienze dell'industria italiana dall'autunno "caldo" alle ristrutturazioni degli anni '80», *Rivista di Politica Economica*, March 1990.

[52] RAMPA L., «Lavoro, produttività, orari: i conti in tasca», *Il Ponte*, n. 2, 1994.

[53] RAPPORTO CEPR, *La disoccupazione. Scelte per l'Europa*, Bologna, il Mulino, 1995.

[54] REGINI M. (ed.), *La sfida della flessibilità*, Milano, F. Angeli, 1988.

[55] RIFKIN J., *La fine del lavoro*, Baldini & Castoldi.

[56] SALVATI M., «Flessibilità ed occupazione», in REGINI M. (ed.) *La sfida della flessibilità*, Milano, F. Angeli, 1988.

[57] SAMEK LODOVICI M., «La valutazione delle politiche attive del lavoro: l'esperienza internazionale ed il caso italiano», Economia e Lavoro n. 1, 1995.

[58] SERGENT T. - WALLACE N., «Some Unpleasent Monetarist Arithmetic», *Quaterly Review*, n. 3, 1981.

[59] SESTIO P., «Retribuziuone, orario di lavoro e dimensione aziendale: un'analisi cross section», in *Economia e Lavoro*, n. 4, 1998.

[60] TADDEI D., «Conseguenze economiche e sociali del tempo di lavoro nella Comunità», *Economic Papers della Commissione CEE*, 1989.

[61] VALLI V. (ed.), *Tempo di lavoro ed occupazione: il caso Italiano*, Roma, NIS, 1988.

[62] VAN DER BERGH R.C. - WITTELSBURGER H., «Working Time Reduction and Unemployment», *Conference Board*, 1981.

[63] VAN GINNEKEN W., «Employment and Reduction of the Work Week: A Comparison of Seven European Macroeconomics Models», *International Labour Review*, vol. 123, n. 1, 1984.

[64] ZENEZINI M., «Esistono veramente le funzioni neoclassiche di domanda di lavoro», *Rivista di Politica Economica*, vol. VIII, n. 1, 1993.

Employment Issues in Banking System

Carlo Salvatori
Banca Intesa, Milano

Introduction

Today I have been asked to discuss employment in the banking industry. The Italian banking system is increasingly exposed to the challenges posed by operating in the European and the international banking arena.

The two *Testi unici* (combined regulations), one regarding banking activities in force as of 1994 and the other regarding financial services issued in February 1998, have placed our banks on a substantially level «regulatory» playing field with their Foreign counterparts.

The same cannot be said with regard to employment. First I will address the problem of the rigidity of the employment structure, which is certainly not an advantage for companies neither does it favour the generation change in the labour market nor new employment.

A second problem is the excessive cost associated to labour, excessive if compared to the average labour cost in the Countries that we must compete with. It certainly represents one of the constraints which reduce the competitiveness of our banking system.

I will try to describe some possible solutions for achieving more efficient personnel management policies and I will sometimes refer to Banca Intesa's actions in this area.

I will then comment the recent — commendable — agreement

stipulated between Associazione Bancaria Italiana (the Italian Banking Association) and Trade Unions for the renewal of the National banking labour contract.

1. - A Brief Introduction on the Evolution Currently Under Way in the Banking World

During the Nineties our sector underwent noteworthy structural transformation processes and important legislative modifications[1]. Changes were caused by: liberalisation of financial services, technological innovation, the disintermediation process, market globalisation and, more recently, the creation of an integrated single currency area in Europe.

Competitive pressures have increased. One of the negative effects on the statements of income is the reduction in the margins on lending and deposit collecting activities following the progressive convergence to the price levels recorded in the large European markets.

All these factors accelerated both concentration processes between banks[2] and internal restructuring programmes promoted by single banks.

In these periods of rapid changes, the possibility and the capability of managing human resources effectively will become cru-

---

[1] Refer to *Testo unico delle leggi in materia bancaria e creditizia (Legislative decree 378/1993)*, in force as of 1st January 1994 and *Testo unico della disciplina in materia di intermediazione finanziaria (Legislative decree 58 of 24th February 1998)*. The two *Testi unici* rationalise and systemise the laws and regulations regarding banks issued in the last few years in order to adopt EU directives on this matter and place Italian banks on a substantially level «regulatory» playing field with the banking systems of other EU Countries.

[2] During the Nineties, the number of Italian banks decreased from 1,156 in 1990 to 921 in 1998 (corresponding to a 235 unit reduction) and the concentration process gained considerable momentum. To quote the Governor of the Bank of Italy in his *Annual Report* presented on 31st May 1999: «Net of operations completed within existing groups, until 1998 aggregations referred to 432 banks, representing a third of the system's total assets. And he went on to state: the disposal of controlling and significant stakes held by the State and Fondazioni [continued]. Market share of state-owned banks which equalled 68% at the end of 1992, decreased to 17%.»

cial in order to ensure the development and the very survival of the Italian financial system as well as its competitiveness.

In recent years, Italian banks have made tremendous efforts in the reorganisation of their activities. They have partly reached their objective of attaining adequate profitability levels.

They have invested in higher value added services and innovation regarding production and distribution strategies and methods.

But all this is still not enough.

The Italian banking system must continue its renovation. There are still constraints weighing it down and putting it at a serious competitive disadvantage in the international arena. In particular, banks — which operate in a sector which is still labour intensive — are penalised by the rules governing out labour market.

I am referring to:

a) rigidity in the hiring process and especially in the dissolution of the labour contract;

b) expensive constraints in the management of existing human resources;

c) social security expenses which also contribute to make overall personnel expenses far higher than the European average;

d) the rare applicability of productivity-based incentive systems.

In the current situation of intense international competition, these problems which have long been affecting the credit sector, must be solved for the very survival of the system, or at least in order to give Italian banks the possibility of competing on equal terms with their international competitors.

The structure of employment must be changed by efficient and flexible management of both human resources and excess personnel. Staff costs must be reduced and re-qualified also through a gradual review of social security and tax burdens.

2. - The First Problem as I Said is the Rigidity of the Employment Structure

Excess personnel is the result of past hiring policies but also of the intense transformation undergone by the Italian banking system. Aggregation processes imply a physiological duplication of head office structures and the consequent need to rationalise.

Bank restructuring, the review of lending processes, technological innovation have led to reduce the need for labour[3], this is due to increased process automation, standardisation of administrative procedures and the possibility to transfer a large portion of contacts with clientele to computer-based and telecommunication-assisted systems.

Few figures are needed to highlight the changes which have occurred: the number of bank employees recorded an approximately 14,000 unit reduction from the beginning of the decade notwithstanding the considerable expansion in operations. At the end of 1998 Italian banks had 312,000 employees[4]. Some observers estimated excess personnel to amount to approximately 10% of personnel employed in this sector. This would mean over 30,000 excess employees. From 1992 to 1996, the last year for which certain statistics are available[5], the balance between new engagements and terminations progressively decreased: in 1996, personnel turnover dropped to 0.54 (that is 5 engagements every 10 terminations). The figure recorded a considerable decrease compared to the previous year.

This trend continued in 1997 and 1998. The reduction in the stipulation of permanent contracts also continued. At the end of 1996 these represented less than half of the new labour contracts (more precisely, 44.8% of the total).

Adapting the employment structure to meet the changing competitive situation also led to a reorganisation of tasks to be carried out and a change in professional backgrounds required.

The evolution of technologies applied to organisational as-

---

[3] Differently from industry, the Italian banking system has had to «suffer» technological evolution without having the possibility of counting on the institutional supports which favour the absorption of the effects of technological progress on employment (e.g. cassa integrazione guadagni, that is subsidised temporary unemployment fund).

[4] See Table 1 in the *Appendix*.

[5] The source of the following data is ABI, *Rapporto su retribuzioni e costo del lavoro nelle banche italiane ed europee* (*1998 Report on Wages and Personnel Expenses in the Italian and European Banks*»), October 1998. To be compared with data contained in Table 2 in the *Appendix*.

pects, distribution models and products, the offer of new services designed to meet new customer needs, the launch of distribution strategies complementary to the traditional branch network imply both the obsolescence of certain professional profiles and the need to turn to new qualified and specialised professionals[6], capable of managing innovation. It is the case of those working in asset management, of specialists in the finance or in the highly technological divisions, such as Risk Management, Asset Allocation and organisational analysis.

3. - The Second Problem is High Labour Cost

Increasing competitive pressures, decreasing interest rates and the consequent contraction in the spread between interest on loans and on deposits have led to a progressive decline in the banking system's traditional sources of profitability. In Italy, in 1998, the net interest and other banking income to total asset ratio equalled 3.35%, approximately one percentage point lower than at the beginning of the decade[7].

The phenomenon affected the whole of Europe, however the Italian banking system has had to face a more substantial contraction than the French and German systems.

Margin erosion was not accompanied by a contraction in costs sufficient to return to adequate profitability levels.

For Italian banks, on aggregate, in the period 1994-1997 the cost/income reached an unacceptable 68%, approximately four percentage points higher than the average ratio recorded in the same period in France, Germany and Spain. Last year the ratio decreased to approximately 60%, thus receding to the levels touched in 1993: nonetheless the improvement recorded by this

---

[6] Data on know how is not available. In terms of qualifications and, in particular, in terms of post graduate courses of bank employees it must be noted that the portion of graduated personnel has continued to increase in the past few years: it reached 18.4% of total employees in 1996 from 17.8% the previous year. See Table 3 in the *Appendix*.

[7] See Table 4 in the *Appendix*. During the nineties, all major Countries in Continental Europe were affected by a reduction in unit revenues: the Italian and Spanish banking systems were affected by a more significant contraction compared to the French and German, which already had considerably lower unit margins.

ratio was still scarcely attributable to costs. It mostly reflected the considerable growth rate recorded by net interest and other banking income[8], especially thanks to the significant capital gains registered on Government securities. Unfortunately, these are one-off effects which are not likely to recur in the future and therefore do not lead to a structural reduction in the ratio.

And the rigidity in operating expenses that, in a still labour-intensive industry such as the banking industry, largely depend upon personnel costs which naturally represent a significant portion of total operating expenses.

In 1997, in Italy the incidence of personnel expenses to total operating expenses equalled 64.7%. It is the highest ratio among all OECD Countries with the exception of Greece[9].

It is undeniable that with regard to labour costs Italian banks are still at a disadvantage compared to their foreign counterparts.

All statistics regarding costs sustained per employee confirmed the gap in competitiveness: in 1996 annual cost per employee[10] in Italy equalled 119 million lire, approximately 32% higher than the average of that in the main competitor Countries.

In the international comparison higher tax and social security charges also negatively affect Italian banks.

In 1997 «social security charges»[11] paid out by companies for

---

[8] Between 1995 and 1996, operating expenses — the numerator of the ratio — recorded a 2.2% reduction (from 61,046 billion lire to 60,038 billion lire), whereas net interest and other banking income — the denominator — registered an 11% growth rate (from 89,208 billion lire to 99,070 billion lire). See Table 1 in the *Appendix*.

[9] See Table 5 in the *Appendix*. Data provided for international comparisons, published by OECD are also drawn from the above-mentioned ABI report. The ABI research refers to the 1998 edition of the OECD report on *Bank Profitability, Financial Statements of Banks*. 1996 is the most recent year for which data on all OECD Countries is available. All international comparisons therefore refer to 1996 figures.

[10] See Table 7 in the *Appendix*. Italy's competitive disadvantage becomes even more apparent if comparisons are carried out using standard purchase power exchange rates and not official exchange rates.

[11] Reference must be made to Tables 9 and 10 in the *Appendix*. It must be noted that: «in order improve comparability of figures between Countries the comparison [of social security charges due] has been carried out including ... pension charges and national health service charges without distinction between those required by Law and those that, for the same purposes, are paid following specific agreements and even non-compulsory payments» (*ABI Report*, 1998).

each branch employee equalled 40.6% of gross wage. It is among the highest in Europe.

On average social security expenses sustained by banks in other EU Countries totalled approximately 30%, with a minimum of 11.5% in the United Kingdom.

4. - And Now Something With Regard to Possible Solutions in Order to Achieve More Effective Personnel Management Policies

In my opinion the system needs new employment and compensation strategies leading the parallel development of improved excess labour management policies via adaptation of professional backgrounds to new requirements.

Operating cost containment cannot occur simply via a reduction in the number of employees.

It must be obtained through more attentive resource management and greater flexibility in the way personnel is employed.

From this point of view training for professional re-conversion[12] must play an increasingly important role. Investments must be made to improve expertise. An efficient reallocation of resources by product and process must be favoured.

4.1 *Banca Intesa's Actions in This Area*

We are trying, I must say successfully, to combine the necessary pursuit of greater efficiency with the safeguard of the human and professional capital present in our Group.

Trade unions have favoured the pursuit of this objective.

From 1998, immediately after the establishment of the Holding company Banca Intesa, we have underwritten a Protocol for

---

[12] Please note active labour policies and, in particular, professional training are among the *Job Strategies* most intensely suggested by OECD for the purpose of combating unemployment in Europe.

the Group's Industrial Relations which proposes more flexible solutions with regard to personnel seconding and mobility.

Under the drive of the *Protocol*, we have started numerous training and human resource development programmes. These programmes will, on the one hand, guarantee our companies better quality services and, on the other hand, also enable members of staff which had till then been less qualified to actively deal with labour market demands without having to resort to state-subsidised or traumatic measures. We are continuing to reserve particular attention to specifically designed training programmes aimed at favouring the transfer of bank personnel from support and back office functions to commercial activities which entail a contact with the customers and are therefore more motivating and higher value added.

But the objective of reducing labour costs cannot and must not be achieved solely via more modern and effective personnel management policies. Improved compensation policies are also necessary.

The importance of automatic promotions and pay rises based on period of service must be reduced.

The weight of the fixed component of compensation must be reduced whereas the variable component must be considerably increased and depend on both the company's overall performance and the person's and the team's capability of attaining predefined objectives.

Opportune incentive mechanisms, enable companies, on the one hand, to increase productivity of individual and team work and, on the other hand, to retain the most talented. This has a beneficial effect on the entire system.

Lastly, a reduction in costs may be obtained by outsourcing certain activities via agreements between banks and specialised suppliers operating in near-credit sectors.

I believe that it is not realistic to expect that traumatic expulsions of workers from productive activities will occur in Italy perhaps with the exception of particularly severe crisis situations. Fortunately it is not the case of the banking industry, for which remedies fine tuned in various experiences in recent years can be applied.

4.2 *The Recent Agreement Between ABI and Trade Unions for the New National Banking Labour Contract to Which we at Banca Intesa, Contributed Various Ideas*

After more than two years from the first generic agreement, the final agreement for the new National banking labour contract, excluding management, was reached on 11th July 1999. It finally seems to contain innovative measures for the solution of the employment and labour cost problems which I mentioned before.

I would like to focus on certain distinctive elements in the new contract because they are particularly important:

— first, greater flexibility of entry via easier use of certain contracts, already amply used in other countries, such as term contracts, temporary labour, part-time contracts, home working, etc.;

— second, a more efficient regulation of flexibility of exit through the so-called «fondo per gli esuberi» (excess personnel fund) which should help solve, without exasperated social conflicts, the more severe cases of personnel which can no longer be effectively employed in the productive process;

— third, greater flexibility within the labour relationship in terms of a more definition of working hours better suited to meet technical, organisational or commercial needs and a radical simplification of the hierarchical structure;

— fourth, greater flexibility in compensation schemes[13], via reduced automatic promotions and pay rises based on period of service and the extension of the possibility of using incentive systems.

There is the hope — and I conclude — that, for our financial system, the new national labour contract may represent a precious

---

[13] More specifically, with regard to compensation, the new national labour contract provides for compensation increases in 1998 and 1999; in the later two years cumulated rises in unit contractual remuneration has been limited to 2.5%, just over the programmed inflation rate. It is worth remembering that the *Accordo quadro* (basic agreement) issued in February 1998 set out the guidelines in terms of cost containment and flexibility. With regard to the first aspect, the *Agreement* set a target of a 3.7-4.1 percentage point reduction in the cost/income ratio by the year 2001 compared to the value recorded in 1997.

instrument for changing a situation which was rapidly becoming unsustainable.

The new contract will lead to good results if banks will be capable of seizing the new opportunities it introduces in terms of greater organisational flexibility with regard to both internal mobility of personnel responsible for support services and the extension and different definition of branch hours.

The labour market in the banking industry will face further globalisation pressures, unprecedented in any other sector.

We can perhaps state that finance is the only market which is really above and beyond national boundaries.

The rise of large financial groups both with national and multinational shareholder base will also contribute to change. This forces us to prepare human resources adequately if we do not wish to become marginal or limited in the definition of future strategies and in the direction of fundamental production processes.

APPENDIX

TABLE 1

THE ITALIAN BANK' AGGREGATED STATEMENTS OF INCOME
(billion lire)

Years	Interest margin (a)	Other income net (b)	Net interest and other banking income (a+b)	Opera-ting expen-ses	Person-nel expen-ses	Total assets	Bank employees (number)
1993	65,224	25,850	91,074	55,364	34,769	2,249,923	335,497
1994	60,164	21,053	81,217	55,684	36,070	2,363,863	333,157
1995	64,893	20,796	85,690	58,340	37,133	2,408,554	332,966
1996	63,621	26,042	89,662	59,976	38,617	2,504,398	322,714
1997	60,179	29,029	89,208	61,406	38,398	2,658,212	318,077
1998*	59,168	39,903	99,070	60,038	36,816	2,785,529	312,153

* Provvisonal data.

Source: BANK OF ITALY, «Assemblea generale ordinaria dei partecipanti del 31 maggio 1999, *Annual Report to the Ordinary Shareholders Meeting held on 31st May 1999*, Statistical Attachment.

TABLE 2

BREAKDOWN OF BANK PERSONNEL *TURNOVER* BY GENDER AND BANK SIZE - ITALY, 1996*

Group	Males	Females	Total
Major banks	0.16	0.94	0.30
Large banks	0.29	0.80	0.37
Medium banks	0.76	1.56	0.96
Small banks	1.14	1.94	1.31
Minor banks	1.02	1.53	1.17
Total	0.39	1.17	0.54

* Turnover is defined as the engagements to terminations ratio.

The breakdown by bank size is that introduced by the 1994 Bank of Italy's *Annual Report*. The parameter used in the classification includes assets collected from residents (deposits and securities), liabilities on foreign transactions, amounts due to state institutions, interbank deposits and Shareholders' equity. Classes have been fixed considering the simple average of the parameter's value per quarter, as follows: 1) major banks: if the parameter's average value is over 60,000 billion lire; 2) large banks: if the parameter's average value is between 16,000 and 60,000 billion lire; 3) medium banks: if the parameter's average value is between 5,500 and 16,000 billion lire; 4) small banks: if the parameter's average value is between 1,500 and 5,500 billion lire; 5) minor banks: if the parameter's average value is under 1,500 billion lire. *Source:* ABI, *Rapporto 1998 su retribuzioni e costo del lavoro nelle banche italiane ed europee* (1998 Report on Compensation and Labour Costs in Italian and European Banks), October 1998.

Table 3

BREAKDOWN OF EDUCATION OF BANK PERSONNEL
BY BANK SIZE - ITALY, 1996
(Percentage values)

Group	Degree	Secondary school	Primary school and lower secondary school	other	Total
Major banks	18.3	65.5	15.3	0.9	100
Large banks	18.2	58.3	22.9	0.6	100
Medium banks	17.4	69.5	11.9	1.2	100
Small banks	20.0	66.7	11.7	1.6	100
Minor banks	19.2	69.0	11.2	0.6	100
Total	18.4	64.7	15.9	1.0	100

Source: ABI, *Rapporto 1998 su retribuzioni e costo del lavoro nelle banche italiane ed europee, (1998 Report on Compensation and Labour Costs in Italian and European Banks)*, October 1998.

Table 4

STRUCTURE OF THE ITALIAN BANKS' AGGREGATED
STATEMENTS OF INCOME
(Percentage of total assets)

Indicator	1980	1985	1990	1995	1997	1998*
Interest margin[1]	3.31	3.05	3.35	2.69	2.26	2.12
Other income, net[2]	0.81	1.07	1.00	0.86	1.09	1.43
Net interest and other banking income[3]	4.12	4.11	4.36	3.56	3.35	3.55
Operating expenses including:	2.54	2.46	2.68	2.42	2.31	2.15
Personanel expenses	*1.86*	*1.68*	*1.67*	*1.54*	*1.44*	*1.32*
Operating income[4]	1.58	1.65	1.67	1.14	1.05	1.40
Net income for the year	0.21	0.46	0.58	0.03	0.04	0.47

* Provisonial data

[1] Interest income - interest expenses

[2] Commissions, fees, profits/losses on securities, profits/losses on foreign exchange

[3] Interest margin + other income, net

[4] Net interest and other banking income - Operating expenses

Source: Calculated using BANK OF ITALY: «Annual Repor», *Statistical Attachment*, various years.

TABLE 5

PERSONNEL EXPENSES TO OPERATING EXPENSES RATIO
(Percentage values)

Country	1990	1991	1992	1993	1994	1995	1996
Italy	65.84	65.45	64.32	63.37	65.19	63.98	64.70
Germany	63.79	63.43	63.22	61.43	60.88	60.42	59.36
France	53.89	53.33	53.11	54.95	54.12	54.20	54.38
Great Britain	56.89	55.35	54.64	55.16	56.04	55.80	54.57
Spain	62.41	60.66	60.75	61.95	60.85	61.39	61.37
Austria	59.33	59.37	59.58	58.78	59.02	52.65	52.51
Belgium	50.74	50.65	50.52	61.00	60.85	60.87	60.10
Denmark	62.23	60.39	61.05	61.02	61.85	61.45	59.66
Greece	76.79	75.76	71.53	69.49	70.31	69.55	69.10
Luxembourg	52.30	52.25	52.03	51.38	52.51	51.39	50.33
Holland	57.82	57.62	58.10	55.47	55.28	55.21	53.96
Norway	47.72	41.97	49.61	48.69	43.79	43.37	45.47
Portugal	61.53	58.80	56.85	56.02	55.57	55.67	54.40
Sweden	31.27	21.82	16.15	14.91	31.08	38.86	44.31
Switzerland	65.57	65.82	64.90	65.32	63.91	62.30	51.58
United States	44.69	42.48	41.78	41.64	42.03	42.35	41.73
Japan	53.19	52.52	52.23	52.62	52.42	52.41	49.80

Source: ABI, *Rapporto 1998 su retribuzioni e costo del lavoro nelle banche italiane ed europee, (1998 Report on Compensation and Labour Costs in Italian and European Banks)*, October 1998.

TABLE 6

INCIDENZA DEL COSTO DEL PERSONALE SUL MARGINE DI INTERMEDIAZIONE
(valori percentuali)

Country	1990	1991	1992	1993	1994	1995	1996
Italy	40.88	42.51	42.38	38.75	44.82	43.64	43.40
Germany	41.31	41.34	40.80	38.32	37.02	38.58	37.85
France	39.00	37.07	35.49	35.58	38.57	35.58	38.02
Great Britain	37.46	36.63	36.13	34.84	35.91	35.61	34.02
Spain	38.10	35.50	36.67	36.96	36.33	38.81	38.16
Austria	38.48	38.54	38.12	37.32	38.42	36.57	36.31
Belgium	36.69	35.49	34.49	41.39	43.64	41.15	39.49
Denmark	42.69	37.79	49.68	31.17	44.85	33.18	33.93
Greece	49.22	38.89	43.67	43.58	41.82	44.70	47.04
Luxembourg	19.52	21.19	20.49	19.51	23.61	23.92	23.41
Holland	39.83	38.90	39.06	36.92	37.07	37.15	36.30
Norway	33.73	36.93	29.93	24.55	28.80	30.03	31.60
Portugal	25.62	26.41	30.40	31.48	34.33	36.15	34.99
Sweden	24.47	26.30	23.66	16.38	25.20	27.81	28.51
Switzerland	39.09	34.42	33.83	31.77	35.55	35.16	34.11
United States	30.25	28.74	27.03	26.58	27.33	26.80	26.10
Japan	35.91	36.17	36.61	39.36	40.02	34.88	37.72

Source: ABI, *Rapporto 1998 su retribuzioni e costo del lavoro nelle banche italiane ed europee, (1998 Report on Compensation and Labour Costs in Italian and European Banks)*, October 1998.

TABLE 7

ANNUAL PERSONNEL EXPENSES PER EMPLOYEE
(Million lire calculated using official exchange rates)

Country	1990	1991	1992	1993	1994	1995	1996
Italy	83.01	91.43	100.31	104.77	108.27	111.27	119.71
Germany	44.86	48.01	53.75	71.63	76.39	91.36	90.81
France	62.92	66.11	74.16	96.93	99.82	112.75	113.83
Great Britain	47.13	52.08	52.30	65.20	66.66	73.55	70.34
Spain	57.33	60.02	65.88	78.09	74.22	84.92	87.94
Austria	60.84	65.94	75.01	92.96	100.46	122.16	120.59
Belgium	55.34	59.16	66.54	103.79	111.30	127.26	126.45
Denmark	48.62	52.53	59.45	70.37	75.67	88.66	89.95
Greece	29.85	31.18	32.21	39.25	43.59	52.56	57.29
Luxembourg	62.23	66.30	73.66	93.81	107.90	126.19	122.84
Holland	54.51	62.20	71.59	97.48	110.42	135.67	141.62
Norway	52.49	57.93	58.44	66.48	69.92	84.49	84.72
Portugal	24.54	30.38	38.98	46.73	48.26	58.00	60.57
Sweden	67.27	75.54	77.80	72.44	75.45	96.11	107.54
Svizzera	74.26	81.71	88.37	119.88	130.12	158.83	166.08
United States	41.27	44.98	46.36	61.79	66.22	70.48	70.50
Japan	66.89	76.47	81.78	119.84	135.3	152.84	133.21

Source: ABI, *Rapporto 1998 su retribuzioni e costo del lavoro nelle banche italiane ed europee, (1998 Report on Compensation and Labour Costs in Italian and European Banks)*, October 1998.

TABLE 8

THE IMPACT OF SOCIAL SECURITY EXPENSED AND PERSONAL TAXES FOR A BRANCH EMPLOYEE - 1997

Country	Gross wage	Labour sustained by the company	Net wage	Differential
Italy	100	140.6	71.7	69.0
Austria	100	129.6	73.2	56.4
Belgium	100	133.7	70.3	63.3
Denmark	100	122.7	62.5	60.1
Finland	100	131.8	60.3	71.4
France	100	146.5	77.8	68.7
Germany	100	131.2	71.1	60.1
Great Britain	100	111.5	76.9	34.5
Greece	100	144.6	81.4	63.2
Holland	100	125.8	70.8	55.1
Portugal	100	131.7	82.3	49.5
Spagin	100	130.8	86.3	44.5
Sweden	100	133.3	67.4	65.8
Switzerland	100	120.0	86.4	33.6

Source: ABI, *Rapporto 1998 su retribuzioni e costo del lavoro nelle banche italiane ed europee, (1998 Report on Compensation and Labour Costs in Italian and European Banks)*, October 1998.

TABLE 9

«SOCIAL SECURITY CHARGES» SUSTAINED BY COMPANIES PER BRANCH EMPLOYEE - ITALY, 1997
(Percentage values)

Country	Figure
Italy	40.6
Austria	29.6
Belgium	33.7
Denmark	22.7
Finland	31.8
France	46.5
Germany	31.2
Great Britain	11.5
Greece	44.6
Holland	25.8
Portugal	31.7
Spain	30.8
Sweden	33.3
Switzerland	20.0

Source: ABI, *Rapporto 1998 su retribuzioni e costo del lavoro nelle banche italiane ed europee, (1998 Report on Compensation and Labour Costs in Italian and European Banks)*, October 1998.

TABLE 10

«SOCIAL SECURITY CHARGES» SUSTAINED BY COMPANIES PER WHITE COLLAR EMPLOYEE OF THE LOWEST WAGE LEVEL ITALY, 1997
(Percentage values)

Country	Figure
Italy	40.6
Austria	29.6
Belgium	37.7
Denmark	21.8
Finland	38.7
France	29.6
Germany	29.6
Great Britain	22.8
Greece	51.6
Holland	30.5
Portugal	33.2
Spain	30.8
Sweden	39.2
Switzerland	20.0

Source: ABI, *Rapporto 1998 su retribuzioni e costo del lavoro nelle banche italiane ed europee, (1998 Report on Compensation and Labour Costs in Italian and European Banks)*, October 1998.

Potential Alliances Between Public and Private Sectors for a New Welfare State: the Foundations Case

Giuseppe Guzzetti

Presidente Fondazione Cariplo, Milano

Our social system is currently experiencing a difficult moment. This difficulty does not exclusively pertain to Italy. The phenomenon is emerging, albeit at different levels and for different lengths of time, throughout the entire Western world. However, the situation in Italy is particularly critical.

This crisis concerns most aspects of social security, from pensions to employment, from health care to housing and to personal and economic security and so on.

Perhaps it is useless to attempt to determine who and what are responsible for this situation, even if they certainly exist.

The fact is we find ourselves faced with evolutionary processes that make the social state much weaker and intrinsically unable, with its objectively rigid — and clearly obsolete — mechanisms, to adequately satisfy the increasingly complex and diversified demand of social security.

From this perspective, I am convinced that Europe will play a much more crucial role, for various reasons.

We must realize that Europe will not be just an economic or political alliance, nor will it merely be a United Europe of nations, markets or governments. It will be the United Europe of the people and their needs, their expectations and hopes, especially for a better quality of life for all.

A comparison of various countries at different levels will inevitably begin: on a cultural level, because different European welfare systems and methods will be examined; on a political - managerial level, because the quality of services provided in each country will be compared; and on an economic level, because each country will be responsible for the level of efficiency of their welfare systems.

Obviously, there are no easy recipes or magic formulas to solve this complex problem. Several paths may be taken, however.

And at this point I can briefly mention the experience of bank foundations, which I am more familiar with and that I believe can offer a few helpful ideas.

I should like to clarify a possible misunderstanding in this regard. Foundations — and I believe any private subject — can be complementary to government, but cannot replace it. No one can ever think of replacing the government in the supply of social services. Foundations are not entitled to do so. What is more, they would not even have the means. However, foundations and private subjects must and can play a very important integrative role.

One must imagine close cooperation between public and private sectors to be able to fully satisfy the demand for social security in Italy and Europe.

No one is questioning the fundamental role of public agencies that protect and assist needier classes, or ones that work in certain areas (health care services, for example).

The problem, however, lies in granting more freedom to people who do not pertain to these classes and allowing them to organize their own pension or health care systems, while ensuring a legitimate and necessary contribution of solidarity to the government. On the other hand, the government must grant private suppliers of services an adequate amount of freedom in carrying out their activities, certainly according to strict game rules and specific skills.

These issues have too often been discussed on the basis of demagogic and populist ideology, without considering the benefits that would derive for weaker classes, upon which more adequate resources could be concentrated.

Resorting to private services would relieve the government

from several duties that objectively compromise operative effectiveness today.

In short, uncontrolled privatization of welfare services is unnecessary. What is needed is mutual and harmonious integration between public and private sectors. It is unthinkable today for government to be entirely responsible for all services offered to all citizens. It must therefore be placed in the condition to be able to focus upon priorities and real needs.

This is not an abstract concept. My considerations are primarily based on the experience of the Cariplo Foundation.

In this regard. I must point out that the government has shown considerable farsightedness with the law on foundations that was approved last year. It has given itself and society the chance to access both economic and project resources. It has also combined the need to respect the operative autonomy of the foundations with enforcement of a strict set of reference laws, which will certainly benefit the country.

Let me mention one aspect of the law that I believe is crucial, in which foundations are allowed to support local economic development. Much bas been said about this topic. In fact, it has triggered a diatribe that was mainly brought up by people who feared that the law was a sort of trick to allow foundations to play an "occult" role as financiers of companies that might be insolvent or on the verge of bankruptey.

That is far from the truth. Interpretation of the law is absolutely clear, and it must be said that, from this perspective, the conduct of the foundations has been — and will increasingly be — exemplary.

What does promoting the development of the local economy mean?

It certainly does not mean "doing banking". It means, for example, supporting applied research, perhaps in cooperation with our excellent university centers. It means allowing entire sectors of local economies to access this research, a transfer of technologies and so forth. All these issues require resources that the government or public administrator cannot — Objectively — always guarantee.

Allowing various economic sectors —- not separate companies, mind you — to access applied research and technologies means giving them a chance to increase their competitiveness, which consequently favors growth and development and has evident repercussions, also in terms of employment.

Restoration of a monument also produces wealth, because it favors tourism. I could continue with other examples.

Clearly, no one can pretend to solve all problems. But apart from its merit, affirmation of the methodological principle is important. Therefore, in our country private and public sectors can coexist and work together to provide an adequate solution to satisfy society's demand for a better quality of life.

Of course, some might rightly object that unlike the government, private entities — foundations, for example — have more possibilities to intervene in an "arbitrary" or more discretionary way.

In other words: why choose to support chemical research in favor of the Lombardy textile sector or restore the Ambrosiana in Milan and not something else? This is a serious issue. Bank foundations manage patrimonies that derive from savings and generous contributions spontaneously donated by society that have accumulated over generations. It is a private patrimony that is always communal and collective, nonetheless. Society, therefore, must receive guarantees concerning the use that is made of this patrimony.

In this regard, besides applying corporate governance rules, in full compliance with the law, that ensure a more effective democratic control of its activities, for over a year now Cariplo Foundation has introduced a systematic redefinition of distribution mechanisms based upon a strict process that monitors and selects needs and priorities. Anyone can verify this process, which has been codified in the maximum trasparency.

Moreover, we have launched in the area of our choice the first community foundations pilot projects (based on the community foundations in the United States) that simultaneously ensure extraordinarily effective actions to satisfy the needs of various communities as well as the full democratic control by these communities of foundation activities. We are counting on this project because it means introducing authentic change in the philanthropic culture and practices of our country.

Entirely new entities will be created that must promote the joint action of public and private organizations, private individuals and society that are involved in activities, in each area, performed in the interests of society.

Of course, implementing these processes is not an easy task. However, if foundations want to be acknowledged and accepted by society and government as intermediate social entities effectively exercising their role as subjects serving the civil and economic development of communities with the maximum effectiveness and according to principles of sponsorship and benefaction, they certainly cannot shirk in their duties and commitment.

With the introduction of the new law that regulates this sector, government has taken a risk and has granted full trust in foundations. Now the foundations have the responsibility, but especially the honor, of repaying this trust in the best way, in the global interests of everyone who is committed to creating for the country conditions of sustainable development and an equitable distribution of services.

The Italian vs the European Union Social Expenditure: a Comparison

Enrico Letta
Ministro delle Politiche Comunitarie, Roma

The six recommendations recently made by the European Union to Italy are the starting point of my considerations. One of them, even though not really new, is particularly important, especially at a time when a major debate on the welfare issue is going on in Italy. The European Union has in fact reminded us that welfare and work are interrelated.

This relation between welfare and work, between welfare and the fight against unemployment has to be developed and given a solution. Our first step is to move from the examination of a general theme, that is how the social expenditure in our country is made up as compared with the European one. Overall, Italy's social expenditure is slightly under the European average and pretty much fails within that figure. However the composition of our social expenditure mirrors an Italy that does not exist any longer, an Italy belonging to the past. More than half of this expense — and this is the only case in Europe — is devoted to social security. This is a well-known fact but it is worth underlining because it is the result of all the important cultural and political choices of a Country.

We have inherited from the past a situation in which 54.5% of the social expenditure is destined to social security. The incidence of social security on social expenditure stands at 31% in Belgium, at 37% in Denmark, at 40% in Germany and at 36% in

France. Within the social expenditure, the maternity leave and family items, on one side, and the unemployment item, on the other — which are two relevant items underlying significant political and cultural choices — have a reduced incidence on our GDP compared to the rest of Europe. For instance, Italy's expenditure on maternity leave and family amounted to 0.8% of its GDP (the figure dates back to two years ago) as against 4.1 % of Denmark, 2.1 % of Germany and 2.4% of France.

Why should any reasoning on welfare and the future of our Country start from this point? Because this picture, if compared to the situation of other European Countries, reflects an Italy which is no more. In that Italy, family and maternity were concepts to which great importance was attached due to our cultural heritage. They were certainly stronger concepts than, on average, in the other European Countries. Nowadays we all know that the cultural impact of family and maternity which made it possible to obtain certain results in our Country has unfortunately ceased to make a difference between Europe and us. It is obvious that the themes of family and maternity not only affect the entire welfare structure but also employment and the compatibility of public expenditure in our Country. Therefore the end of that cultural impact and the absence of any public measure on the family and maternity issues have created the negative situation that we all know: record birth rate lows with all the ensuing consequences.

The same reasoning applies to unemployment. As long as the Country has had redistributive mechanisms which allowed social measures to be taken through other systems, the need for active policies to solve the problem of unemployment was not felt. Now, on the contrary ......

Behind the picture described above there are precise choices, the same choices we should make today if we want that picture to remain still. We should, for example, let workers retire at 55 years of age rather than help young people to enter the labour market, families to consolidate or the Country's demography to improve. Everyone knows that adding something here means taking away something there: parameters have to be respected, today more than yesterday.

This is why from this point of view it is paramount and essential to reach a new balance and this is why it is so fundamental that our Country is now debating such an issue. Some steps forward have indeed been taken, at least in the recent past: the Dini pension reform was very important and, a few days ago, Minister Livia Turco, on behalf of the current government, did launch a series of important measures for large families and maternity.

Nevertheless the problem has to be tackled comprehensively since we have to make cultural choices that respond to a different model of Italy with respect to the past. Some far-sighted measures, the call for a possible change in social security made by the secretaries of the DS and the CGIL, Veltroni and Cofferati, testify to a great courage and point to us the important way we have to follow through.

Sticking to this issue, we should carefully consider the proposal to separate social security and welfare which professor Modigliani launched some weeks ago. This is the right way. In our Country the separation between social security and social welfare is extremely important. We should clearly state that there is a need for two types of measures. There is the need for the State to grant a pension which is not as high as 80% of the last salary, as it is now the case, sometimes even at 55 years of age. The ratio should be decidedly lower. Then we should make another important choice that is so clearly stressed in Modigliani's proposal: creating, framing a market for pension funds. This is the enormous difficulty encountered by our Country but this is not a choice that Italy can make on its own. We are a member of the European Union, our market is amongst the most hapless ones but this is the way along which we should advance.

It is not by chance that we are working hard at a Community directive on the market of pension funds which was one of the last proposals by Commissioner Monti before he changed Directorate. This is the prospect that allows us to intervene at European level where choices are made that have decisive impact on our Country. If a Community directive on the European market of pension funds is enacted within this year, in the much touted 2001 we will be in a condition to cope with severance indemni-

ties and pension funds within the framework of a European market of pension funds and on the basis of Community rules which
will enable us to operate in a bigger market. A market of fifteen
Countries creates greater expectations and offers higher revenues
to the investments of pension funds. It is also a guarantee of fiscal harmonisation, a prerequisite for the take-off of pension funds.

There is one more thing to say. A system like ours, going
through a transitional phase, should be characterised by a commitment to explain the existing generational gap. To ignore this
gap is the worst response we can come up with. As regards unemployment and welfare, it is necessary to invent new forms of
action and solidarity rooted in our Country's traditions and to offer greater transparency and information. It would really be important, for instance, to tell any young citizen who is beginning
to work or has been working only for a few years: «Take care of
yourself because with just your employer contributing for you, you
will get a small pension at the end of your working life». It would
be important if we could tell this by sending them a fake pension
allowance with the figure clearly stated on it. From this point of
view education is the only way by which we could push through
a supplementary pension scheme, even culturally.

There would be nothing wrong if we could kick-start the same
mechanism the other way round. To explain how much seniority
pensions cost to the new generations and to explain to the retir-
ing workers who are granted those pensions how much damage
they do to the young should at least morally discourage their use.
If we do not succeed in taking any action on this matter, everyone will still be able to benefit from seniority pensions. In any
case the explanation of the social burden will be the sort of information that may raise some scruples.

As everybody knows, the other big problem of our Country is
the rigidity of the labour market. From there the need to act on
flexibility arises. Two are the fronts we can intervene in: the first
front is that of atypical contracts. Hardly anything is new here except for the need to find the correct definition. During the last
four, five, six years there has been a boom of collaboration contracts, the so-called "12% people". Employers are well aware of

this because they know how many more jobs they can create with this instrument. Even those who start working at 25, 26, 28, 30 and, in 50% of the cases, do so thanks to the 12% contracts, are aware of this fact. This is the Italian way to flexibility, an Italian approach to flexibility whose success we should recognise if we do not want to underestimate it.

It is not possible to increase social insurance, taxation and contributions to this work typology without adopting other measures, since this kind of work functions as it is. It would be meaningless to tell the young people who have been offered an atypical contract, even a precarious one, at 12%: "We increase taxation to protect you". And then, maybe, they will lose their jobs as a consequence of that form of taxation. Vice versa, a comprehensive approach is required and needs to be adopted very cautiously, as it is the case for the other typology of work, which is not the 35 working hours. We are talking about part time. We still have to take many steps forward in this direction, since part time means flexibility, and this is a very serious issue in Italy. Let's then forget 35, 38, or 30 working hours. We can learn from experience that this is the right direction, and that part time is a way to flexibility.

Another element reminds us of our responsibilities. It originates from the comparison between European countries as regards two different aspects: the delay with which Community regulations are absorbed in the various countries and unemployment rates. No direct link can be scientifically hypothesised, but it is remarkable to note that the tables compiled on the basis of these figures list countries in the same order. This means that the countries whose structural capacities make it possible to absorb community regulations, directives, rules on the liberalisation of public utilities, of labour markets — that is all countries capable of implementing these rules and therefore of eliminating fictitious barriers of privileges — are the countries where the unemployment rates are the lowest. Conversely, countries suffering from greater structural dfficulties — among which Italy and Germany are to be mentioned — are the countries where the highest unemployment rate is recorded: Germany and Italy, indeed. In addition, at least Italy finds it very difficult to try to speed up the implementation of Community directives.

It is therefore immediately necessary to include the Community regulations on the liberalisation of public utilities, of the labour market, of jobs, to liberalise professional associations, to share the various forms of the labour market. There are still, those who believe that national barriers favour employment: on the contrary, in the long term, they hinder it.

My conclusions are drawn from last year manifesto, that is the need that the European Central Bank takes an interest not only in inflation, but also in unemployment. The outcome of its first nine months of work is exactly the opposite. It is true, however, that one must consider things in terms of complementarity: in fact, it is difficult to think that the European Central Bank may deal with unemployment before the European Union creates the institutions which are needed for the economic and monetary Union, that is during the next Intergovernmental Conference — this is at least my wish. Another difficulty is related to the fact that only eleven countries out of 15 have entered the Euro area. As a consequence, the ECB governor, for example, in establishing contacts with all other Community institutions, should be accompanied by the governors of the central banks of the non-Euro countries (United Kingdom, Sweden, Denmark and Greece).

We know that this does not make sense and we hope that the Euro area may be soon, very soon, extended to all 15 countries, since this may allow us to establish the institutions of the Economic and Monetary Union which do not yet exist. This is vitally important, if we want the ECB to deal with unemployment in addition to inflation.

However, there is still room for optimism, at least if we consider what the situation was like just a few months ago. From a political point of view, big steps forward have been taken during the last period. As proof of this, just imagine that today, when debating about welfare, we start from results which have already been attained (for example, maternity benefits and large families benefits), we come to an agreement on the shift to the contributory system, we talk about severance indemnity, about the spreading of pension funds and their take-off, just when the relevant Community directive is being prepared. All this came out in a few months' time and it is absolutely meaningful.

Of course we should go on, we should do more, but feeling prouder of Italian achievements, avoiding provincialism and giving up continuous references to France and Spain, which were typical of the past. At the beginning of one of our television newscasts, the following piece of information was given: "There is much debate on the Spanish model". A Spanish TV newscast, on the contrary, would never have opened its edition by saying "There is much debate on the Italian model".

The "jospinisation" or "aznarisation" of our political debate is really a very provincial attitude; we rank third among European economic powers, and thanks to our economic and political strength we have the political leadership of the European Union, in the person of Romano Prodi. It is really harmful to go on believing that we need to copy other models because of our sense of inferiority. We may still feel this inferiority, but it must stimulate us to do what we have to, what we can do and are able to do to create the adequate political environment. It is thanks to the political engagement of this period that some results are being achieved. And they may encourage us to take further steps forward in this direction in the months to come.

II - HOW TO REFORM
SOCIAL SECURITY

Welfare State and Pensions in Italy: Who Benefits? Who Pays?

Mario Baldassarri
Università «La Sapienza», Roma

Introduction

The economic debate on the meaning of the terms *welfare* and *workfare* is always very fertile; sometimes experts oppose these two words, other times they assimilate them, and at times they distinguish them according to upheld theses. Here I would like to refer to their simplest and most real meaning, by calling *welfare* (Social Security) "to do well" and *workfare* (employment policy) "to create or produce jobs".

Of course the two terms can be synergetic or opposite and this fact introduces the first problem I want to face: to analyze Italian data of the last twenty years in order to assess which *welfare* has been realized in Italy and how it has impacted on the *workfare* of this country.

As for *workfare* — to create or produce jobs — a second distinction sounds suitable: the debate among economists has mainly associated the *workfare* concept with microeconomic policies that are actions or ways aiming at looking for or finding job opportunities, improving the profession and joining the labor market again. However, it is necessary to clarify that a macroeconomic *workfare* also exists: it is job production that depends on the structure of the economic system and the impact of economic policy.

Therefore, I will primarily focus my analysis on the *workfare* concept referred to in macroeconomics and I will try to formulate a specific economic policy proposal in order to realize a macroeconomic *workfare* in Italy.

I will point out that this *workfare* concept, that is, the conditions for an increase in employment and for economic growth, must be joined up with a microeconomic *workfare*, that, in my opinion, is mainly and strictly concerned with labor market flexibility. In fact, without the microeconomic measures permitting labor flexibility, the demand-supported development conditions are running the risk of changing into inflationary impulses caused by labor market bottlenecks and, in general, by contraints on the supply side.

An example: if, under equilibrium conditions, we produce 100 units of output with a labor force equal to 10 workers, what happens if the demand temporarily increases to 150 (other things being equal)? If there is a sufficient flexibility, during the period when the demand is higher, we will be able to increase the number of workers, by setting up a "real" and lasting growth cycle. On the other hand, without suitable flexibility, we will have to increase the labor force over a long period, so that, when demand eventually decreases to 100, the cost of the increased labor force will bear on prices, thereby producing no real growth. This paper is an attempt to use the Italian economy as an example to study the implementation of the measures we have being trying to disseminate all over Europe in the *Manifesto* against Unemployment[1]. In fact, I remember that the leading lines of the Manifesto speak about raising the demand, based on the certainty of the existence of flexibility conditions on the supply side. In order to achieve this goal, these conditions should be such that the demand pressure does not impact on prices but produces higher real growth and employment.

Finally I will refer to Modigliani and Ceprini's analysis and

---

[1] See Various Authors «Manifesto Against Unemployment in Europe», *BNL Quarterly Review*, no. 206, Sept. 1998.

proposal, because I strongly believe that the main, structural and underlying topic (regarding not only our social assistance and security system, but our entire economy as well), is the historic passage from the pay-as-you-go to the fully-funded system.

According to their calculations, this passage requires a transition period lasting about sixty years before it will become fully operational and produce the desired results. This does not imply that it is less urgent; on the contrary, it is a decision to be taken as soon as possible because the transition is likely to be lengthy.

After this brief outline of macroeconomic implications and microeconomic links, let's come back to our question: which *welfare* and which *workfare*?

By these terms I do not mean an economic system that makes men poor and then saves face by trying or pretending to help them, but, in my opinion, social assistance and security and *workfare* mean to create conditions leading to higher growth and employment by offering opportunities to reduce the number of the poor and, thus, getting resources to support the "real" poor.

In any case, in order to answer the previous question, I will try to follow a new path, even by making use of some elements provided by generational accounting.

I will divide the discussion into two different parts.

In the first part a synthesis of the empirical analysis of the historic situation will be shown, with reference to the most notable items in public expenditure and their impact on different generations.

In the second part, a synthesis of the "inertial" outlook of the Italian economy during the next five years will be proposed without taking serious and structural measures into account. On this basis, a specific proposal of economic policy will be suggested, aimed at realizing, after the "miracle" of zero inflation[2], a second seeming miracle, that is, the fall in unemployment.

---

[2] See MODIGLIANI F. - BALDASSARRI M. - CASTIGLIONESI F., *Il miracolo possibile*, Bari, Laterza, 1996.

1. - Public Expenditure: What it is, How Much it is, Who it Addresses

Now we try to read the Italian public budget figures by introducing generational accounting criteria too, with particular attention paid to the pension item. Nowadays — from a theoretical viewpoint — every time a bill involving public finance is proposed (hence, almost always), it is compulsory to include technical analysis in order to assess its economic impact from the viewpoint of borne costs and achieved benefits. However, under the present rules costs are measured in "static" terms and, especially, in "closed" terms. "Static" means that they do not incorporate long-term impacts and the effects on future conditions of employment and growth in the economy, "closed" because their evaluations refer to the effects that a bill might have on the present generation, whereas a modern state should benefit from a dynamic and open *welfare* and *workfare* system and assess the middle-long term impact of measures on the dynamic trends in the economic system.

As far as pensions, specifically, are concerned, I will mainly stress one aspect: the "future hump" which was illustrated in the well-known document by the State General Accounting Office. This department tends to explain the social security problem by the fact that, starting from 2005, the relation between pension expenditure and Gross Domestic Product will rise from 14% to about 16% and drop back only after 2035. In my opinion, that "hump" is not only a future concern but might even be misleading because it diverts attention from the real problem. Instead, I will focus on what I think the real anomalies of the Italian pension system are: they have originated in the past and have already created heavy present burdens and will seriously influence the future.

Now we can wonder about what we have created. What is what we call the Welfare State in our country nowdays?

To answer this question I have calculated the essential data in public expenditure during the last twenty/twenty-five years. In Graph 1 the different items in public expenditure from 1980 up to 1996 — as a percentage of GDP — are shown. I believe that it is not necessary to point out analytical comments to highlight what expenditure structure we have adopted during the last two decades.

Therefore, I shall confine myself to the three expenditure items in which an intergenerational evaluation is possible: education, health and pensions.

GRAPH 1

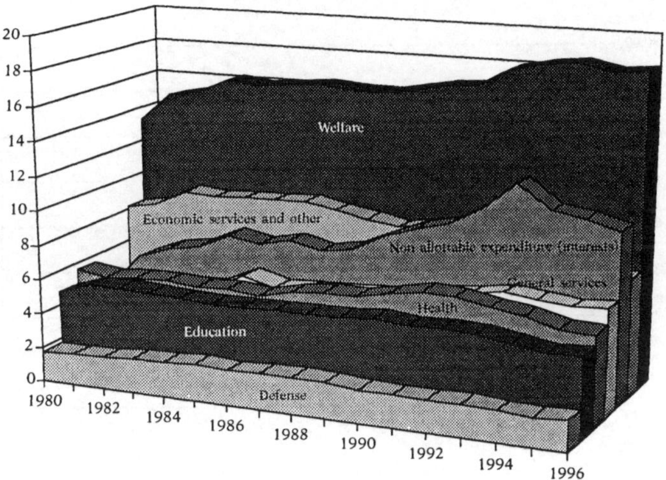

PUBLIC EXPENDITURE BREAKDOWN IN 1980-1996
(as a percentage of GDP)

1.1 *Education Expenditure*

As to their amount, education expenses have varied between 4.5-5 as a percentage of Gross Domestic Product in this country during the last sixteen years. It should be noted that some control of expenditures has existed for this item from 1993 to the present.

From a theoretical viewpoint, we should say that spending for education benefits young people and represents a human capital investment. Looking at Graph 2, however, we realize that spending for education primarily covers personnel and teachers' wages and salaries. Only a little money is spent on goods and services in school, even less for investments. A relevant question arises from this: are the wages and salaries paid to teachers and non-teachers and other personnel in the education sector real human capital accumulation profiting young people or do they represent, to some extent, corporative protection ensuring jobs or salaries to those who are hired as employees?

GRAPH 2

EXPENDITURE IN EDUCATION
(billions of 1997 liras)

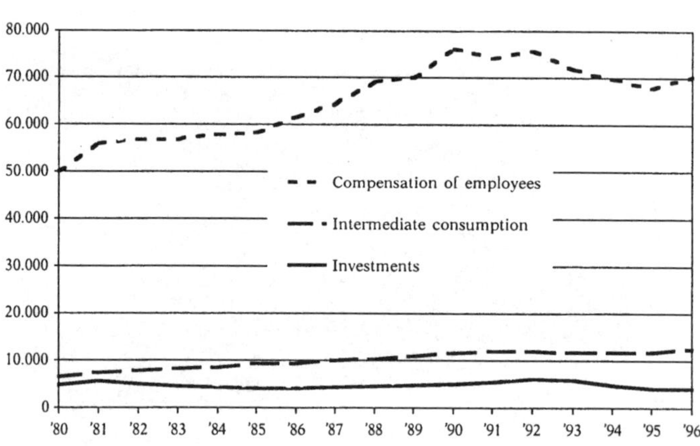

Let's look at per capita expenditure for each student at the different school levels during the last twenty-two years from 1975 to 1997 in Graph 3. The cost for each child in primary school exceeds 5 million lira a year; in middle school about 7 million per capita; in high school it amounts to 6 million. It should be noted that in 1997 high school cost a little bit less than the middle school, owing to the fact that the latter has experienced a reduction in the number of school children, as we shall see, whereas high school is still influenced by the baby boom wave. Finally, each university student costs over 12 million a year, even if he directly pays only 1.3 million lire for matriculation fees.

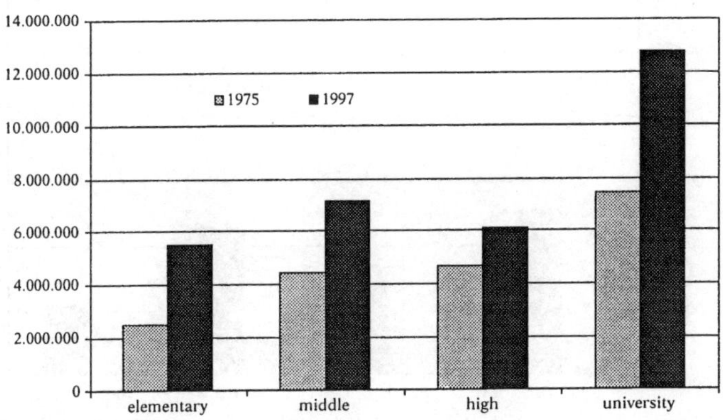

Facing these increasing costs, the student population in primary school has fallen, as illustrated in Graph 4. In fact it has decreased from less than 5 million to about 2.5 million pupils, with a reduction of about 45%. Even the middle school has experienced a 30% enrollment drop. Seemingly, the student population seems to grow at the high school and university levels, even though the annual time series points out that, during the last two years, enrollment started decreasing in higher education as well.

However, the overall student population has decreased by about 12% on average, as shown in Graph 5. It is easy to realize that the current reduction in the student population in primary and middle education will be reflected in high schools and universities between 2005 and 2010. This phenomenon could be partly offset by external factors which cannot presently be precisely evaluated and are mainly related to immigration.

Now let's examine Graph 6, the age-grouped redistribution of wages and salaries in the school sector. It is worth reminding that all data used here are expressed in real terms, at constant 1997 prices and, therefore, they are not affected by inflation. It is extremely interesting to notice that the greatest salary outlay is for

STUDENT POPULATION

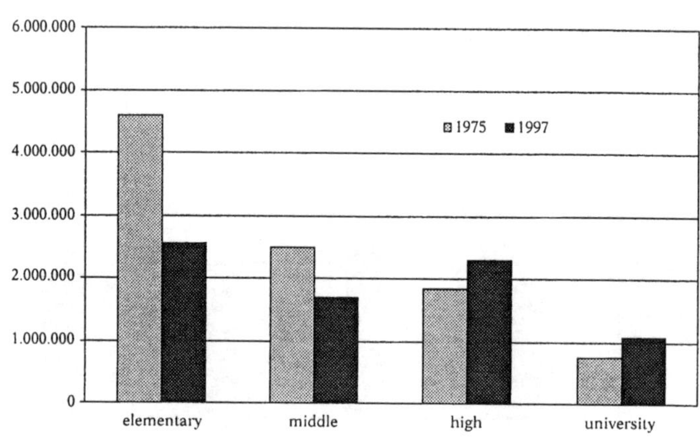

STUDENT POPULATION (% CHANGES)
1975-1997

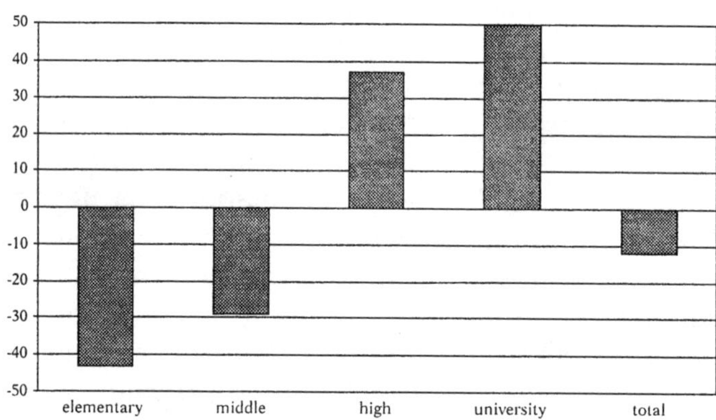

45-to-49-year-old employees; afterwards, expenses due to school-sector wages are strongly reduced.

This trend can be simply and meaningfully explained if we examine the average per-employee salary, always by age-class, in

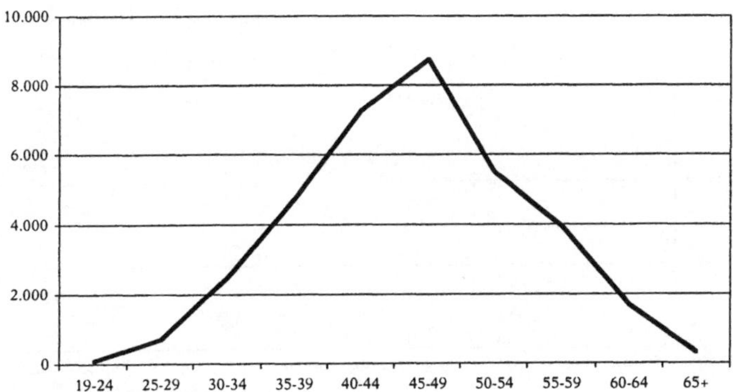

Graph 7. Hence, it can be noted that when an employee (teacher and non-teacher) starts working in this sector, at about the age of twenty-four, he earns about 2 million 300 thousand lire a month at 1997 prices. After forty years, when he stops working, his salary amounts to about 3 million 300 thousand lire. However, we have to realize that the growth of his salary, which is quite moderate throughout his working career, stops when he is fifty-years old in any case. It is obvious that someone who can retire at the age of 50 finds it greatly advantageous to leave school, in the presence of definitely favorable conditions represented by:

(i) the little chance in career and wage increases after 50;

(ii) the small difference between salary and retirement pension;

(iii) the decreasing possibility of finding other jobs as his age rises, since he has already got another steady source of income, that is, a pension.

Everything is confirmed in the previous graph that underlines how salary expenses in the school sector shrink for people older than 50. In fact, it does not appear economically reasonable either for teachers or non-teachers to prolong their job activity at school over that age.

                         Mario Baldassarri

**AVERAGE MONTHLY WAGE
IN THE SCHOOL-SECTOR BY AGE-CLASS, 1995**
(thousands of 1997 liras)

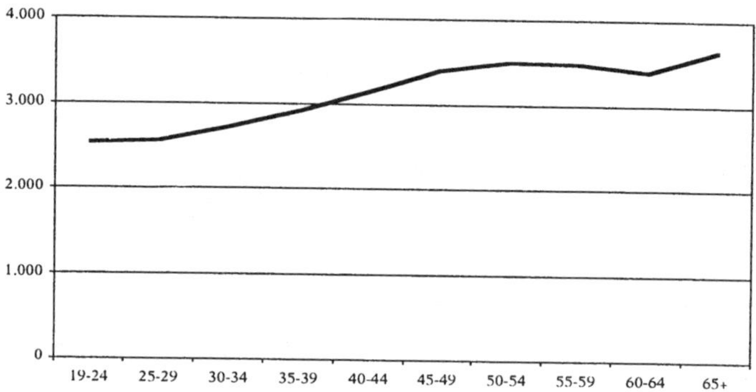

1.2 *Health Expenditure*

Now let's examine the health sector and consider the period from 1980 to 1996. As it can be seen in Graph 8, expenditures until 1986 fluctuated at about 5.5% of Gross Domestic Product: they rose to 6.5% in 1992 and then, from 1992 to 1996, returned to about 5 and 5.5%, in line with Eighties' values. What kind of welfare state does it represent?

To analyze the allocation of health expenses, let's look at Graphs 9 and 10. In the first one, outlays by economic end-use are represented and divided into wages and salaries, social services (to a large extent medicines and hospital admissions), and direct consumption (goods and services purchased by health operators). In the second one function-disaggregated spending is reported, that is, medicines, hospitals and medical examination costs.

A comparison among the various items makes it clear that the greatest outlay, over 55% of the overall amount, is for wages and salaries of medical and paramedical personnel in hospital structures, which is about 3-3.2% of GDP, as shown in Graph 11.

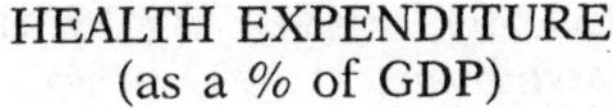

HEALTH EXPENDITURE
(as a % of GDP)

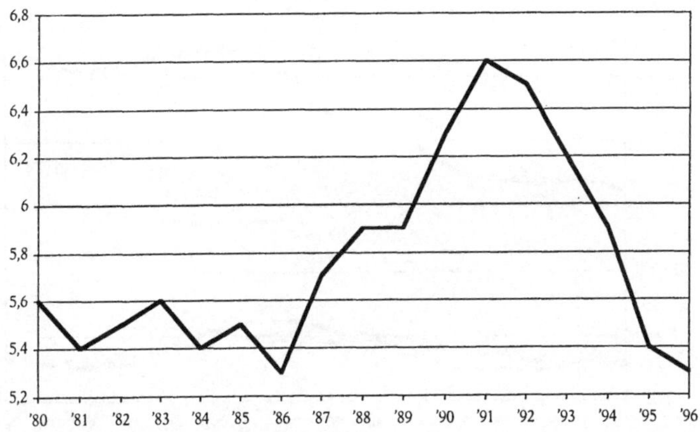

HEALTH EXPENDITURE
(billions of 1997 liras)

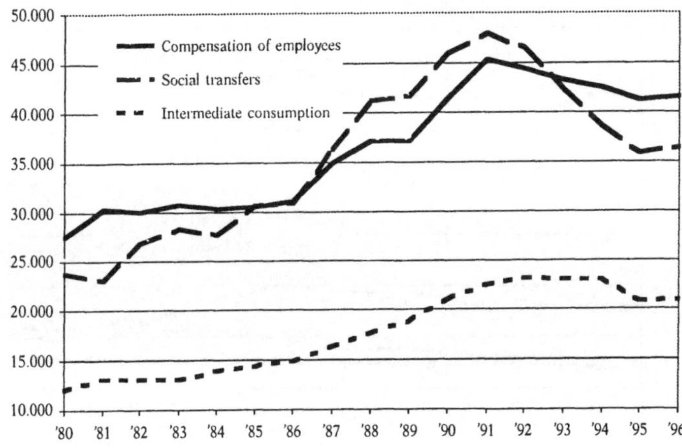

Let's see now (Graphs 12 and 13) how much of the health expenditure is allotted among the various age groups, in order to introduce some principles in intergenerational redistribution. Ex-

HEALTH EXPENSES BY PURPOSE
(billions of 1997 liras)

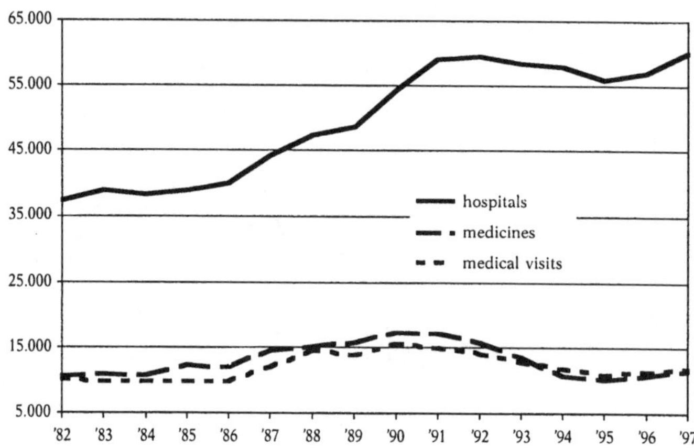

HEALTH EXPENSES BY PURPOSE
(as a % of GDP)

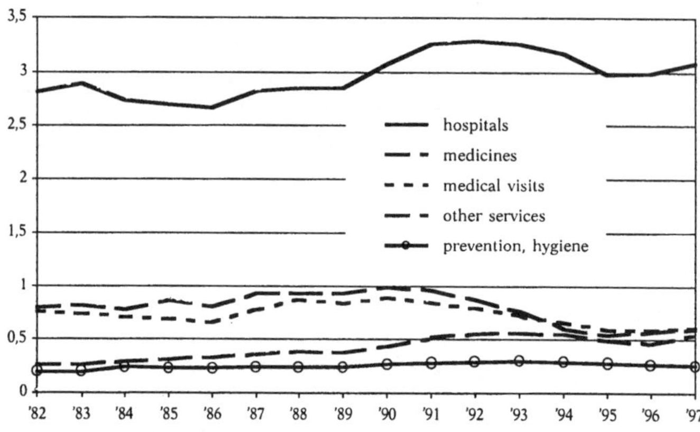

penses for medicines and medical examinations do not show great differences: each examination provided by the national health service costs about 27-29 thousand lire, regardless of age. The per capita expense for medicines rises for people over 45 and decreases a little for those over 75. Therefore, from this viewpoint, health represents a clear intergenerational redistribution benefitting the elderly.

GRAPH 12

HEALTH EXPENSES BY TYPE OF SERVICE AND AGE-CLASS
(billions of 1997 liras)

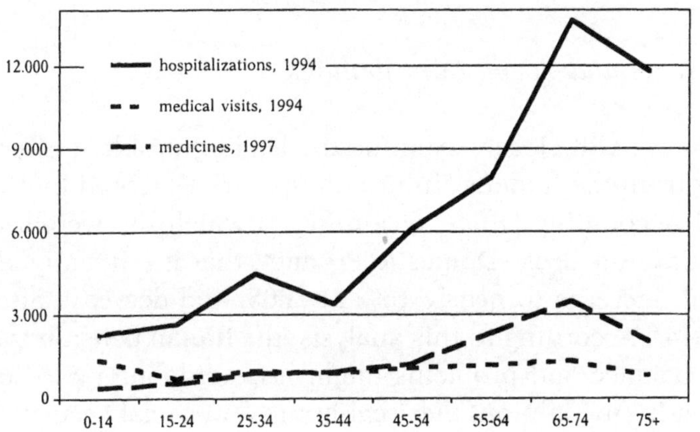

GRAPH 13

PER CAPITA HEALTH EXPENSES BY TYPE
OF SERVICE AND AGE-CLASS
(billions of 1997 liras)

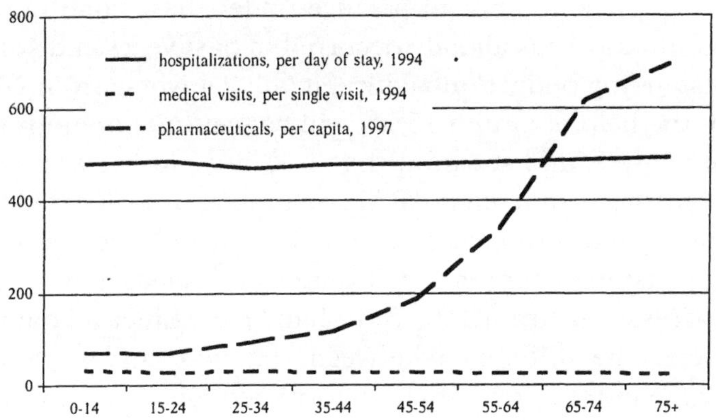

Finally let's look at the cost for every service: 27/29 thousand lire per examination; 220 thousand lire (a year) for pharmaceutical expenses; 500 thousand lire a day in 1994 — increased to 650 thousand by 1998 — per admission to a public hospital. Up to now, every day of hospitalization costs about 800 thousand lire on overage, and the cost changes according to the different supplied service (surgery and technically advanced treatments), even though the patient has the impression that the service in free.

1.3 *Pensions and Social Contributions*

Now we will closely examine the leading problem of pensions starting from the famous "future humps" underscored by the State General Accounting Office, according to which the weight of pension outlays on Gross Domestic Product, that is currently at about 14%, will increase to nearly 16% in 2005, and decrease after 2035 (Graph 14). According to this analysis, the Italian pension system is now in balance and problems might arise only after 5 or 6 years. However, in my opinion, the "real humps" of social security expenditure do not only belong to the future: they have already caused a problem, which we have been dragging along for years. Today, 300 thousand billion in pensions are disbursed and only about 200 thousand billion in social security contributions are received. The difference — equal to about 100 thousand billions — is covered by transfers from the public budget in order to finance the deficit in social security. The system is not in balance under these conditions. And since this situation has already occurred in past years and still causes an outstanding budget unbalance, it will get worse from 2005 on.

With the help of Graph 15 we will concentrate on an intergenerational analysis and see how, the disability, old age and survivor (I.V.S.) pensions disbursed in 1975 and in 1997 are allocated by age-class. The expenditure peak rises for fifty-year-old people who entered the pension system in the Seventies. It is clear how such peak shifts progressively toward the right-hand side. Since all data are in 1997 prices, the difference between the two curves shows the greater expenditure for inflation-corrected pensions in the last twenty two years in Italy. It should be observed how this difference becomes smaller and smaller for recipients getting on in years.

GRAPH 14

PENSION EXPENDITURE
(as a percentage of GDP), 1999 forecast

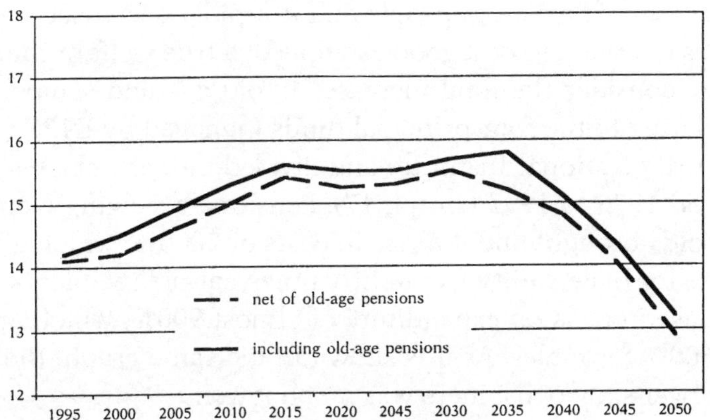

GRAPH 15

DISABILITY, OLD-AGE AND SURVIVOR PENSIONS:
TOTAL AMOUNT BY AGE CLASS
(billions of 1997 lira)

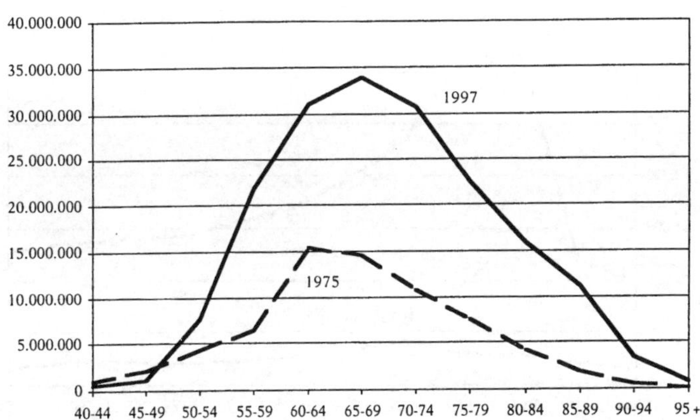

Source: INPS Data.

Let's examine the average amount by age in Graph 16. In 1975, the average pension did not differ much among the various age classes, because the problem of early retirements had barely begun. In fact, we refer to the pension reform introduced in 1969 concerning seniority pensions and baby pensions in the public service legislated by the Andreotti-Malagodi Government in 1970/1971. We notice what happened in the 1997 data: the average pension was higher among 50 and 55-year-old people and it rapidly decreased with age. This does not seem to be a good example of a true welfare state at all.

Now consider the total increases in old age and seniority pensions relating to the four principal funds managed by INPS (the Social Security National Institute) and divided into age classes during the period 1975 to 1997 (Graph 17). Pensioners ranging from 50 to 54 year-olds brought about a rise in costs of 2000%, which amounts to 2300% for males. Fifty-five to fifty-nine-year-old recipients caused an increase in pension expenditure of almost 900%, which amounted to 2600% for males. As it is shown in the same graph, the rise in cost for over-sixty pensioners was much lower.

GRAPH 16

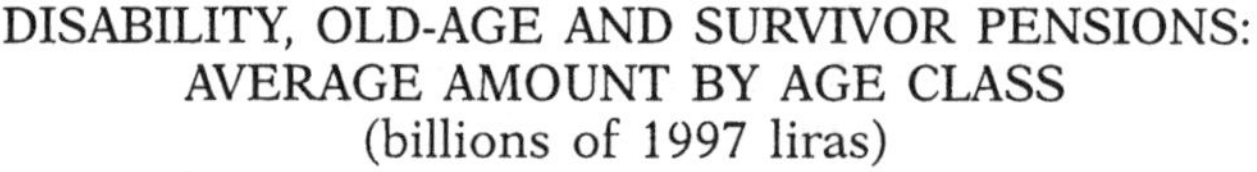

DISABILITY, OLD-AGE AND SURVIVOR PENSIONS:
AVERAGE AMOUNT BY AGE CLASS
(billions of 1997 liras)

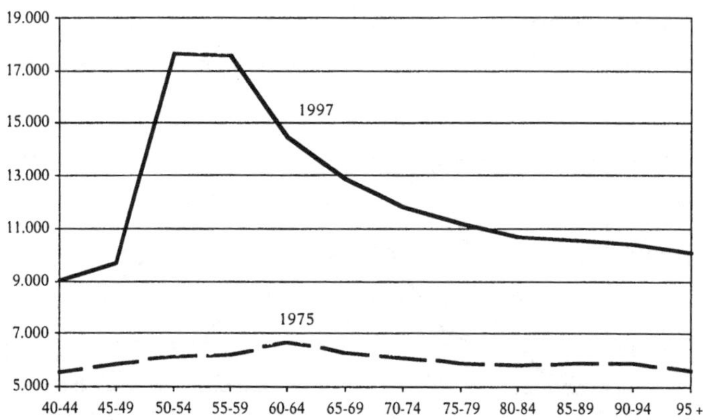

Source: INPS Data.

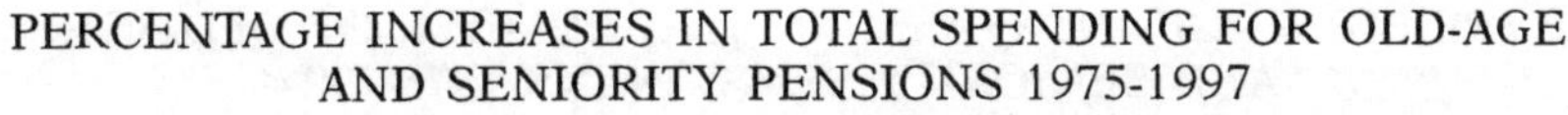

PERCENTAGE INCREASES IN TOTAL SPENDING FOR OLD-AGE
AND SENIORITY PENSIONS 1975-1997

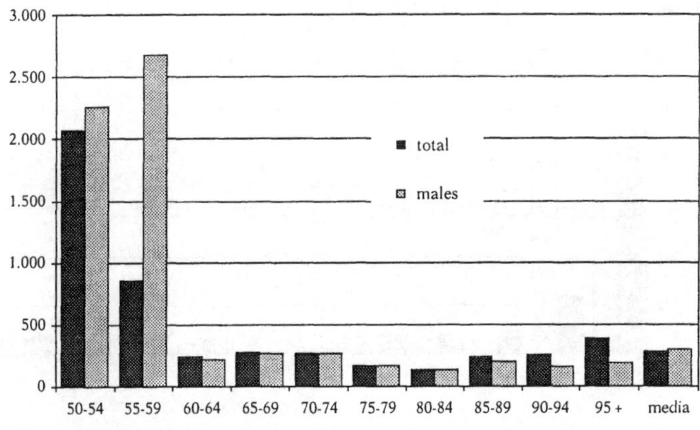

Source: INPS Data.

Such increases in total expenditure were due to the rise in
the number of retirees and the average pension amount. Hence,
examine Graph 18: It represents the increase in the number of old
age and seniority pensioners by age-class between 1975 and 1997.
As the graph show, such increases were lower for people over sixty but really considerable for fifty-year-old retirees, whose number experienced a nearly 1000% increase.

Such a growth in the number of recipients must be added to
the rise in the "total average" amount (Graph 19), which is inversely proportional to age, that is, the increase was bigger for
younger pensioners and much smaller for older ones.

The same phenomenon occurred in the most important fund
managed by INPS: The Employees' Pension Fund. In 1995 (Graph
20) the peak in the average pension amount refers to 50-to-54
year-old people. This phenomenon is outstanding even if we consider only the increases recorded for old-age and seniority pensions, hence leaving out disability survivors' pensions. The expenditure for pensioners over sixty involved very little increases but

                    Mario Baldassarri

GRAPH 18

PERCENTAGE INCREASES IN THE NUMBER OF OLD-AGE AND SENIORITY PENSIONERS 1975-1997

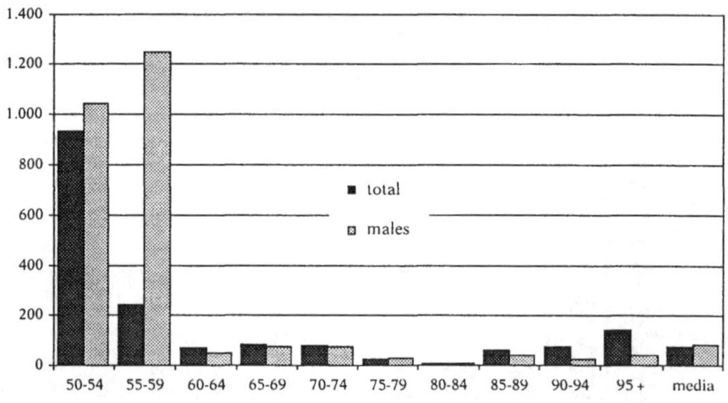

Source: INPS Data.

GRAPH 19

PERCENTAGE INCREASES IN OVERALL AVERAGE PENSION AMOUNT 1975-1997

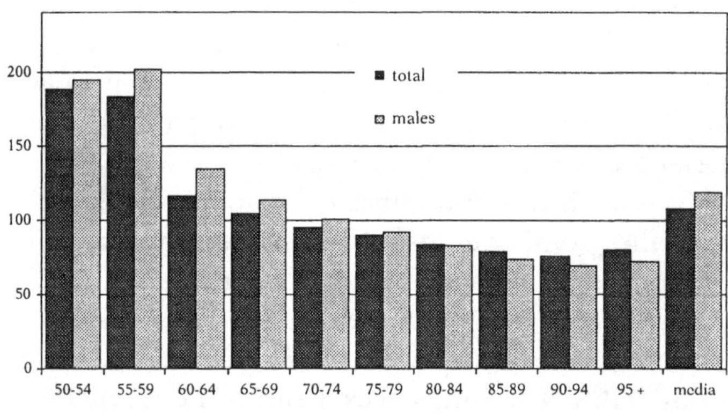

Source: INPS Data.

the one for fifty-year-old people (Graph 21) jumped by nearly 2000% (males 2300% and females about 1000%). On average, the increase for the same classes reached a 200% peak that decreased

GRAPH 20

AVERAGE DISABILITY, OLD-AGE AND SENIORITY PENSIONS PAID BY THE EMPLOYEES' PENSION FUND
(billions of 1997 liras)

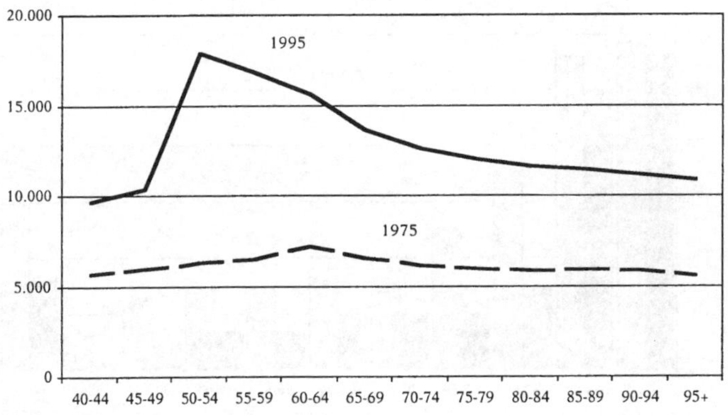

Source: INPS Data.

GRAPH 21

DISABILITY, OLD-AGE AND SENIORITY PENSIONS PAID BY THE EMPOLYEES' PENSION FUND
(percentage increases of total amount, 1975-1997)

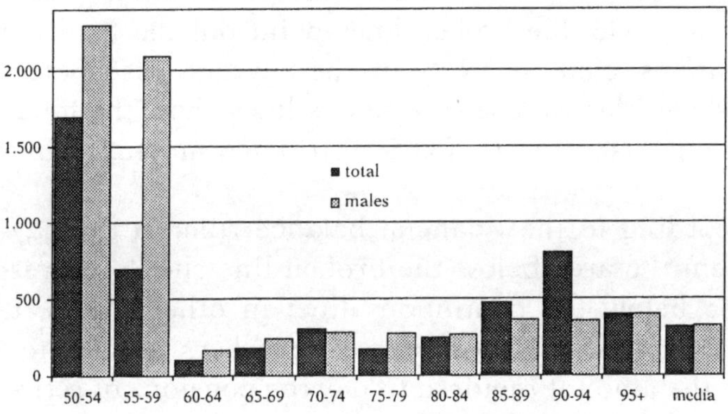

Source: INPS Data.

inversely proportional to the increasing age of the recipients, as it is shown in Graph 22.

                           Mario Baldassarri

AVERAGE OLD-AGE AND SENIORITY PENSION AMOUNT
PAID BY THE EMPLOYEES' PENSION FUND
percentage increases, 1975-1997

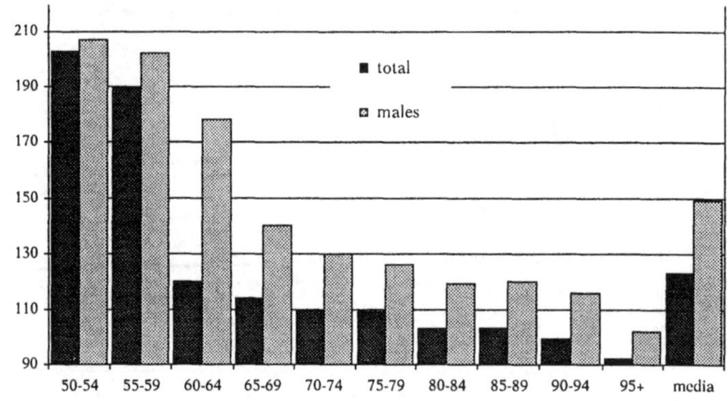

Source: INPS Data.

Hence, a last important remark must be made in order to better understand Modigliani-Ceprini's problem regarding the transition from the pay-as-you-go to the fully-funded system. In Graph 23, representing the relation between contributions and pensions in 1975 an 1995, the broken lines point out the total amount of contributions paid to INPS in these years, distributed among workers' age classes. The continuous lines show the total amount of pensions disbursed by INPS distributed among recipients' age classes.

According to the financial balance rule, in the pay-as-you-go system the area below the broken line should correspond to the area below the continuous line: in other words, the total amount of contributions paid by workers should to able to finance the amount required to pay the pensions of retired workers. As it is shown, the difference between the two areas (pensions and contributions) is much smaller in 1975 than in 1995. In fact, the nine thousand billion difference in 1975 became 65 thousand in 1995. The gap between total contributions and total pension expenditures (including all private sector funds and the

GRAPH 23

COMPARISON BETWEEN EMPLOYEES' CONTRIBUTIONS
AND PENSIONS 1975-1995, ABSOLUTE VALUES
(millions of 1997 liras)

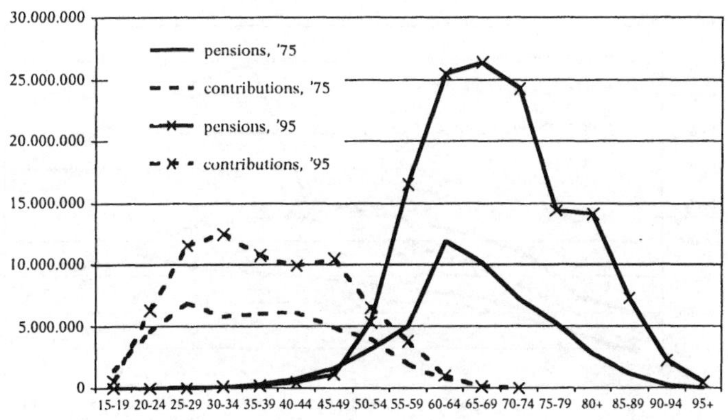

Source: INPS Data.

pubblic administration) was estimated at about 100 thousand billion in 1997, a burden which lies heavily on the public budget every year.

Therefore, the pay-as-you-go system, in contrast with the fully-funded one, implies a "shifting" of resources, and causes contributions currently paid to finance today's pensions. Instead, in a fully-funded system, contributions that are paid today are invested today to finance tomorrow's pensions.

Graph 24 shows that, although the average amount of social contributions notably increased, the relationship between pensions/contributions went up much more proportionally. Even this redistribution, therefore, benefits today's fifty-year-old people and is quite unfair from the intergenerational viewpoint.

This incontrovertible data proves that the Italian pay-as-you-go system has not been on balance for years and it does not make any sense to postpone the problem to a future time. In fact, the broken line of Graph 23 defines an area much smaller than the continuous line for pensions. Therefore, it is inaccurate to affirm that social contributions in Italy are equal to 32.7% of salaries

COMPARISON BETWEEN EMPLOYEES' CONTRIBUTIONS AND PENSIONS 1975-1995,, PER CAPITA VALUES
(thousands of 1997 liras)

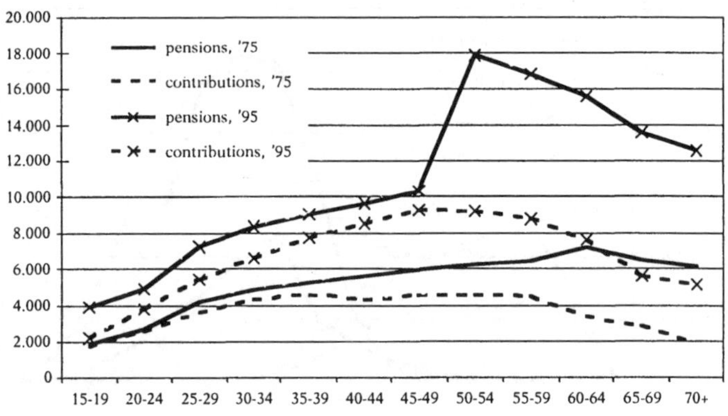

Source: INPS Data.

plus (about) 7% of the TFR (retirement allowances), because Italian pension expenditure would have been in balance only with contributions at 46% and not 32.7% like it is today, according to INPS data. This imbalance reaches its maximum for the fifty to sixty-year-old age-class.

In my opinion, this steady situation only benefiting 50 to 60 year-old people cannot be defined as a "welfare" state. On the contrary, the welfare state has to be dynamic and consider the impact of long-term social security policy on the conditions of economic growth, in addition to safeguarding the over-sixty elderly more serously.

2. - "Inertial" Outlook and Proposals for Economic Policy

First of all, it is necessary to rid our minds of a great misunderstanding which has arisen in Europe and Italy. People say: "Since we have signed the Maastricht Treaty and the Stability and Growth Agreement and agreed that it is not possible to run a public deficit any longer, both the public finance policy and the demand-side economic policy are no longer feasible".

This is a statement I disagree with because it implies a dangerous concept according to which the demand-side policy and the support policy aimed at promoting development and employment can be carried out only through deficit and public debt accumulation. Instead, I will demonstrate that a true public budget policy can be performed, even pursuing the objective for the deficit and controlling the level and composition of public expenditure and fiscal revenues. This public finance policy will determine, after the first "miracle", which together with Modigliani, we identified in the zero inflation objective, a second "miracle", that is, full employment.

As for pensions, the transition from the wage-based to the contribution-based system, proposed by trade unions, does not imply a structural change. In fact, two elements are needed to carry out a serious pension reform in our country and, partly, in the rest of Europe:

1) raise the minimum retirement age to more than sixty, matching it to the average lifetime increase;

2) pass from the "pay-as-you-go" to the "fully-funded" system.

This can be done so as to let a worker retire at the age when he wants: this way, he benefits by a "private" pension proportional to contributions paid and compounded, without taking advantage of the public system that will intervene only starting from the attainment of the minimum retirement age.

Without these two elements we cannot speak about pension reform seriously; without them, any proposal is only an expedient to putting the problem off. In fact, this happened in 1995 with the Dini reform, which was worthwhile in order to avoid a short-term crash, but it has only changed what was an "earthquake" into a form of "bradyseism", where the country does not collapse unexpectedly but slowly sinks, year after year.

                     Mario Baldassarri

2.1 *"Inertial" Outlook*

Even if everything goes well all over the world, if we do not implement structural measures, inadequate growth and high unemployment will always be recorded in Italy. Furthermore, if in the next five years, international interest rates increase, we would be the first to suffer from this situation (Graphs 25-26).

Estimates made under inertial conditions indicate that the Gross Domestic Product would rise at about 2%-2.5% a year and the rate of unemployment would drop from 12% to 11% in five years. If the rates of growth of GDP return to under 1.5%, unemployment would increase over 12%. With a public deficit to Gross Domestic Product ratio like ours, we will be able to respect the Stability Pact only if conditions are favorable in the rest of Europe and all over the world. If average interest rates go up a point and a half, the ratio between the deficit and Gross Domestic Product could even increase again above 3% in two years' time, owing to the expirations of public debt (Graph 27). In spite of its decreasing trend, we have a public debt that will be over 100% of

GRAPH 25

GDP GROWTH

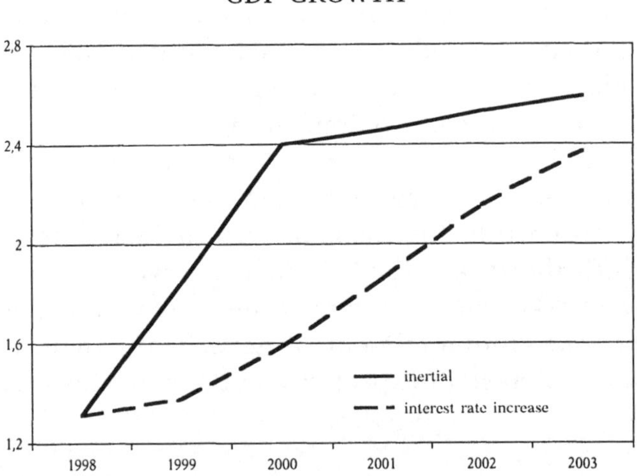

UNEMPLOYMENT RATE

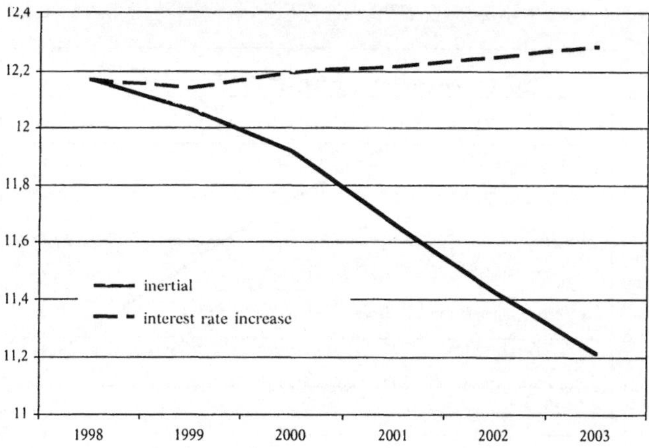

NET DEFICIT/GDP RATIO

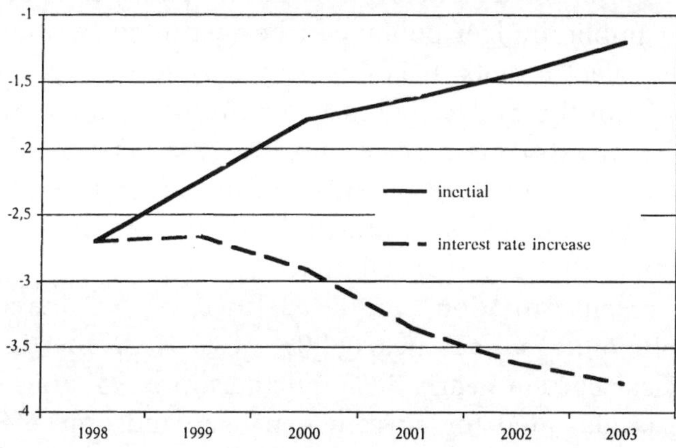

Gross Domestic Product until 2003 (Graph 28). As long as the level of our debt remains this high our economy will always be at risk because any increase in interest rates on the international markets will become a double burden for us, in comparison to Germany or France, for example.

PUBLIC DEBT/GDP RATIO

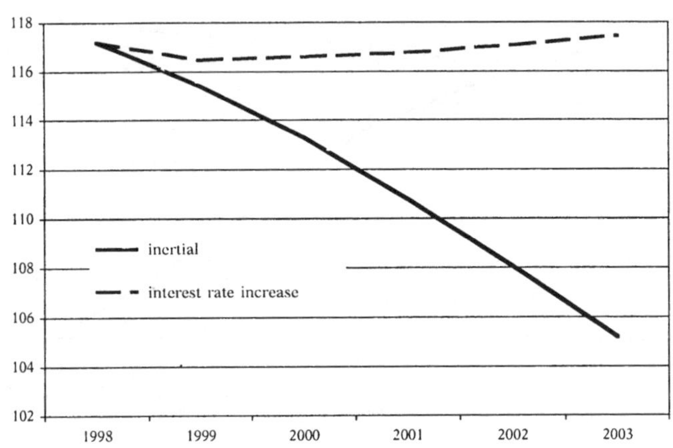

2.2 *Proposals for a Structural Economic Policy*

My proposal for a structural economic policy is based on the fact that a public budget policy can be instituted by maintaining the Stability Pact targets. It is not necessary to exclude public investments from the budget balance requirements for the Stability Pact. Public investments can be and must be performed through structural reforms of current expenditure so that resources between the State on one side and individuals, families and enterprises on the other are redistributed.

The present situation can be defined as a "sharecropping pact". Public outlays reach nearly 50% of Gross Domestic Product and the fiscal burden nearly 48%. Furthermore, 94% of public expenditure is allocated for current expenses and only 6% for the capital account, supposing that capital account expenditure represents real investments.

In my opinion, a public budget policy can be implemented by fixing a deficit target and cutting down simultaneously public expenditures and fiscal revenues, which will be reduced from 50% to 40%, in four or five years' time. This does not mean to either destroy the state, or the welfare state, but it rather means to create enough resources so as to cause the economic system and employment to grow and strengthen both the state and the welfare state in the middle-long term. This can happen through an economic policy approach aimed at establishing a pact with families and enterprises and at introducing greater flexibility in the labor market.

In addition to adequate monetary policies and unified employment and growth policies among the different European countries, in my opinion flexibility in the labor market represents the basis for the *Manifesto Against Unemployment in Europe* applied to the Italian economy.

The pact with families has to consist of lower taxes, fewer social contributions, the extension of the retirement age and more flexibility in the labor market. Regarding this subject I want to include a specific proposal in a comprehensive project to redefine the fiscal revenue policy. It deals with an intervention on IRPEF (the personal income tax) rates consistent with a balanced budget, or rather — as it will be shown — with a public deficit/gross domestic product ratio in compliance with the Stability Pact that is better than it is today. Tax rates would be reduced to two only: 15% under 60 million and 30% over 60 million (Graph 29). The elimination of all allowances and current deductions would be replaced by an income deduction of 5 million a year for every family component.

Now consider what would happen, for instance, in a household composed of three people, on Graph 30. A strong tax relief could be obtained through a very progressive IRPEF rates structure, particularly in favor of the poorest classes, but with a small rising curve for contributors whose income is over 125 million.

A tax reduction of this size could act as a strong deterrent against tax evasion, particularly for high incomes since the ratio between the implied risk in tax evasion and the profit from it would be less favorable, and at the same time stimulate private entrepreneurship.

This effect becomes stronger as family members increase;

INCOME TAX RATE STRUCTURE BY INCOME BRACKETS
(Three-Member Household)

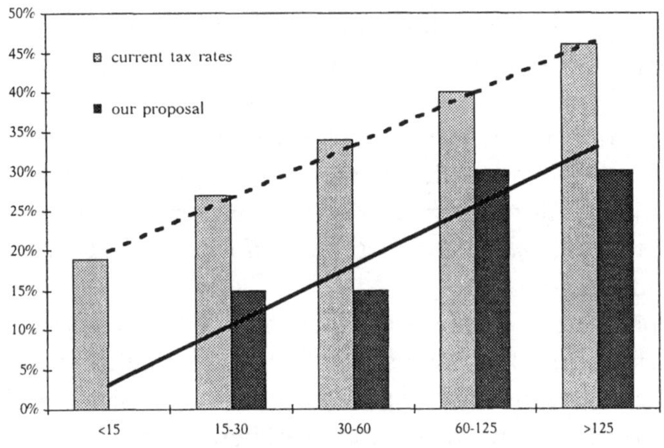

ACTUAL TAX CUT BY INCOME BRACKETS

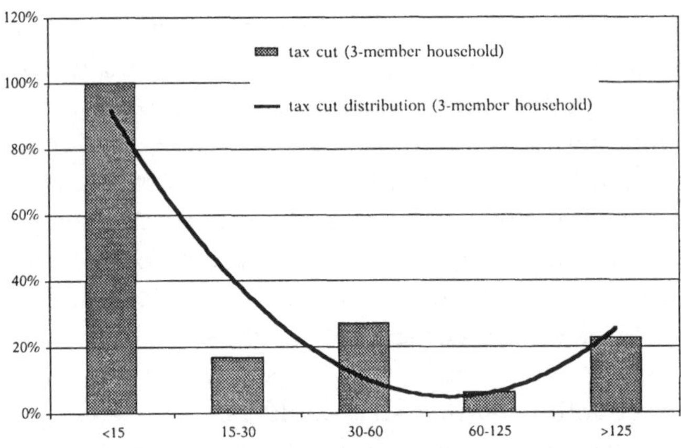

for instance, six members whose income is 30 million would pay zero IRPEF and, if their income were greater, only 15% from 30 to 60 million and 30% of their remaining income (Graph

31). In this case, the tax relief is strongly progressive, almost linear for low incomes and much less linear for midle-high incomes (Graph 32).

GRAPH 31

INCOME TAX RATE STRUCTURE BY INCOME BRACKETS
(Six-Member Household)

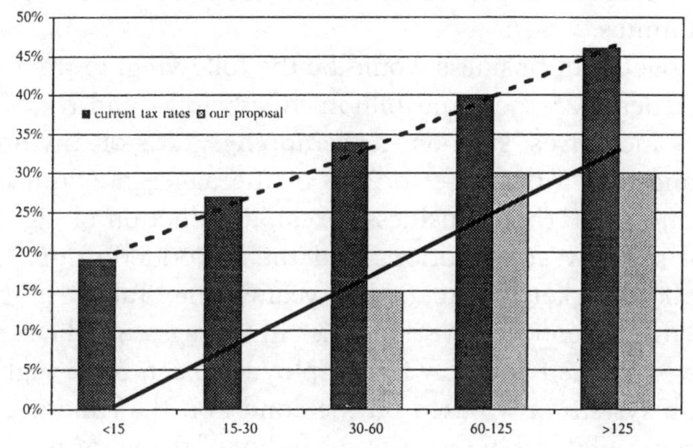

GRAPH 32

ACTUAL TAX CUT BY INCOME BRACKETS

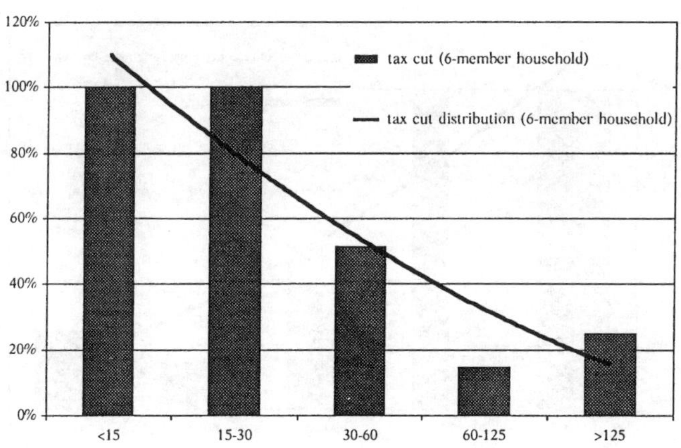

According to this chart, fiscal pressure on families could be reduced or even eliminated for both lower incomes and for the most numerous families. As it is shown in Graph 33, the difference between the unbroken line and the broken line represents the tax gap between a three-person household and a family of six people; the different combinations between the two lines highlight the effects on various household structures. By consequence, a Pact that would cut down fiscal pressure and would be equitable to lower incomes and more numerous families can be agreed upon by families.

The pact with business would be the following: to progressively replace at least 25 thousand billion in subsidies and transfers disguised as incentives, such as car scrappings, aids or anything else, in exchange for a decrease to 25% of the aggregate sum between IRPEG and IRAP (both business taxes), a reduction of eight points in social security contributions and the introduction of flexibility in the labor market in four or five years' time (Table 1).

The macroeconomic workfare lies in this system. The zero inflation rate is reached and now full employment can be brought about through a system only based on the condition that microeconomic workfare be achieved in terms of flexibility of the labor market.

Graph 33

ACTUAL TAX CUT BY INCOME BRACKETS

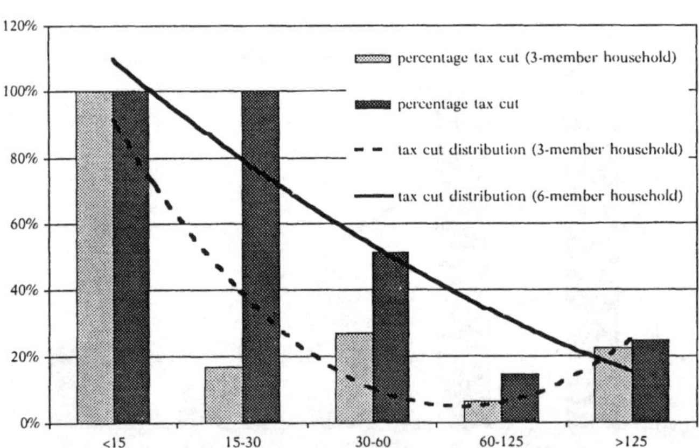

TABLE 1

TAX RATE STRUCTURE

		Current (1998) (%)	Our proposal* (2003)
Irpeg		53	} 25.0
Irap**			
Irpef	(income brackets)		
	up to 15 million	29.0	}
	from 15 to 30 million	27.0	} 15.0
	from 30 to 60 million	34.0	
	from 60 to 125 million	40.0	} 30.0
	over 125 million	46.0	}
Social security contributions (Tfr included)			
	Industry	40.0	32.5
	Construction	30.0	22.5

* 5-million exemption for each household member.
** for previous years Ilor.

In the last two years new agreements have been drawn up. In fact, today, the entrepreneur can hire a worker under one of five or six different forms of contracts: alternative, atypical, etc... Yet, at the same time, contracts have become more rigid: a fixed-time contract cannot exceed a year's time or be renewed more than once and the grounds must be either fixed by law or provided for in collective agreements; a part-time contract cannot be modified, once the schedule has been arranged.

In short, the realization of our economic policy proposal would bring about higher growth and a great reduction in unemployment, through an increase in demand that would not hamper the achievement of public budget objectives which would be guaranteed by the introduction of further flexibilities in the supply side, and, hence, in the labor market. Under stable conditions Italian unemployment could achieve the 6% "miracle" (which can be defined as full employment) in comparison to the current 12% (Graph 34).

In conclusion, the real problem, already dealt with by Modigliani-Ceprini, is a long-term problem requiring immediate decisions: in fact, it is that of the transition from the pay-as-you-go to the fully-funded system.

UNEMPLOYMENT RATE

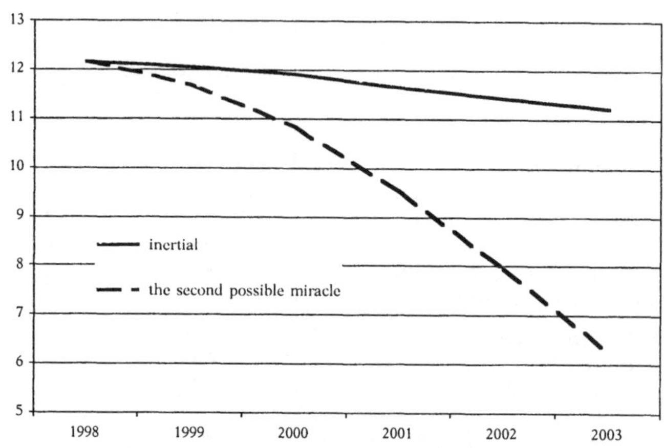

We say that the pension system should not be privatized nor should it exclude solidarity and introduce an individualistic system. However, two basic concepts must be clear:

a) through the pay-as-you-go system the compulsory savings of the workers immediately changes into consumption by the pensioners so as to remove indispensable financial resources for development from the economic system;

b) through the fully-funded system the compulsory savings of the workers changes into investments in enterprises which bring about development and employment and guarantee the pension afterwards.

Hence, we point out that the problem lies in changing one pension system into another one. The difficulty mainly consists in the fact that it is not only necessary to go on ensuring pensions for the present retirees through the pay-as-you-go system but to also begin capitalizing funds for future pensioners.

On this subject, the only resources that could be available in Italy result from future capitalization of the TFR, a suitable system to cause pension funds to grow, on condition that it represents the way to reduce social security contributions in the pay-as-you-go system. In fact, the main goal must be to replace the system and not add another one. In my opinion, Modigliani-Cepri-ni's proposal must not be interpreted as an integrative pension system simply because the INPS is replaced with a new fund at the end of the process. Of course, the balance point between the pay-as-you-go and the fully-funded system depends on political choices.

How to Save the Pension Reforming the Financing of the European Social Security System. The Case of Italy

Franco Modigliani - Marialuisa Ceprini
MIT, Cambridge (Mass.)

1. - Introduction[1]

We wish to make clear that our proposal does not mean to reduce the pensions, which remain the same, but to finance them rationally by capital investments. Ours is the reform of pensions financing and not the pension reform.

In early analysis, we review the critical shortcoming of the currently prevailing method of financing public pension systems, the so-called paygo scheme, and we explain why this system must be discarded promptly, arguing that the system best suited to replace it is a fully funded public system (pillar of mandatory saving), constructed to guarantee defined real benefits. Such a system is the most promising alternative from the point of view of: *(i)* Efficiency (cost to participants per unit benefit); *(ii)* Reliability (stability of contributions needed to deliver the promised benefits for realistic variations in the relevant parameters), and *(iii)* Maximum certainty (about the pension entitlement).

---

[1] A synthesis of the project was presented by Marialuisa Ceprini at the Hearing on the "Commission's Broad Guideline of the Economic Policies of the Member States and of the Community" of the European Parliament on Tuesday 4 april 2000, Brussels

The authors thank the Ragioneria Generale dello Stato (RGS) for making data available in the course of drafting.

The main reason for the immediate shortcoming of paygo is the decline in economic growth, both demographic and in productivity, and growing life expectancy. These developments are undermining the ability of paygo-financed systems to deliver the promised benefits because they reduce the income, and hence, the contributions of the working generations relative to pensions matured. In a funded system, these developments cause no problem because the pensions are not paid from the contributions of the workers, but out of the assets accumulated in the pension fund of the new funded system.

Since most countries in the European Union rely on the paygo method, and all face to a degree the danger of bankruptcy associated with that method, they all need to consider soon a major overhaul of the existing public pension system. We suggest that this circumstance provides a unique opportunity for undertaking coordinated reforms resulting in a common public pension system, for the entire European Union, possibly of the type proposed herein. This would contribute strongly to encourage the mobility of labor, which is so vital for the maintenance of full employment under a fixed exchange system. Furthermore, it would make easier to invest the substantial amount of assets accumulated by the system in a diversified portfolio of all marketable assets in the Union, whose return would be far more stable than those obtainable from a purely national portfolio. Obviously, the existence of transition problems implies that the achievement of a unified system, though a highly desirable goal, might require some time for completion. We suggest that the time to begin working toward that target may well be right now!

2. - The Problems of the New Welfare in Europe

Two are the serious concerns that Europe has to face in the 21st century. The first is *Unemployment*, a short-term problem; the second is *Financing of the Public Pension System*, a very long-term problem, that we discuss hereafter since the first is considered in a separate cover.

3. - Analysis of the European Pension Schemes

3.1 *The Real Problem*

Pension liabilities are an issue for almost all *European Public Pensions Systems* since they are mostly unfunded paygo schemes. The real problem is the financing of the system and not, as is widely believed or asserted, in the fact that they are managed by a public structure. In our view, the mandatory saving, (first pillar) should properly be managed by the Government, and it should cover a reasonable portion of the desired retirement income. The remaining part should be covered by voluntary saving in a private funded system (second pillar), where an individual is free to decide how, when, and whether to deposit his/her saving, as suggested in the *Life Cycle Hypothesis* of saving model *(LCH)*[2].

3.2 *The European Scenario*

Looking at the European scenario, we find out that on average 88% of pensions are provided for by public schemes. Only 7% of pension payments come from occupational schemes, and 1% from voluntary pensions offered by Life Insurance Companies. With a partial exception of Denmark, Finland and Sweden, characterized by a system that gradually will be partially paygo and partially pre-funded, public systems are unfunded paygo schemes representing the main or sole source of retirement income.

From Table 1 we see that, in countries like Italy and Spain, the mandatory contribution is oppressively high; it largely exceeds 25% (compared with some 12% in USA) and it supports very generous benefits, measured by the replacement rate and the retirement age, (50% and 65 respectively in the USA). The oppressively high mandatory contribution, devoted today to maintain an unreliable and inefficient paygo scheme, does not leave to the workers adequate room for voluntary contributions supporting viable private plans.

---

[2] See MODIGLIANI F. [4].

TABLE 1

STATISTICS OF SOCIAL SECURITY SISTEMS IN THE EU

	Replacement ratio[1]	Average contribution	Retirement age[2]		Life expectancy[3]			
					M		F	
			M	F	2000	2020	2000	2020
Austria	79,5	22,8	65	60	74,4	77,6	80,8	83,7
Belgium	67,5	16,4	65	60	74,4	77,1	81,1	83,6
Denmark	56,2	1,0	67	67	73,4	73,5	78,5	78,6
Finland	60,0	17,9	65	65	73,6	75,1	80,6	81,5
France	64,8	19,8	60	60	74,6	78,0	83,0	86,5
Germany	55,0	18,6	65	65	73,7	75,7	80,1	81,9
Greece	120,0	...	62	57	...	...	...	...
Ireland	39,7	15,7	66	66	73,7	76,4	79,4	82,4
Italy	80,0	32,7[4]	62[5]	57[6]	75,9	78,3	82,3	84,7
Luxembourg	93,2	...	65	65	...	...	...	...
Netherlands	45,8	14,5	65	65	75,3	77,8	80,6	81,6
Portugal	82,6	13,9	65	63	...	...	...	...
Spain	100,0	28,3	65	65	74,1	76,0	81,9	83,7
Sweden	74,4	19,8	65	65	77,2	79,6	82,0	83,8
UK	49,8	13,9	65	60	75,1	77,6	80,1	82,6
average	71,2	17,9	64,5	62,7	...	...	...	...

[1] The replacement ratios are changing due to pension system overhaul in Europe.
[2] Retirement age is fixed by law.
[3] Eurostat Estimates of Life expectancy from birth computed in the EU.
[4] Contribution rate of the public employees fund. Labor's categories are subject to different contributions.
[5] At steady state, the retirement age will be 65 years.
[6] At steady state, the retirement age will be 60 years.
Source Data: EUROSTAT and OCSE 1998.

3.3 *The Serious Defects of Paygo Systems*

The paygo system must be discarded promptly because of its serious inferiority in many respects compared with a funded system.

1) *Onerousness:* in a funded system, contributions are gradually invested at a compound return rate, and that usually allows reducing the contribution for stated benefits. The amount of saving depends on the gap between the investment return rate and the implicit return offered by the paygo system (which is the long-run growth rate of the real wages). Undoubtedly, the available information supports the conclusion that actually, and in the near

future, the investment return rate will be above the growth rate of wages. We have demonstrated in a program developed for the USA that, with reasonable estimates of return on capital and productivity growth, the required contribution with full funding could be as much as 2/3 lower than under paygo.

2) *Insolvency:* the endemic uncertainty over its future ability to deliver the pensions promised. This is because under paygo scheme the contribution/benefit ratio (dependency ratio shown in Table 2) depends crucially on growth rate of real wages, in that future pensions have to be equal to the amount of contributions collected at that time, which are obviously proportional to income.

Thus, if real wages rate decreases more than that used to compute contributions, due to a drop in wages growth rate or productivity, promised pensions will be proportionally greater than the pensioners' past contributions. As known, a slow down in population growth does affect the dependency ratio (workers and young over elderly people). The estimates 1990-2050, shown in Table 2, confirm the worsening of this ratio. It is a scaring increase, which mainly reflects a longer average life expectancy of retirees.

TABLE 2

ESTIMATES 1990-2050 OF THE DEPENDENCY RATIO[1]
IN THE INDUSTRIALIZED COUNTRIES

	1990	*2010*	*2030*	*2050*
Belgium	28.4	30.5	49.2	54.5
Canada	21.0	25.2	47.2	52.9
France	27.6	31.5	49.0	58.3
Germany	27.1	33.3	47.6	62.1
Japan	22.0	38.3	53.0	70.1
UK	30.9	31.0	45.0	49.3
Italy	27.4	35.7	55.8	82.8
Netherlands	24.1	27.2	50.3	57.3
USA	24.1	24.3	41.6	44.2
Sweden	35.2	35.0	46.9	49.3
Switzerland	26.2	29.9	53.4	61.5
average	22.8	26.9	39.6	52.4

[1] Ratio of working age persons (25-64) over young (<24) and elderly people (65>).
Source: G-10.

Therefore, when a scheme sets its contribution rates and benefits on the assumption of given long-run growth rates and life expectancy, it follows that if growth slows, or life expectancy lengthens, the system's revenue will no longer suffice to pay promised pensions.

This is exactly what has been happening for years now. Any further major adjustments would not assure lasting of pension schemes financed by paygo. No question about it, paygo scheme is in trouble wherever it was adopted.

It appears clearly, looking at the statistics of Table 3, that the aging population trend, in all OECD countries, leads to an increase in the share of GDP needed to pay the pensions promised under the present paygo scheme. In this Table we see that the pension cost projections, in 2040, for countries like Finland, Germany, and Spain exceed 15%, while, for Italy are higher than 20% which is consistent with the generosity of paygo schemes (see replacement ratios of Table 2), with the predicted fall in population growth,

TABLE 3

PUBLIC PENSION EXPENDITURE IN OECD COUNTRIES
AS A PERCENTAGE OF GDP IN 1994 PRICES

	1995	*2020*	*2040*	*2070*
Austria	8.8	12.1	15.0	13.5
Belgium	10.4	10.7	15.0	14.3
Denmark	6.8	9.3	11.6	11.7
Finland	10.1	15.2	18.0	17.8
France	10.6	11.6	14.3	14.0
Germany	11.1	12.3	18.4	15.5
Ireland	3.6	2.7	2.9	2.2
Italy	13.3	15.3	21.4	17.0
Netherlands	6.0	8.4	12.1	11.0
Norway	5.2	8.6	11.8	11.1
Portugal	7.1	9.6	15.2	14.8
Spain	10.0	11.3	16.8	16.0
Sweden	11.8	13.9	14.9	15.1
UK	4.5	5.1	5.0	3.1
US	4.1	5.2	7.1	7.4
Japan	6.6	12.4	14.9	14.4

Source: Aging Populations, Pension Systems and *Government Budgets. Simulations for OECD Countries 1996.* Copyright © OECD. All rights reserved.

and with the life expectancy lengthens. Today In Europe, on average three and half active workers contribute to the retirement income of one pensioner. This ratio is expected to be worst by 2020 when there will need to be two and half active workers per pensioner. Data confirm the strong pressure put on paygo schemes, providing to Europe the clear message of an urgent need for taking a common action right now.

3) *Inefficiency:* the large compulsory saving contributes nothing to the accumulation of National Wealth or investment, because it is used exclusively to pay current pensions and is thus consumed. In contrast, in a fully funded system, those savings are invested entirely in all financial assets of the European Union that, in turn, will support new investments realized through fresh saving.

4) *Illiquidity:* the trust fund nature of paygo does not allow any accumulation of assets because contributions are immediately «consumed». Therefore, it is an illiquid credit that workers cannot utilize to finance personal temporary investments until retirement.

4. - From a MIT Team How to Save the Pension Reforming the Financing Method of the European Public Pension Schemes

The new mandatory public system, that we advocate, is characterized as follows: *(i) fully funded financing* (contributions are totally invested in financial assets quoted in the European Union); *(ii) maintenance of the existing defined benefits,* based on the; *(iii) guarantee of fixed rate of return on contributions,* using the «swap», an innovative financial transaction, by which the new funded system swaps with the Treasury the uncertain return of an indexed market portfolio for a fixed real interest rate.

The proposed system directs all contributions into a common market-indexed portfolio with a certain return, and maintains a Defined Benefits (DB) scheme.

To manage a means-tested «pooled» portfolio is much less costly than managing many individual small portfolios (as in the case of privatization). The new system could pursue such a simple investment objective directly or assign the task, at a minimum cost, to private managers selected through a tender procedure; while, the passive indexation immunizes the new system from the critique that the politicians will manipulate the fund's growing assets.

4.1 *Transition Phase*

In the past, a major obstacle in moving from an unfunded to a funded scheme has been the presumed high cost of transition that must be paid by the current and/or future generations. As is well known the contribution necessary to build the new fund cannot simply come from diverting the contributions to paygo to the new public funded system because paygo needs those contributions to pay the pension to those who have acquired the pension right through earlier contributions. It would seem, therefore, that during the transition participants would have to double their contribution, one for the old system and one to build the new one.

Drawing on the basics of pension finance, we have developed an operational method for carrying out the transition at small and bearable costs for every generation.

4.2 *In United States*

We apply our approach to the United States[3] and show that it is possible to complete the transition from paygo to a fully funded system without increasing contributions, by relying on a series of favorable circumstances: *(i)* reserves accumulated in the Social Security Trust Fund by old surpluses; *(ii)* the future surpluses for the next ten years; *(iii)* contributions by the government (using

---

[3] As the approach is general, it can be applied to other countries as well. For the application of this approach to the case of Italy, USA, and Europe, see Modigliani and Ceprini (1998a, 1998b, 1998c, 1999b, 1999c, 2000, 2000b), Modigliani, Ceprini and Muralidhar (1999a, 1999d, and 2000c).

budget surplus already promised to Social Security in the President's proposal in the Mid-Session Review of the Budget), and *(iv)* investment policy (investing efficiently the future contributions).

4.3 *In Italy*

In Italy, the serious defects of paygo are magnified due to: 1) very generous replacement rates (amount of pension). At least recently the pension was equal to 80% (Table 1) of the final wage, which is about 20% higher of the average wage (in USA, the pension is on average equal to 50% of the average wage. Beyond that limit individuals provide directly by voluntary saving); 2) the additional contribution necessary to cover the seniority pension (or length-of-service), phenomenon typically Italian and unknown everywhere; 3) low return of TFR, the so-called *Deferred salary* that, in a system with so high pension, while increasing a lot the mandatory contribution (7,70%), it contributes very little to increase the pension because its real return is very low (the current value, about $1\text{-}1^{1/2}\%$, is based on a fixed rule); 4) one of the lowest dependency ratio, toward a foreseeable worsening (within the 2020 is forecasted a negative birth rate).

To the foregoing, it should be added that the contributive evasion of the shadow economy (black work), discovered only in the small industries, was of 1% of the entire pension system (more than two thousand milliards of current Lire).

Some of the above defects have been correcting by the reforms that have imposed a gradual cut to replacement rate, from 2000 to 2050, and a linkage of contributions to the average of life wages (in 2050, when the Dini reform will be at steady state, the retributive principle will be changed in contributive, feature maintained in our proposal). Unfortunately, the ratio benefit/contribution will be variable because the implicit return is not fixed but it remains dependent on the actual income growth. *In other words, the system becomes Defined Contribution (DC) scheme, because the Government has decided to keep the paygo system with its aberrant defects.*

TABLE 4

FORECASTING 2000-2050 OF DINI REFORM (FUND INPS/FPLD)

year	pension amount[1]	Dini Reform							
		INPS forecasting (in %)				RGS forecasting (in %)			
		equilibrium level[2]	mandatory contribution[3]	deficit[4]	average R.R.[5]	equilibrium level[2]	mandatory contribution[3]	deficit[4]	average R.R.[5]
2000	163.094	45.01	32.70	12.31	60	45.30	32.70	12.60	62
2005	197.208	46.77	32.70	14.07	51	46.40	32.70	13.70	54
2010	233.693	47.78	32.70	16.08	50	47.10	32.70	14.40	56
2015	274.021	48.27	32.70	15.57	44	48.00	32.70	15.30	52
2020	318.854	48.40	32.70	15.70	38	47.90	32.70	15.20	48
2025	370.609	48.47	32.70	15.77	36	48.30	32.70	15.60	45
2030	428.971	48.35	32.70	15.65	33	48.70	32.70	16.00	42
2035	474.170	46.05	32.70	13.35	31	48.40	32.70	15.70	41
2040	505.542	42.30	32.30	10.00	29	47.00	32.70	14.30	42
2045	528.912	38.14	28.14	10.00	28	44.80	32.70	12.10	43
2050	552.000	34.44	24.44	10.00	29	41.40	31.40	10.00	43

[1] Amounts in milliards of current Lire.

[2] and [3] The equilibrium level and the mandatory contribution do not include the TFR.

[4] The Deficit of INPS (Istituto Nazionale della Previdenza Sociale) and RGS (Ragioneria Generale dello Stato) include the GIAS (Gestione degli Interventi Assistenziali e di Sostegno alle gestioni previdenziali) amount (about 10%), which remain in 2050.

[5] The replacement ratio is the average of the four pension categories: Elderly people, Seniority, Disability, and Survivor.

Source: Own Forecasting on data INPS and RGS 1999 of the FPLD (Fondo Pensione Lavoratori Dipendenti).

Indeed, today the mandatory contribution is 40.4% of the gross salary (32.7% plus 7.7% of TFR) but is not enough to cover the equilibrium level of 52.7%. The remaining part of 12.3% is a deficit covered by general taxes on the entire population.

Looking at Table 4, in 2050, without an adequate reform, the bitter effect will be nothing less than few points in the mandatory contribution (that, TFR free[4], decreases from 32.7% to 24.44%

---

[4] Actually at the Italian Parliament is blocked a proposal of Law relative to TFR, that we hope it will be definitely stopped. Briefly, the government would like to transfer all TFR (mandatory saving accumulated by the industry on behalf of

(for INPS forecasting) or to 31.40% (for RGS forecasting which we consider more realistic), a tiny decrease of deficit, and a substantial cut of benefits (measured by replacement ratio).

4.4 *Inception of the New Public Funded System in Italy*

We have seen that in USA the transition relies on the existence of surpluses and a big contribution from the Government. In Italy, failing these conditions, the use of TFR could be the unexpected «Surplus» that, covering the supplemental contribution necessary to support the transition cost, should allow the way for changing to the new system without further sacrifices for workers. In other words, we propose to use at least two third (5%) of TFR as annual contribution for the new public mandatory system, making easier the transition towards a more efficient and reliable system financed by funding.

From the inception, the new funded system will work together the current paygo system that would continue to collect and pay the promised benefits (with the Government subsidy if necessary).

4.5 *Operational Phase of the New Public Funded System*

The growing surplus of the new system will be used *(i)* to increase gradually the initial contribution to the new system up to the steady state (that, for USA, we figure out around 7%; while, for Italy, around 14% included TFR), then, *(ii)* partially to pay pensions still due from paygo, and *(iii)* partially to decrease the pension deficit (case of Italy and all those countries of European Union with the same situation).

When the new system reaches the «maturity» (working years plus retirement years), the steady state contribution plus the inter-

---

the worker and temporary used for self-financing) to the supplemental pension funds. Up to now, the Law 164 decided only for 1/3 of TFR (about 2,50%) hoping the launch Supplemental funds, without considering that those could not and cannot start properly due to the heavy tax pressure and high mandatory contribution (we already discussed the matter in the article "Pension Fund: Italy is on the wrong path", Il Sole 24 Ore n. 49, February 1998).

est yielded will be sufficient to pay all the defined benefits promised by the old paygo system (and, for the case of Italy, to give back the TFR to workers at time of retirement). The paygo system would then have no pension to pay and hence no contributions to collect and it could be replaced from the new public funded system.

4.6 *The Payoff of the Proposed New Public Funded System*

The «miracle» relies on a very gradual and slow transition (albeit 6-8 decades) and occurs without increasing contribution or cutting benefits. The contribution is dramatically reduced (for USA from 12,7% to around 7%, for Italy from 40,4%, included TFR, to around 14%, included TFR), a substantial cut of almost 2/3.

4.7 *Portability of the Portfolio in the Euro Market*

Our approach lends itself to portability and portfolio diversification over large cross-sections of Euromarket. Not only will European countries benefit from economies of scale and international diversification, but also, pooling diversified groups of participants, will lower liability risk, typical defect of paygo systems.

4.8 *New Confidence in Public Pension System*

The funded structure should recreate confidence in the public pension system. This is especially relevant for youth, who are inclined to think that the pension fund will have run dry when their turn comes to draw benefits.

4.9 *The Second Pillar of the Pension System*

Regarding the second pillar of the supplemental pension system, which is voluntary saving, the workers should feel free to enter in Open or Category Fund, receiving the same benefits. Any participant should have the right to manage personally the portfolio of his/her fund, and the right to self-funding a personal loan, according to specific rules. Obviously, the contributions to the fund should have the exemption of income tax (according to rules defining ceiling and limits).

The exemption should also apply to the return of the capital invested in the fund; while the benefits are under the criteria defined by current European Tax Laws.

5. - Review and Criticism of Alternative Solutions

The reform of the paygo system has been a major issue for some time and accordingly there is by now a vast literature on the subject that contains numerous suggested solutions. However, for our present purpose, we will concentrate on the few that have elicited the greatest attention. These can be classified into two major categories.

The first class of suggestions aims at «fixing» the current paygo system by changing a variety of rules so as to avoid, or at least substantially postpone, the «insolvency» toward which the system is heading. The measures considered include increasing contributions, decreasing benefits, raising the standard retirement age, or indexing it to life expectancy, counting on immigration that, fairly controlled for not interfering with the policies for the unemployment, could be helpful to increase those low dependency ratios changing substantially the age structure of the adult population.

The last two measures should be considered even in connection with our 100% funding proposal, but they are, realistically, insufficient on its own to solve the problem. Moreover, the first measure is not practical in the light of the already exorbitant contribution prevailing in Europe and the second too unpopular to be considered, unless unrivaled to participants. In addition, even if these measures could get us over the immediate threat of insolvency, they would result in retaining the paygo system which is much inferior to a funded system because: *(i)* it is unreliable in view of its high sensitivity to changes in economic and population growth; and *(ii)* it is prospectively much more onerous for the participants in the foreseeable slow growth economy.

The second class of suggestions consists in moving to a funded system (totally or partially); but with the funding, accomplished trough a mechanism, which is, in spirit and philosophy, profoundly different from ours, and is frequently advocated in the name of privatization of Social Security. Basically, it requires participants to shift (some portion of) their mandated contribution from the paygo system to a *personal portfolios*, generally managed by a fund selected from a list approved by the government. At retirement, the amount in the account is converted in an annuity. This form of funding was first introduced as an innovative total replacement for paygo in Chile, coining the term «privatization» of Social Security (although the only thing that is privatized is the management of the portfolios). The *fundamental difference* is that our system of a common fund with *a guaranteed return* results in a *Defined Benefits* (DB) scheme with a predictable relation between contributions and benefits, while the reliance on individually managed accounts inevitably results in a *Defined Contribution* (DC) system, in which the pension outcome for given contribution is an aleatory quantity, a compulsory «gambling casino» because depending on the luck in choosing managers or even on the date of birth, which determines the date of conversion of the assets in the portfolio into an annuity. The first feature is clearly highly undesirable in a world of prevailing risk aversion. The second has the effect (generally regarded as undesirable) of creating artificial inequalities in the distribution of income. Moreover the dispersion of the outcomes, for equal contribution, is further magnified with the private accounts in that even the average outcome is variable and uncertain, whereas in our «common fund» the return is guaranteed, at least for long periods, by the swap with the Treasury, which for a price assumes the responsibility of smoothing the market «bumps».

A further inferiority of personal portfolios is that the available evidence (e.g. from South America) suggests that the fee to be paid to private account managers, especially for small accounts, is far larger than the negligible cost of managing our fully indexed portfolio.

The above considerations suggest that our fully funded approach is to be preferred to the many proposals that favor a mixed system, partially funded and partially paygo. In such a system, the required contribution is a weighted average of the contributions required under each system, which in turn depends inversely on the «rate of return» corresponding to each system.

The main justification for a mixed solution relies on the assumption that a mixed portfolio is more efficient than only one of its components. But this is not true when one of its components (the funded portion) does have a return enormously higher and a variance enormously lower than the other one (the paygo portion). In this case, the better portfolio is the first alternative (the funding).

However, more important, our analysis clearly implies that, if one were to adopt a mixed system, the funded portion should take the form of our common funding defined benefit type. Here the return is certain and vastly higher than the foreseeable rate of growth of (real) income. Hence, the rate of return rises, and the required contribution falls monotonically as the funded share of the mixture tends to 100%.

The Table 5 compares advantages and disadvantages of our solution with the current paygo system, and «privatized» systems, fully or partially funded.

6. - Conclusions

6.1 *From 2000 to 2050*

The conclusion is that the rational long run solution to the question of how to finance a Public Pension in the foreseeable future is to rely entirely on a «Common Fund - Defined Benefit» (CFDB) system as we suggest.

The only questions still opened are related to the methods and timing of transition. These questions can be answered only in a specific institutional context (as we already have done for the U.S. and Italy).

The decision to realize a common European Social Security reform urges now. Right now Europe has the unique opportunity for undertaking coordinated reforms resulting in a common public pension system while reducing significantly the scourge of the high mandatory contributions. Acting now means that the workers of 2050 will thanks us for our brave courage.

COMPARISON AMONG CURRENT PAYGO SYSTEM, MIT TEAM SOLUTION, AND «PRIVATIZED» SYSTEMS: ADVANTAGES AND DISADVANTAGES

Current Paygo System	*M.I.T. Team Solution*	*«Privatized» Systems*
1) *Public Mandatory Pension Fund* (one or more mandatory funds); 2) *Fund financing: (paygo)*; this 'ingenious» mechanism does not accumulate contributions but uses it to pay the current pensions guaranteeing the tacit intergenerational understanding; 3) *Type:* The majority of the schemes in Europe today are DEFINED BENEFIT type. For the ongoing reforms many schemes, at steady state, will be DEFINED CONTRIBUTION; 4) *Methodology:* all European countries, except two, at steady state, will be gradually: *Contributive Paygo.* Contributions will be tight to average life wages. Unfortunately, the relation will be variable because the implicit yield is not fix but dependent on the current growth of income.	1) Public mandatory pension fund; 2) *Fund financing: fully funded, capitalized 100%*; 3) *Type: REAL DEFINED BENEFIT;* 4) *Guarantee of DEFINED BENEFIT scheme by SWAP* transaction between the new funded system and the Treasury; 5) Methodology: *Contributive accumulation:* 1st Phase: The current paygo continues to raise contributions and pay pensions. The new funded system starts «to pay» pensions based on contributions. The entity of such «payments» grows very fast until maturity (third phase); 2nd Phase: The pensions «paid» by the new funded system are not given to pensioners (who continue to receive it from paygo system) but used to raise the initial contribution of the new system to the equilibrium level (which varies according to the differences of the current European pension systems), while the remaining part, continuously growing, is transferred to paygo system to gradually reduce its original contributions; 3rd Phase: After several decades the new funded system enters maturity. At that point, the transfers to paygo equal the pensions to pay. The paygo contribution equals zero and paygo can be replaced by the new fully funded system with a reduced contribution of almost 2/3 compared to the original contribution (details for USA proposal are in the SWAP # 4051, May 2000 revision; while for ITALY proposal are in the article «The possible future» #3, April 1999).	1) «Privatized» mandatory pension fund; 2) Fund financing: fully or partially funded, 3) Type: DEFINED CONTRIBUTION; 4) Methodology: Contributive accumulation; *DISADVANTAGES of «Privatized» System* 1) No guarantee of the benefits obtainable at retirement because it depends on portfolios performance; 2) The risk, born by the participants, is tremendously high due to a DC scheme, creating inequalities in pensions for equal compulsory contributions caused by differences of portfolios return; 3) The system is less efficient because the mandatory saving is invested in small individual diversified portfolios managed by private managers at very high cost (in South America costs raised to 20% of contributions);

DISADVANTAGES
of the current system

1) The system is inefficient because the mandatory saving is used to finance the pensions, thus is consumed;
2) The system is insolvent because workers contributions are not sufficient to pay the current pensions;
3) The steady state contribution remains too high, because at steady state maintaining paygo the high cost is estimated to be 25% of the gross salary with a heavy cut to benefits;
4) The contribution requested for given benefits is unstable because largely depends on population structure and on productivity growth. Unfortunately, *the heavy and painful adjustments: a)* reduce benefits, and *b)* do not offer a permanent and stable solution;
5) Lack of confidence in the Social Security, particularly for youth who think no benefits will be available for them by their retirement time;

ADVANTAGES
of the current system
1) Progressivity is possible.

ADVANTAGES of the M.I.T. Team Solution

1) The system is efficient because the mandatory saving is used to finance productive investments. Therefore, does make an addition to national saving and capital stock. The fund return contributes to cover the pension cost;
2) The new funded system invests its capital, mandatory saving and accumulated yield, in a diversified «indexed» portfolio of all marketable financial assets;
3) The new funded system is solvent because the compulsory saving accumulation (contribution + real fixed yield) guarantees pensions payment;
4) The steady state contribution is reduced, a substantial cut of almost 2/3 since capitalization replaces paygo;
5) The structure of the new funded system guarantees the stability of the pension system, since is independent from population growth and relatively independent from productivity growth;
6) Real DB are guaranteed by a SWAP between the new funded system and the Treasury for which the uncertain market return of the funded system portfolio is exchanged with a real fixed rate;
7) Risk is born by the Government by the DB scheme;
8) Restoring of new confidence;
9) Liquidity of the capital accumulated in the fund makes possible for the participants to get personal temporary financing, as already tested for the American supplemental pension funds 401(K);
10) «Privatization» of some mandatory saving functions giving to the industry the possibility to offer pension funds if only they provide benefits competitive with the new funded system.
11) Progressivity is possible.

4) Difficult and too expensive to offer means-tested pensions under DC scheme;
5) The steady state contribution is very high;
6) The progressivity is difficult.

FURTHER DISADVANTAGES
of Partial «Privatization»

1) They are incomplete reforms because they stop at half way and loose *a big portion of the advantages of funded system;*
2) The steady state contribution is higher than that of full privatization.

BIBLIOGRAPHY

[1] DIAMOND P., «Investing in Equities — The linear case», Center for Retirement Research, *Working Paper*, 1999.

[2] FELDSTEIN M., «Transition to a Fully Funded Pension System: Five Economic Issues», NBER, *Working Paper*, no. 614-9, 1997.

[3] HELLER P., «Rethinking Pension Reform Initiatives», IMF, *Working Paper*, April 1998.

[4] Modigliani F., «The Life Cycle Hypothesis of Saving, the Demand for Wealth and Supply for Capital», ed. *Social Research*, no. 2, 1966.

[5] Modigliani F. and Ceprini M.L., «Pension Funds: Italy is on the Wrong Path», *Il Sole 24 Ore*, February 19, 1998.

[6] — — - — —, «Social Security: a Proposal for Italy», Roma, Banca di Roma *Economia Italiana*, Rivista Quadrimestrale, n. 2, May-August 1998, pp. 275-305.

[7] — — - — —, «A Gradual Changeover from a Paygo to a Funded System», *Il Sole 24 Ore*, December 17, 1998.

[8] — — - — —, «Social Security Reform a Proposal for Italy», Roma, Banca di Roma, *Review of Economic Conditions in Italy*, n. 2, 1998, pp. 177-201.

[9] — — - — —, *A Comparison Among Pension Systems: Proposals for Italy*, Proceedings of the seminar held at Banca di Roma and University of Rome, June 1999.

[10] — — - — —, «How to Save Returns and Decrease Contributions, *Il Corriere della Sera*, September 1999.

[11] — — - — —, «Welfare, The Solution is In Europe. Unfortunately, the Government Burns the TFR and Postpones the Pension Reform», *Il Sole 24 Ore*, February 17, 2000.

[12] — — - — —, *Pension System Reform: An intergenerational Understanding, a Challenge for the Country*, Proceedings of the Conference held at Confcommercio, March 2000.

[13] MODIGLIANI F. - CEPRINI M.L. - MURALIDHAR A., «A Solution to the Social Security Crisis from a MIT Team», Sloan, *Working Paper*, n. 4051, May 2000 (Fourth revision).

[14] — — - — — - — —, «The Possible Future», *Realtà*, May-June, n. 3, 1999.

[15] POTERBA J., «The Rate of Return to Corporate Capital and Factor Shares», *Carnegie Rochester Conference on Public Policy*, n. 48, 1998.

Welfare: the British Proposal

Baronessa Hollis of Heigiham
Parliamentary Under Secretary of State
at the Department of Social Security (UK)

In Europe we are all concerned about the future of our social protection systems; how we can reform them to meet changing needs. There is no one-size-fits-all solution. What I would like to point out is firstly why we need welfare reform in the UK, and secondly what shape it will take. Some statistics in the Appendix show my effort as a politician to pretend I'm not a politician and that it is rooted in solid information and not party views.

These three pages of statistics compare the situations: 1945, 1979 when the Wilson Labour Government came back and then when firstly the Thatcher Govemment came in 1979 and the situation now, analyzing the changes in demography and particularly, as you will see, the growth in the number of elderly. Secondly, changes in family structure, particularly the growth in divorce and, above all, the growth in one-parent families in Britain, so that a quarter of all children in the UK are being brought up in families headed by a lone parent/mother. Thirdly, changes in the labour market and again particularly women's entry into the labour market on the one hand and the reduction in the number of people over the age of 50 on the other hand. Finally incomes and particularly the growth of private funded pensions which has meant that pensioners are no longer the poor in Britain, but the poor in Britain are children.

The situation our Government inherited in 1997, when the Blair government came to power, was that we were spending more and more on social security — social security is obviously part of social protection — for less and less benefit. In other words, we were spending more and more to keep people poor. Compared, for example, to 1979, when one penny in five, 1/5 of government expenditure was on social security, today, it is 1/3 and yet poverty has grown, inequality has grown and more and more people are consigned to poverty and to failure. We are spending more and getting less, and the question is why. We are spending a hundred billions a year to keep people dependent on benefit and everlastingly poor. They are born poor, live poor and die poor. Why is this the case in Britain?

I want to take you back to 1942, when a distinguished thinker in Britain called William Beveridge and Beveridge together with John Maynard Keynes shaped the development of post-war British society and the country decided that we must win the peace as well as win the war and introduced the Beveridge Report in which he wrote we must slay the giants that stalked the land of Britain and those 5 giants were want (poverty), squalor, disease, idleness (unemploynient) and ignorance. These were Beveridge's 5 giants and the policy of the first great Labour Government in 1945 was to develop education, reform, national insurance, national health service, local authorities strengths in order to slay Beveridge's five giants.

The social security system was therefore shaped in 1945 in a society where jobs were for life, marriages were for life and where life was not lived very long after retirement, and this was common across Europe. It was a situation where men had forty-year jobs and forty-year marriages and where there was full employment; where women were married, did not enter the labour market, lived in the home and mediated their relationship to the State through their husband and other men; where lone parents, single parents, were mostly widows; where families only had one wage-earner; where 95% of all children were brought up in one-earner, two-parent families; and where, significantly, people on average only lived two years beyond retirement. That Beveridge family (working man, non-working wife, children) in Beveridge's time was about 3/4 of all families. Now, it would be about 1/5 of all families. Yet our welfare state in Britain is still modelled on that pattern of Beveridge's society and because of the demographic changes, the family changes, the labour market changes, and above all the inequality changes, we in Britain, under Blair, need to reform the welfare state.

Three crucial changes have marked our lives. The first has been *the emergence of women into the labour market*: 8 in 10 married men work in Britain, 7 in 10 married women work in Britain, usually or very often part-time, and they are willing to take low paid flexible part-time jobs, but taking those jobs does not mean poverty for them, but lifts their families out of poverty. Secondly, *those same women are not willing anymore to remain in unsatisfactory marriages* and particularty will get rid of men who are unemployed and as husbands are simply yet another child to look after.

Thirdly, *the growth of the number of elderly people* and also the worsening of the ratio between those who arc dependent and those who are working. But also, associated with that, the more married women go into the labour market, the less informal and family care support there is for those elderly dependent people. On the other hand, the opportunity for more waged work in the fields of care. Again this is reflected in the statistics, tables 1*a* and 1*b*.

Fourtly, *the growth* of course *of young people who are dependent*. In Beveridge's time you went into work at the age of 14-15, now it is 18, maybe 21, maybe later. Therefore, the worsening of the ratio of non-workers to workers in the labour force has not only been at the elderly end, it has also been at the young end, with falling birth rates and longer periods of dependent childhood.

So, the British welfare state was built on a perception of men in full-time work, sole earners, married for life, ensuring themselves against the risk of unemployment (because there was full employment) not the certainty of unemployment, against the risk of old age and not the certainty of old age. And that was the concept of insurance: actuarially it worked while you were dealing with quite slender risks. The moment it becomes certainties, as it has done, then the actuarial basis of social insurance begins to go into a black hole.

Today, old age is not a risk, but a certainty, and the insurance scheme is not sufficiently robust. In any case given the changing labour market, people cannot build up insurance records. Perhaps only half of all jobs are the traditional full-time 37-hour stable jobs on which you can build up social insurance. And in any case, those with the greatest need, those at most risk of sickness or chronic unemployment, women and youngsters are least able to build the insurance records for social protection. So that we are faced with problems of black youngsters who have double the unemployment of white youngsters; we are faced with problems of the chronically sick and disabled who have grown in four-fold, 400% in numbers on benefit since 1979; with women who persistently receive only 70% of male pay; with areas of high unemployment (there are two «Italies», we have several «Britains»), particularly in areas of the traditional heavy industries of coal, iron and steel, like Wales, Scotland, Liverpool and some inner-city areas which are like Washington (DC) of poverty and deprivation and of heavy concentration of Bangladeshi families.

We therefore have a society in which the bottom 1/5 are in and out of the labour market; in which low pay and low *skills* makes no pay; in which they have repeated *spells* of unemployment separated by periods of low paid work. They churn: if this year they are in the bottom fifth of income next year they go into work, they will go up into the second fifth of income, but after two years half of them have fallen back again; in other words, mobility out of poverty is short range and for a very short time, and those people cannot therefore build up insurance.

This means we have growing inequality of income, not so much by social class, as in the past, as within each household type — as for instance that of pensioners: most of them are confortably off and only a few are poor but those are very poor —. Most families in work are comfortably off, but a few families with large numbers of children are very poor. The main division in

British society is between those in work and those not in work and that is our poverty line. If He is in work, She will be in work, if He is not in work, She will not be in work.

In Britain today 60% of all families have two earners, 30% have one earner, 10% have no earners. We are either work-rich or work-poor. The only way to spring people out of poverty so they are not born poor, live poor, retire poor and die poor, is to get them into work. The poorest of all in the UK are not pensioners, not the disabled, they are not even the unemployed — most people who are unemployed are unemployed only for six months — they are children. The face of poverty in Britain is the face of a child: one child in four has persistently low incomes. Double, three times the number in 1979. They are firstly the children of families where there is no worker in the family and, secondly, where there is no father in the family. Poor children are children in workless families and in fractured families because in lone-parent families women — unlike Europe — are less likely to work than married women. So those children have the double disadvantage to overcome. A quarter of all children live in workless families and in single families. So children in Britain inherit poverty as they inherit wealth and they are both equally unmerited, unearnt and underseved and they pass their poverty on. While in Italy, only 7% of families with children are headed by a lone parent, in Britain the percentage rises to 20.

So what are we going to do about this? The problem, as I mentioned, is workless families. We have to reform the welfare state: 1/3 of our budget is going on social security and yet we are not meeting needs and poverty and inequality are growing in Britain and that is because work is concentrated in rich families and denied to poor families. And that in turn is because of the interaction of work with the welfare benefit system.

Our budget for social security, in Britain is a hundred billion pounds: of that, pensions account for about 36 billion pounds, that is, for just over a third; disability benefits for about 20 billion pounds; income support for families not in work for 12 billion pounds; support for widows, 1 billion pounds; support for housing costs about 12 billion pounds; support for those who are unemployed but expecting to go into work is about 3 billion pounds. So you will see, I think, that in Britain we see the problem not as that of supporting pensioners — only a third of our social security budget goes into state pensions spending — it's about how we use that money to bring workless families over the poverty line, into work which will allow them to come out of the bottom quintile of income, move up into the second quintile and stay there so they do not churn around bumping along at the bottom of income, bumping along at the bottom of our society and with children inheriting the deprivation of their parents. We know that, for example, three million people in Britain have spent more than two years on benefit. They cannot get out: it is a «benefit trap». Now the answer of course could be to cut benefit levels and make work more attractive. We are not, of course, as a Labour Government or any government, going to do that. Our primary concern in Britain is to make workless households have a worker in them, to bring families into the labour market. And if the jobs are too poorly paid to live on — because those are the only jobs available for unskilled manual men and women with poor education in areas of chronic underemployment — if those are the only jobs available then we will support those jobs by in-work benefit that top up their pay to a living guaranteed wage. Our tax credit system which is paid weekly or monthly — unlike the American or Canadian system — allows us to have a flexible labour market without exploiting individual families, because the risk is laid on the State.

So hence our strategies for getting workless families and their children into work. Four things we are doing. The first is to coin a cliché, the 'new deal', modelled of course on the concept of America in the 1930s. We are tightening up access to unemployment benefit because in Britain, young single people get generous unemployment benefits, through a gateway of compulsory interviews, personal advisors, compulsory training, childcare support for lone parents, job search activity, so that getting benefit becomes a contract, it becomes a conditionality, it's about rights, your right to benefit is matched by your responsibility to seek work. Government is not making it compulsory for lone parents, or disabled people to seek work. They are making it compulsory to have interviews, and develop their work skills. We do not believe that someone who has a bad back as a construction worker at 40 must be consigned to unemployment for the next 25 years. If we invest in him with his consent, we can spring him off benefit and off poverty into decent and fulfilling later years and therefore into decent old age.

So the first thing is our 'new deal': everybody going onto benefit must be interviewed and helped back into work and develop work strategies. The second thing we are doing is looking at the interface between the benefit system and work because obviously if you have high replacement social security benefits there is less attraction, particularly for families with large numbers of children, in going into work. So we are anxious that our benefit system should not subvert our efforts to go back into work, without, however, cutting back on the benefits. We are doing things like rolling over benefits so that for your first month in work you can continue to claim your benefits so that you do not have gaps with your money. Equally, particularly for disabled people whose benefits get more generous the longer they are on benefit, we are laying the risk away from them and onto the State by ensuring that they can return to their former higher level of benefit if in the first 12 months in work, either their health deteriorates or their job collapses. They can return back to their benefit. In other words one of the biggest difficulties we find — and roll-over too for lone parents — is the perception of risk, that somebody who has lived for several years on benefit has a terror of losing certainty of income; they would rather have low but secure income from the state on benefit than take the risk of going into jobs, losing jobs, going onto benefit and being weeks without money while the system catches up. We are trying to make sure that there is a smooth transition across, so if they lose their work, people can come back onto benefit, people going into work can carry some of their benefits for a short while with them, so we smooth that entry into work. The first point is the new deal, the second point is the interface between benefits and work.

The third thing we are doing is that when they look at work, we want to make sure work pays for them even if it is low paid work. In Britain, the social security system has low replacement value compared to average wages but high replacement value to entry wages. In Britain entry wages are 40% lower than average wages. It takes you four years to build your average wage. So our problem is how do we overcome that perception that it is not worth working to start with and how do we get people on the escalator of work and income. We want to make sure work pays, but we definitely do not want to price jobs out of the labour market. Hence, our Chancellor, Gordon Brown, and this is our third strategy, has developed the working families tax credit which is an income related top-up to low pay, paid weekly or monthly, based on family size. That means the problem of low pay is removed from the employer, because we want to keep the jobs in the labour market, the problem of low pay is removed from the employee, and laid on the state. Full-time work here is over 16 hours a week, that is our definition, and if you work over these hours you will always be better off in work than on benefit and you'll have an ensured minimum income of at least 10,000 pounds a year. There are problems, there are high taxation rates effectively as the more you earn the more you lose your income related to working families tax credit. These are problems we have to overcome. It means that we are going to spring one and half million families into work that pays. Half of those will be families that are headed by a lone parent so we will not only be benefiting them, but their children as well. Half will be families of a couple where either usually the wife is in work because the husband is sick and she is low paid or he has temporary short hours and poor pay.

The fourth part of our strategy is, for the first time in Britain, a minimum wage. It is only modest, it is £ 3.60 an hour, over 21, but the reason for the minimum wage is that it is not only decent in its own right to stop sweater employers, exploitative employers, but it is to put in a floor underneath the working families tax credit so employers know that they cannot cut wages wherever they want — because there is a minimum wage they must pay, because otherwise, all that would happen is that the employer would cut wages and taxpayers and other workers would take the strain —.

Our first concern in addressing the problems of the welfare state we inherited — which is of men in work for life, married for life and not living very long and all of that has changed as the statistics show — is to ensure, as a result, that we have large numbers of workless families. One family in five in Britain is without work, and if you are without work then you cannot build a decent pension. We want to tackle the pension problem by tackling the work problem in your 20s, 30s, 40s. Therefore we want to ensure that families come into work and the way we do that is our 'new deal', smoothing the interface between benefit and work, going for the working families tax credit, going for the minimum wage. That is the core of our strategy so that if we can get that right then we lift pensions and we lift children out of poverty because those are the other two related areas of concern. But it all starts with workers' capacity to find work and that work pays.

Our second concern is obviously with pensions. In the longer term the situation in Britain is quite good compared to examples in Europe. Only 35% of our social security budget is spent on state pensions. We have a modest, rather low universal state pension. But in Britain and the US and unlike much of Europe, I think, we have a very large private funded pension industry: 650 billion pounds, i.e. 2 thousand trillion lire, is in pension funds in Britain, about six times our annual state social security budget. If therefore people have access to an occupational pension schemes, as 70% of men do, 60% of women do, 60% of self-employed buy themselves a pension, they are comfortable and, in the longer term, as we ensure people are in work and remain in work and pay in contributions, not only to get their basic pension but their second private funded pension they will be comfortably off. Our problem are those people who are pensioners now or who will soon be pensioners without access to a private funded occupational pension. Largely women, largely the elderly, largely the poor and the chronically sick and disabled who have been in and out of the labour market. And increasingly there are going to be black families and ethnic minority families. I am sure this is a common experience for most societies.

So that is why we are this year and next year passing the legislation which I am involved with in constructing an alternative pension system which is funded but shaped by the state for those people who do not have access to schemes funded and run by their employers. In Britain the traditional occupational scheme is made for 5%-6% from employees, 8%-10% from employers, and about 5% or so from the state, which is insurance or rebates which are credited back to the system. But if you are self-employed, if you do not have an occupational scheme, if you do not have an employer who runs the scheme, if you do not have access, you will be poor in old age and you will be poor for thirty years in old age. That is why we are, under this govemment, developing two new pension schemes which will come into effect in 2001-2002 that produce funded pension schemes called 'stakeholder pension schemes' for those who are self-employed, who are too poor or whose employment history is too erratic to go into private schemes as well as a more generous safety-net even for those like carers of disabled people who will never be in the waged labour market.

Another concern for us is children. The face of poverty in Britain is not a disabled person, not a pensioner, but a child. 4 million children, 1 in 4 is unacceptably poor and Tony Blair is determined that we will eradicate child poverty in 20 years. We are increasing child benefit, which is our basic family allowance, that still is not enough. It is universal and therefore you cannot help and our problem is how you target help without having the means, testing which means, there is a disincentive to earn more and which has stigma. We are also extending the tax credit system, the top up payments, to focus on children and help their parents into work and then the other part, which I am particularly responsible for, is that the poorest children live in workless families and in fatherless families. Families where the father does not support the children but asks other fathers or taxpayers to do so. I am trying to ensure that maintenance is paid by fathers who no longer live with the mother. Only one child in three who should gets maintenance from the non-resident father: they've always got other more important things to do, like looking after their dogs or sailing their dogs or cutting their garden than looking after their children. We are going to make child maintenance a tax on their income and not a voluntary payment effectively, which is what it is at the moment so that our strategy for children we hope will be they will live in families where there is someone in work so that we break that cycle of deprivation and they will live in families where they and their mother are getting maintenance, that is our strategy.

We are focusing on work for families who can and security with decent benefits for those who cannot. We have problems and let me just end with addressing some of our issues that we still as a government, as a country, as a society have to face.

The first is to ensure that by getting people who can work into work, that we do it without worsening the condition of being out of work, that is, to make work more attractive and more financially rewarding. And how we get tight gateways onto benefit — I think in the States they have the phrase 'tough love'—. A professor in California was instrumental in developing the 'beacon schemes' that we have followed, in terms of trying to get families without work into the labour market. How you do that, by getting tight gateways onto benefit without however stigmatising families.

Our second problem is that half of all poor families live in the areas, defined as poor areas, and turn them into special help areas. Half of poor families are scattered among the prosperous and are not visible. In other words, when you have poverty you not only have poor families, you very often have a concentration of poor families in poor communities. They are deprived communities with poor housing, high rates of crime, truancy in school, teenage pregnancies and all of these problems are in poor areas. Now how do we tackle those area and we have new units, new policies devised to tackle areas, communities of deprivation as well as families of deprivation. How do we ensure that those who do not live in deprived areas, but live among the wealthy, invisible and silent, how do we give them sharp elbows so that we can make sure we hear their voices.

It's clear thirdly that if we want to get people into work, we've got to ensure that the jobs are there and the problem is that we know that growth, particularly in traded jobs and financial services, may actually reduce jobs. We also know that growth in untraded services, like healthcare, and the demand for labour is almost infinite, so we have got to get the job problem right.

Then, our problem is with working families tax credit and making sure that work pays; we have got to get the balance right between ensuring that employers are socially responsible without adding so many burdens on them, as in Italy, that they are not willing to take on new workers. These include problems of the rights for disabled people to be employed and the cost for the small firms can be very heavy, the rights of part-time workers for job security, and maternity leave but the cost for small employers can be very heavy. Trying to get that balance right, that we ensure that for employees it is worth them working and that they have rights at work, without discouraging small employers, but ensuring that they keep going, pay jobs and take on risks.

Our fourth problem is how we address the problems of high unemployment and we are developing regional development agencies with the help of the EU to tackle those issues. Overall unemployment in Britain is about 6%, but in our poorest areas it is 30%, 40%. In some families there has been no-one in work for three generations; in Liverpool, the grandfather, father and now their teenager children never worked or will work. How do we tackle those problems of high unemployment? We need obviously to ensure incentives. We need as a society to re-think strategically our basic approach which since Beveridge has been based on the social insurance contributory principle — which is increasingly redundant, irrelevant —. How do we replace that with the tax credit system to make work pay, because work will ensure that people save and invest?

Finally, and here I will finish, the last problem is with us, and I speak now as a politician; when we were not in government and did not have the public administration or scientific research department, we worked across the front together so that we each stood on each other's shoulders as politicians. I was working with social security, I worked with my colleagues in health, concerned about poor child health, low birth-rates, poor families and so on. Once in government we get captured by the 'departmentalities, the territorialism of benefits, the clients and the like. One of the things that Tony Blair is very insistent on is what in Britain we call 'joined-up govemment', joined-up thinking, joined-up policies so that we get value added rather than pulling away.

We are doing a poverty auditing in our country and each year we will be measured by our success in tackling poverty which is rooted in workless families where the children are therefore poor and you therefore cannot build up a decent private funded pension ...

Let me finish with a quotation from the same Beveridge who in 1942 sought to slay those five giants. When he published his Report, people queued all around the streets to buy copies of this Report, as I say, to see how Britain would win the peace as well as the war.

Beveridge wrote in 1942, and the language is old-fashioned but I'm sure you'll understand: 'The five giants want (poverty), squalor, disease, ignorance and idleness are common enemies of us all, not enemies with which we may individually make a separate peace leaving one's fellows in their hand ... that one should refuse to make a private separate peace with social evil'.

APPENDIX

TABLE 1

THE SOCIAL REFORM
Changes in Demography

Population in England 1945-1999 (in thousand)   1a)

	1945	1999	percentage changes 1945-1999
0-14 (a)	9.996	10.984	9,9%
15-64 (b)	32.453	37.605	15,9%
65+ (c)	4.861	9.049	86,2%
all ages (a+b+c)	47.310	57.638	21,8%
reference percentage* (b/c)	6,7	2,5	

* Defined as the population aged between 15 and 64 divided by the population aged over 65.

Life Expectation (years)   1b)

	1901	1945	1999
men			
at birth	45,3	63,0	74,9
at the age of 65	10,6	12,3	15,1
women			
at birth	49,2	68,0	79,9
at the age of 65	11,6	14,3	18,6

Source: GOVERNMENT ACTUARIAL DEPARTMENT.

TABLE 2

SOCIAL AND FAMILY CHANGES

Percentage of Divorces   2a)

	1951	1971	1998
rate per thousand married women	2,6	5,9	13,0

cont.

TABLE 2 *continued*

SOCIAL AND FAMILY CHANGES

One-Parent Families   2*b*)

	1951*	1971	1996
number of one parent families	0,3	0,6	1,6
number of children in one-parent families	0,5	1,0	2,8

* 1951 data exclude households where the lone parent is not at the head of the family so the number is underestimated.

Type of Household   2*c*)

Distribution of Type of Household
in England in 1951

type of household	all families (%)	families with at least one child aged less than 16 (%)
married	76	94
widows/divorced	17	5
single	7	1
total	100	100

Source: 1951 CENSUS.

Distribution of Type of Household
in England in 1995

type of household	all families (%)	families with at least one child (%)
married couples	61	77
single	39	23
total	100	100

Source: 1995 general survey on families excluding households with more than two families or two or more adults not linked by a relationship. These two categories are 3% of families.

cont.

TABLE 2 *continued*

SOCIAL AND FAMILY CHANGES

Type of household

2c)

Families with Children Divided by Marital Status, 1995

marital status	proportion	proportion
	all families (%)	lone parent (%)
married/living together	78	N/a
single never married	8	38
widows	1	5
divorced	7	33
separated	5	24
total	100	100

Source: 1995 general survey on households.

TABLE 3

THE JOB MARKET

Employment

3a)

employment rate	1951	1971	1999
total in working age	73	76	74
men in working age	100	93	79
women in working age	46	57	69
men 16-24	90	71	65
men 25-49	99	94	88
men 50-64	93	87	69
women 16-24	72	55	59
women 25-49	36	51	73
women 50-59	32	52	63
proportion in part-time employment	4	16	25
proportion in self employment	8	9	12

Employment Rate in Female Job Market per Marital Status

3b)

tipe of household	1977-1979 (%)	1994-1996 (%)
lone parent	36	32
widows	50	52
divorced mother	52	52
separed mother	44	41
total lone mother	47	42
married women	52	66

Source: General survey on households.

TABLE 4

INCOMES AND INCOMES OF PENSIONERS

*Proportion on Population with
Income Below Half Average Income*   4a)

percentage	1961	1971	1996/1997
excluding housing expenses	10,5	10,7	19,1
after housing expenses	11,1	12,4	25,1

Source: INSTITUTE FOR TAX STUDIES (1961, 1971); DEPARTMENT FOR SOCIAL SECURITY (1996/1997).

Income of Pensioners According to Different Sources of Income   4b)

lone pensioners		
	1979	1996/1997
gross income (pounds per week July 1996 prices)	92	146
of which (%):		
benefits	70	62
social pension	12	21
investments	11	13
profits	8	4
others	1	–

couple of pensioners		
	1979	1996/1997
gross income (pounds per week July 1996 prices)	181	286
of which (%):		
benefits	53	45
social pension	20	30
investments	10	15
profits	16	9
others	–	–

*Percentage of Children Living in Families
with Income Below Half Average Income*   4c)

	1968	1979	1995/1996
% of children	10,0	12,6	32,9

Source: GREGG HARKNESS & MACHIN (1999).

The Italian System of the Social Security

Alberto Brambilla

Consigliere di Amministrazione INPS, Roma

My paper will centre on the Italian social security system, a topic which is known to be closely linked with the subject of employment. I shall dwell upon three main points: 1) the extent of the Social Security problem in Italy; 2) the most critical elements of the system; 3) the objectives of the new welfare system.

1. - The Extent of the Social Security Problem in Italy

First of all, let us look at the extent of the problem - unfortunately, now I shall give you a vast pile of data that will certainly not be easy to swallow, but these are the facts.

The Italian pension system in 1997 — the data refer to 1997, because all the relevant state accounting has been completed and therefore we have the complete data available — cost about 300 thousand billion in benefits, equivalent to 15.3% of the gross national product (Table 1).

The total amount of contributions which support these welfare costs added up to 195 thousand billion, so that the total overall deficit is 105 thousand billion. As a matter of fact, taking into account the IRPEF — income tax — deductions that weigh on most of the services, the actual deficit adds up to about 76 thousand billion.

TABLE 1

ITALIAN PENSIONS SYSTEM
1997
The Extent of the Problem

Total cost of benefits	300.683 billion	15,3 of GNP[1]
Total income from contributions	195.193 billion	
Deficit	105.490 billion	
Number of persons in work	21.385.000[2]	1,32 workers for each pensioner
Number of pensioners	16.204.000	
Number of pensions	21.602.473	1,33 pensions for each pensioner
Number of inhabitants (in Italy)	57.500.000	1 pension for every 2,66 inhabitants
Mean annual cost of pensions	13.880.000	
Cost corrected per head	18.500.000	
Mean contribution rate	28,5%	

[1] GNP 1997: 1,950,680 billion
[2] Including 1.281.000 self-employed contracted 958.000 among them without a previous registration.
Source: ISTAT, INPS.

The second block of data identifies the beneficiaries of the welfare system. There are twenty-one million, three hundred and eighty-five thousand workers in employment, including the so-called «self-employed contracted» ones — I mean those who have to pay 12%, and taking away that number from the ones who have a double job and who therefore cannot be considered «self-employed contracted», there are sixteen million, two hundred and four thousand pensioners, so that the ratio between workers and pensioners is equivalent to 1.32 workers for each pensioner.

Unfortunately, this ratio is destined to become worse, because life expectancy is increasing; this is undoubtedly a fine prospect, but while the number of workers remains more or less stable, according to INPS' projections, the number of pensioners is increasing.

However, the number of pensions paid — and here I come to

the first anomaly in the Italian welfare system — is 21 million, 600 thousand. This means that there are 1.33 pensions for each pensioner, but the even more striking fact is the information on the ratio between the population resident in our country and the pensions paid: out of 57 million, 500 thousand inhabitants, we have in practice a pension for every 2.66 persons, including children. This means that each family in Italy is involved in the problem of pensions.

The average amount of the pension is, nominally, 13 million, 880 thousand lire per year, but owing to the effect of the so-called plurality of pensions, we may say that the average pension adds up to 18 million, 500 thousand lire, so that the figure is not as modest as some say.

Finally, to finance the system «the average rate of funding» — it's an average between employees and the self-employed — equals 28.5%, which means that 28,5% of our income goes to finance welfare, but nevertheless there is still a shortfall of 105 thousand billion that must be financed from general taxation.

What does this slide show us? While the system is expensive, the number of benefits is too high and the rate of funding, although insufficient, is extremely high; but it also tells us that the «pensions problem» is a phenomenon to be treated with all possible caution, just because it concerns all Italian families. It is a truly «open wound» which, as we shall see in due course, differs from one region of the country to another.

2. - The Most Critical Elements of the System

Obviously, at this point one may ask what has led to this situation. To cut the story short, considering the time available, I shall focus on three causes: 1) the excessive burden of welfare payments; 2) the lack of balance between the contributions paid during a person's working life and the benefits paid; 3) the lack of balance in regional payments.

Now, social security has been used almost everywhere not only for welfare purposes but, above all, to capture the electorate's votes, to gain political and social consensus. In our country, this practice has reached truly alarming proportions, especially over the last twenty years.

2.1 *The Excessive Burden of Welfare Payments*

If we take a look at the data about the welfare burden, we find out something that leads me to a particular difference of opinion because it is not true that pensions, taking 100 as the overall cost of welfare, account for 60%; if only it were true! There would be real pensioners! In actual fact, the real pensions, that is, the ones «supported» by national insurance contributions, even if these are sometimes insufficient from the actuarial point of view, weigh much less heavily. The welfare total in Italy in 1997 came to 451 thousand billion, about 24% of the gross national product; 300 thousand of this accounted for pensions, so if we limit our-selves to a ratio of 300 thousand billion to 451 thousand million, taking out the 300 thousand from old-age pensions and other small items, an apparently huge burden of the social security sys-tem is evident, which is close to the 65% communicated by the «Onofri Commission» (it was evaluated at 61.5% for 1995).

But let us try to examine this system; we shall discover that if we re-classify the budget of the social security institutions in a better way, the amount of benefits to be found within what we call «pensions», but which are not so-called abroad, is much less, accounting for about 48%. Thus, while it is still higher than the European average, which is around 44%, the differential is more acceptable than the one supplied to us by the «Onofri» official da-ta. Besides, these data, resulting from the processing of data con-tained in the report on the country's economic situation, strike me as an «own goal» for the whole Italian system. In 1995 in fact, I had re-classified the national welfare budget, and the incidence of «pensions» on the total proved to be 49% (Table 2).

A lot of examples could be given to prove the foregoing; let us look at some of them.

We have 6 million, 100 thousand disability pensions in Italy,

SOCIAL PROTECTION BENEFITS IN 1995
(billion liras)
(reclassification according to the 3rd hypothesis)

	V.	%
expenditure for pensions and incomes	246.765	
less: benefits components of expenditure with regard to INPS	44.979	
integration with minimum benefit	24.226	
welfare upgrading of minimum pensions	994	
CDCM pensions beginning before '89	10.028	
Increase for «pensioni di annata»[*]	3.656	
early retirement pension rates	2.927	
war pensions upgrading	1.012	
family benefits	1.820	
levelling the financial year's deficit	316	
social security expenditure	201.786	51,5
less: benefits components of costs with regard to the Public sector	8.000	
social security expenditure	193.786	49,4
expenditure on health	86.382	22,0
expenditure on welfare benefits	111.878	28,6
total expenditure in 1995 for social security	392.046	100,0

Source: BRAMBILLA A., *Dalla riclassificazione dei conti INPS: il peso specifico della previdenza* (*From the Reclassification of INPS Accounts: the Specific Weight of Welfare*).
[*] Pensions garanted before 1.7.82 and up to 31.12.88 according to Law n. 59/91.

costing a total of 54 thousand, 400 billion lire — they cost that in 1997, now it's a little more — but we also have 500 thousand, 500 war pensions, so that even today — in the year 2000 — we are spending 2 thousand, 800 billion on these benefits.

Furthermore, about 20 thousand billion «basic supplementary benefits» are paid, which cover the differential between the pension calculated on the basis of contributions paid and the «basic» pension (that is, the fact that not enough contributions have been paid to arrive at 630 thousand lire a month, in spite of the generous method of calculation adopted by INPS!).

Finally, the fund for «farmers of their own land, tenant farmers and sharecroppers», which has 900 thousand working members and 2 million, 100 thousand pensioners, costs more than 10 thousand billion; it has a shortfall of about 100 thousand billion, since most of the benefits are not covered by contributions.

But the following datum is the one that best demonstrates the situation: INPS, which manages 75% of the entire Italian social security system, is responsible for 12.5 million income-linked benefits. What does this mean? It means that for all these 12.5 million benefits there is a chunk of assistance, to a greater of lesser extent.

As you may observe from the figures, I think that the problem of the excessive burden of welfare should be clearly perceived by the legislator. On the contrary, I find that in current debates they talk of the availability of 4 thousand, or even 8 thousand, billion to finance the new «social shock-absorbers». I believe that it is absolutely out of place to discuss availability of new resources to finance further benefits using these figures; if anything, the resources are to be found to support the output of the small-to-medium businesses, research and, above all, to reduce the burden of contributions that weighs upon production and incomes.

It is equally useless, in my opinion, to attempt to reduce the differentials between contributions paid by the self-employed and those paid by employees, by thinking of increasing the self-employed workers' contributions to a rate of 20%, or perhaps even more, and bring up the «self-employed contracted» workers from their present 12% to 20%; we should trigger a mechanism that, if anything, allows for a reduction in the employees' national insurance payments, so as to lower labour costs — I shall leave on file a suggestion of mine to reduce national insurance contributions to between 8% and 10% — at least with regard to Small and Medium-sized Businesses and at least with regard to newly-employed young people, starting from 01.01.2000 (the firs of January, 2000)[1].

---

[1] See BRAMBILLA A. - LEONI S., «Primi passi verso il riequilibrio tra previdenza pubblica di base e complementare» (First steps towards restoring the balance between basic and complementary state welfare), Banca di Roma, *Economia Italiana*, n. 3, 1998.

In brief, this proposal envisages that the employees' burden of contributions will be reduced from the present 32.7% (33% is the calculated rate, 0.30% of which is paid by the state) to 22.7%, while self-employed workers will go from the current figure of about 16% (20% is the calculated rate used for calculating the pension, of which about 4%!! is paid by the state) to 18.7%. The same applies for the «self-employed contracted» workers.

This would immediately do away with all the manoeuvres to «evade» payment of contributions practised today (passage of employees to a self-employed or «self-employed contracted» status) to save on national insurance contributions, since the proposed rates are quite similar to one another. Furthermore, such a measure would lead to substantial savings for the State, both at the stage of contributions (the reduction of the 0.30% and 4% contributions) and also at the stage of benefit payments, which would be equivalent to the contributions paid. This latter point is vitally important to guarantee the financial/actuarial balance of the new «contributory» method introduced by the «Dini Reform», by Law 335/95. Moreover, within this framework, new resources would be freed to favour complementary welfare.

2.2 *The Lack of Correlation Between Contributions Paid During the Working Life and the Benefits Paid*

The second critical feature — I must speed up, because I'm running slightly late — is the lack of correlation between contributions paid and benefits received. Only one thing needs to be said: if a man works for thirty-five years and then retires, he will receive a pension equal to 70% of his last salary (2% for each year for 35 years) — in actual fact, since the pension is calculated on the average salary over the last 10 years, it is no longer 70%, but about 64-65%. But the problem is that this worker, according to the old method, could pay one lira for thirty years, then if he paid 100 lire in the last five years, the only years valid for calculating the pension, how much pension would he get?? 70% of 100 lire. And then what can we say about self-employed workers, who paid 14,928 lire a year in contributions until 1973 (see Table 3)? If these

TABLE 3

HISTORIC SERIES OF RATES OF DISABILITY, OLD AGE, WIDOWS CONTRIBUTIONS AND CONTRIBUTIONS PER HEAD

Years	Employees' pension fund[a]		Craftsmen		Tradesmen[b]		Annual inflation[d] %	Income from public bonds[e] %
	total %	paid by employee %	fixed annual contribution (lire)	annual contribution %[c]	fixed annual contribution (lire)	annual contribution %[c]		
1960	14,41	4,75	7.778				2,6	5,3
1961	14,41	4,75	7.778				2,9	5,0
1962	16,42	5,42	7.778				5,1	5,1
1963	19,10	6,32	7.778				7,5	5,2
1964	18,80	6,17	7.778				5,9	5,7
1965	18,58	5,95	7.778				4,4	5,4
1966	18,56	5,95	14.928		14.928		2,0	6,5
1967	18,91	6,30	14.928		14.928		2,0	6,6
1968	19,67	6,55	14.928		14.928		1,3	6,7
1969	20,56	6,85	14.928		14.928		2,9	6,9
1970	20,56	6,85	14.928		14.928		5,1	9,0
1971	18,91	6,30	14.928		14.928		5,0	8,3
1972	19,01	6,30	14.928		14.928		5,6	7,5
1973	19,01	6,30	14.928		14.928		10,4	7,4
1974	19,95	6,30	30.528		30.528		19,5	14,1
1975	20,77	6,72	72.528		72.528		17,2	11,0
1976	23,31	7,15	87.408		87.408		16,5	16,6
1977	23,31	7,15	99.672		99.672		18,1	15,2
1978	23,31	7,15	119.112		119.112		12,4	12,2
1979	23,31	7,15	290.428		286.928		15,7	12,5
1980	23,90	7,15	432.736		429.236		21,1	15,9
1981	24,01	7,15	635.220		632.720		18,7	19,7
1982	24,17	7,15	601.660	4	598.161	4,20	16,3	19,4
1983	24,51	7,15	759.940	4	756.441	4,20	15,0	17,9
1984	24,51	7,15	857.500	4	854.001	4,20	10,6	15,4
1985	24,51	7,15	944.620	4	941.121	4,20	8,6	13,7
1986	24,51	7,15	1.194.980	4	1.191.480	4,20	6,1	11,4
1987	24,51	7,15	1.255.100	4	1.251.600	4,20	4,6	10,7
1988	24,51	7,15	1.302.980	4	1.304.160	4,20	5,0	11,1
1989	25,92	7,29	1.358.780	4	1.355.280	4,20	6,6	12,6
1990	25,92	7,29		12,00		12,00	6,1	12,4
1991	26,09	7,46		12,75		12,75	6,4	12,5
1992	26,49	7,86		13,50		13,50	5,4	14,3
1993	26,97	8,34		14,29		14,29	4,2	10,6
1994	26,97	8,34		15,00		15,00	3,9	9,2
1995	27,16	8,40		15,00		15,00	5,4	10,9
1996	32,70	8,89		15,00		15,09	3,8	8,5

[a] Mean annual rate calculated taking additional payments into account.

[b] Management of tradesmen began in 1996.

[c] The rate for 1990 is the one in force since July 1st for 1991, 1992 and 1993, the mean yearly rate is given.

[d] ISTAT cost of living indexes for employed workers' households.

[e] For 1960 to 1965, the yield from medium-term fixed income bonds is given; for subsequentl years, the mean rate of Treasury bonds.

Fonte: BRAMBILLA A., «Primi passi tra previdenza pubblica di base e complementare», (First steps between basic public and supplementary welfare) *Economia Italiana*, 3, 1998.

are the regulations — as indeed they were until 1995 — and if we consider that in the public sector, which now has an annual shortfall of 20 thousand billion, the pension was calculated on the basis of the last month, — I'm not talking about some sectors of the Civil Service and the Army, where someone about to retire was first promoted from colonel to general and therefore received a pension worth 120% of his last salary — it is obvious that there is a total lack of correlation, which is reflected above all in the line of balance of the various social security departments.

Graph 1 shows the evolution of the rate of equilibrium for the management of employees (Employees' Pension Fund), that is, what I should take from the incomes of people in work to pay pensions.

So that the system is self-financing and therefore balances out, the rate today is calculated at 46% (that is, I should take 46%

GRAPH 1

EMPLOYEES' PENSION FUND
RATES OF EQUILIBRIUM UNDER DIFFERENT PROPOSED NORMS

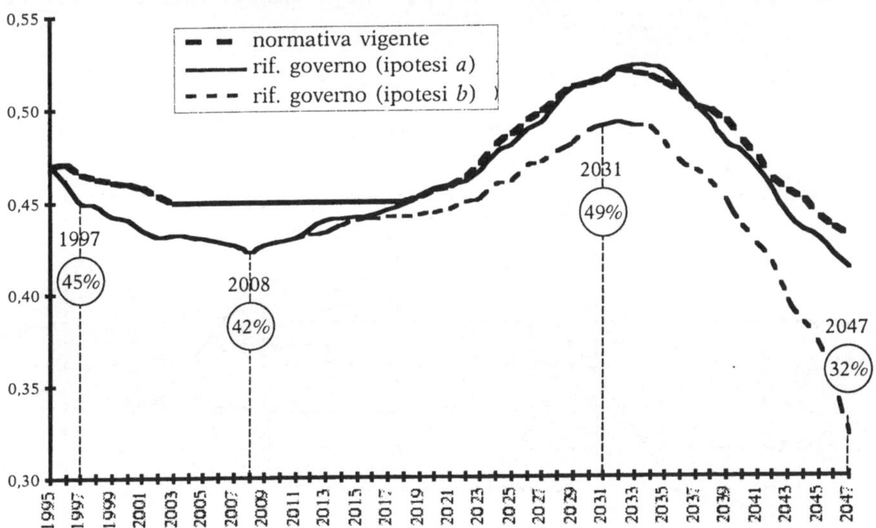

proposal *a*: conversion coefficient of inadequate contributions
proposal *b*: adjustment of conversion coefficients of contributions at ten-yearly rhythm
Source: CER, *Report.*

from people's incomes to finance the pensions paid to today's pensioners). In the period 2006-2030, it will go over 48% and deign to settle at around 34% by 2050. Bear in mind that the calculated rate today is 33%.

To keep things brief, I shall also show you the curves relating to self-employed workers, craftsmen, tradesmen and agricultural entrepreneurs. If possible, the situation is even worse than that of employees; craftsmen start from a rate of 21% for the year 2000 (today they pay about 16%) which will soar to a peak of 34% in 2025, and then settle at 23% in the far-off 2050 (graph 2).

Although the situation is slightly better, but only because the tradesmen's fund was set up a few years later than that of the craftsmen, in terms of rates and balance it is more or less identical, as graph 3 shows.

The curve relating to farmers, tenant farmers and sharecroppers, of whom we spoke earlier, has no need for comment; it is emphasized in graph 4.

What do these slides tell us? They tell us that probably too many promises have been made, perhaps the welfare system has

GRAPH 2

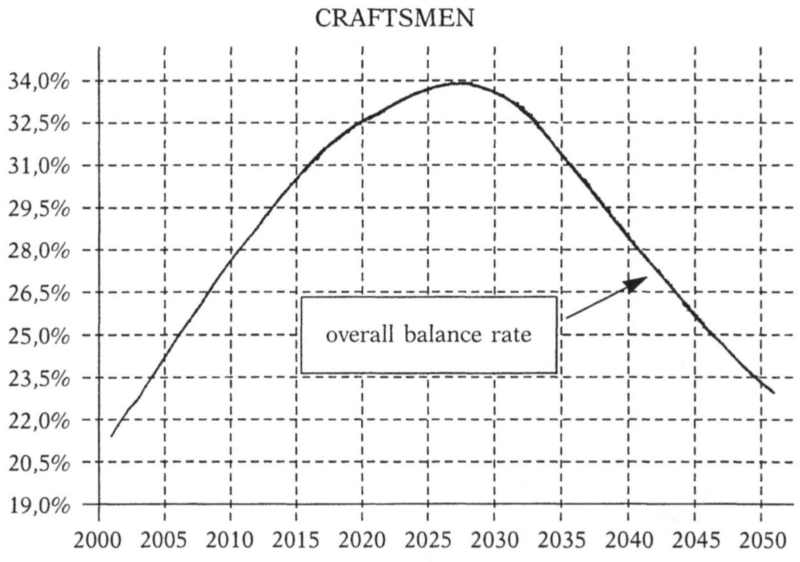

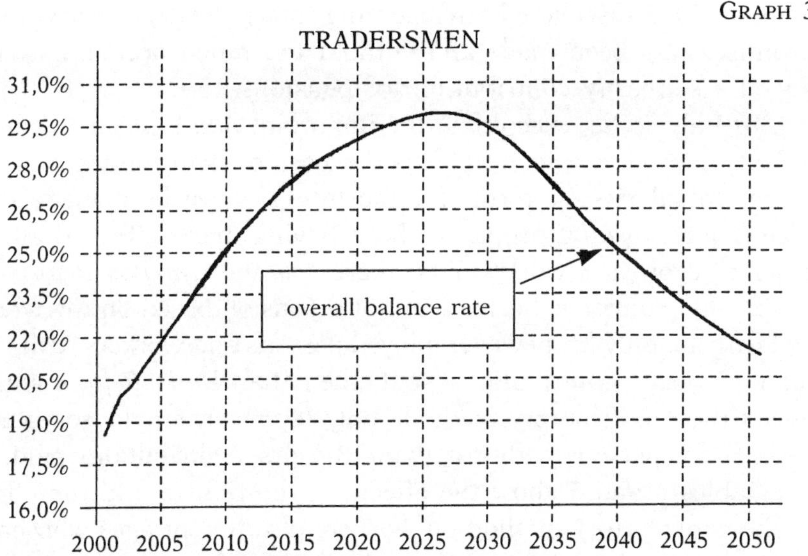

FARMERS WITH THEIR OWN LAND, SHARECROPPERS AND TENANT FARMERS
Overall balance rate

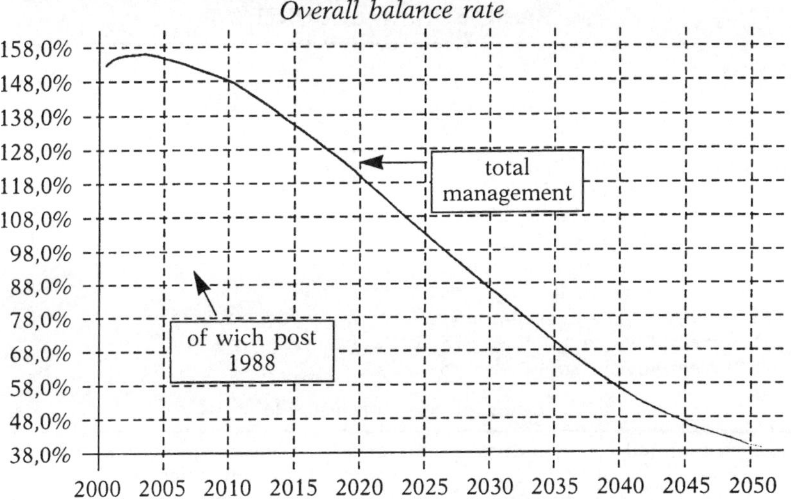

been stretched too far, perhaps we are guilty of not being able to plan for the future, not foreseeing that low funding would result in these breakdowns. However, the first Dutch centre-left government in 1993 discovered after coming into power that very grand promises had been made and without too much uproar it introduced a solidarity contribution for pensions, too.

In Italy so far, except for the important *Amato Reform*, which linked indexed pensions only to the cost of living index and no longer to salaries, «reforms for the future» have been made that mainly affect young people, without having much effect at all on other categories of worker. First there was the «*Amato*» *Reform* in 1992, which envisaged calculation of a pension based on the whole working life only for newly-employed persons and workers with less than 15 years' contributions paid; then the «*Dini*» *Reform* introduced the «contributory method» only for newly-employed youngsters or for persons with less than 18 years' contributions paid.

Tables 4 and 5 show the effects of the reform and the effect of the contributory method on workers of different ages who have paid contributions for a different number of years. As you can

TABLE 4

BASIC SOCIAL SECURITY

employee

example:
— age starting work
— starting salary: 30 million
— age upon retirement: 57
— individual salary increase: 2%
— rate of contribution: 33%
— income: 1,5% (for the contributory part)
— years before retirement:
  - 37 for newly-appointed employee
  - 20 for employee appointed < 18 years of age
  - 5 for employee appointed > 18 years

extent of cover on last salary

newly-appointed employee	seniority < 18 anni	seniority > 18 anni	newly-appointed employee with managerial career
52,70%	58,8%	66%	44,7%

17 payment+   all 37
20 contribution   payment

Source: BRAMBILLA A., «Capire i fondi pensione», *Il Sole 24 Ore.*

TABLE 5

BASIC SOCIAL SECURITY

self-employed workers

examples:
— age starting work
— starting salary: 30 million
— age upon retirement: 57
— individual income increase: 2%
— total rate of contribution: 20%
— social security income: 1,5% (for contributions)
— years to retirement:
   - 37 (starting work)
   - 20 (work < 18 anni)
   - 5 (work > 18 anni)

extent of cover on last income

commencement of occupation as of 1 january 1996	years working < 18 anni	years working > 18 anni
31,9%	47,6%	66%

Source: BRAMBILLA A., *Capire i fondi pensione*, «Il Sole 24 Ore».

see, the differential between young people and workers with 20 or more years of contributions behind them is considerable, even more so if we take into account the fact that young workers pay vastly higher rates that their fathers do.

2.3 *The Lack of Balance in Regional Payments*

Now let us go on to examine the third critical point: the imbalance in INPS' budget between revenue and expenses, by regions. At last I have concluded the first study in Italy on regionalization of INPS Budgets, not from the desire to prosecute anyone, but only to understand and know exactly what the situation is throughout the system[2].

---

[2] Compared to the provisional data given to the Conference, the definitive data are supplied in this paper, calculated after the '98 accounts were drawn up.

It has been a very lengthy task — it has lasted for more than two years — because the contributions have had to be calculated by workplace and the benefits by residence of the welfare beneficiaries. Thus, the overall INPS budget system has had to have all its various anomalies weeded out: such as the fact that the Fiat workers in Melfi are paid in Turin, and so for the General Accounting Department, the contributions are paid in Turin, not Melfi[3].

In this way, huge differences have emerged at a regional level. As you can see in the last column of Table 6, there are some regions that show very high «cover rates» (that is, the ratio between total contributions paid and benefits received), while other regions find themselves in serious difficulties. In 1998, the contributions/benefits ratio was 106.6% in Trentino Upper Adige (which means that for every 100 lire received in benefits, the inhabitants of this Region paid INPS 106.6%), 105.5% in Venetia, 95.8% in Lombardy. On the other hand, other regions can't manage even to achieve 50%. For example, Sicily's ratio is 32.7%, Calabria's is 25%.

This is reflected in the balance between receipts and payments; still with reference to 1998, the most notorious cases are — for example — Sicily that showed a differential of over 8,700 billion between contributions and benefits and Campania, with over 8 thousand billion. Generally speaking, all the South of Italy is in the same situation but there are critical cases in the North, too, notably in Liguria, where the shortfall adds up to 3,400 billion.

In 1997, the imbalance between revenue and expenses cost over 55,000 billion and the eight Regions in the South were responsible for about 34 thousand billion, 62% of the total. Sicily, a truly symbolic case, had 12,854 billion with a shortfall of 8,845 billion: almost the whole amount of the budget for 1998. The sit-

---

[3] See BRAMBILLA A., «Il sistema previdenziale italiano. Il problema degli squilibri regionali nei saldi tra contributi e prestazioni: il caso Inps» (The Italian welfare state system. The problem of imbalance between contributions and benefits in the regions. The case of Inps), Banca di Roma, *Economia Italiana*, n. 1, 2000.

BALANCE BETWEEN DEBIT AND CREDIT AT «CURRENT VALUES»
(in billion of lire)

region	revue from contributions		welfare payments		balance		progressive total[1]	% contrib./ benefits 1998
	1997	1998	1997	1998	1997	1998		
Piedmont	14.771,00	15.140,84	18.619,76	18.784,01	–3.848,76	–3.643,18	–62.656,63	80,60
Valle D'Aosta	319,37	345,59	510,44	512,89	–191,08	–167,30	–3.311,39	67,38
Lombardy	36.605,72	36.979,27	37.837,24	38.582,32	–1.231,52	–1.603,06	49.785,70	95,85
Liguria	3.901,78	4.138,87	7.517,16	7.585,69	–3.615,38	–3.446,83	–56.465,75	54,56
Trentino A.A.	2.929,48	3.125,75	2.914,98	2.930,92	14,51	194,83	–3.606,87	106,65
Venetia	14.704,44	15.639,20	14.924,94	14.811,20	–220,50	828,00	–8.511,66	105,59
Friuli Ven. Julia	3.483,31	3.665,70	5.123,04	5.078,60	–1.639,74	–1.412,90	–26.595,77	72,18
Emilia Romagna	13.897,47	14.702,36	16.494,84	16.583,31	–2.597,37	–1.880,95	–55.028,24	88,66
Tuscany	9.487,69	9.793,45	13.482,53	13.417,15	–3.994,84	–3.623,70	–62.969,33	72,99
Umbria	1.703,81	1.821,36	3.163,52	3.133,52	–1.459,71	–1.312,16	–23.258,71	58,12
Marches	3.630,34	3.867,52	5.032,49	4.901,75	–1.402,15	–1.034,23	–26.129,37	78,90
Latium	14.408,34	14.827,00	15.279,39	14.849,18	–871,05	–22,18	12.099,03	99,85
Abruzzi	1.909,68	2.285,37	3.810,50	3.786,16	–1.900,82	–1.500,79	–29.450,59	60,36
Molise	349,61	407,90	982,45	971,09	–632,85	–563,19	–10.782,80	42,00
Campania	5.480,91	5.614,04	13.454,74	13.744,30	–7.973,83	–8.130,25	–115.228,58	40,85
Apulia	3.866,62	4.092,28	10.847,93	11.008,25	–6.981,31	–6.915,97	–111.378,59	37,17
Basilicata	595,13	660,17	1.744,53	1.721,37	–1.149,41	–1.061,20	–21.199,42	38,35
Calabria	1.394,09	1.414,48	5.625,80	5.641,53	–4.231,71	–4.227,05	–75.919,07	25,07
Sicily	4.008,87	4.264,69	12.853,80	13.024,47	–8.844,92	–8.759,79	–142.809,53	32,74
Sardinia	1.931,35	2.066,29	4.239,59	4.165,35	–2.308,23	–2.099,06	–38.698,47	49,61
not divided					0,00	0,00	–11.416,81	
total for Italy	139.379,00	144.852,12	194.459,66	195.233,07	–55.080,66	–50.380,95	–823.532,84	74,19

[1] Summary of surpluses / deficits from 1980 al 1998 at 1998 values.

Source: BRAMBILLA A., «Il sistema previdenziale Italiano. Il problema degli squilibri regionali nei saldi tra contributi e prestazioni: il caso INPS» (The Italian welfare system: The problem of regional imbalances between contributions and benefits: the case of INPS), Banca di Roma, *Economia Italiana*, n. 1, 2000.

uation in Campania is more or less the same. Compared to 5,481 billion in contributions, it paid out over 13,455 billion, with a negative balance of 7,974 billion.

In 1998, the imbalance between revenue and expenses cost over 50,000 billion. Almost all the Regions in the North reduced the negative balance and the overall shortfall fell by almost 2,200 billion compared to the previous year. Some Regions got out of the red: Trentino (+194 billion) and Venetia (828 billion). In Central Italy, the deficit was 5,992 billion, about 2,000 billion less than in 1997; all 4 Regions did better, with Latium reducing its negative balance from 871,05 billion to only 22 billion. The shortfall in the South was 33,257 billion. Almost the same as in 1997. However, the GAP between revenue and costs is widening more and more with the passage of time and this calls for hefty corrective measures. Such measures however have been disregarded by the various Governments; we might well wonder how long it will be before the whole country may take upon itself this heavy burden that is worth more than a «tough» Budget every year?

The table also shows the progressive total, which represents the algebraic sum of the surplus or adverse balance from 1980 to 1998, calculated on 1998 monetary values. The overall shortfall of the «INPS System» adds up to about 823.000 billion.

From the data it is evident that there are some Regions, such as Lombardy, that have accumulated a surplus of over 49 thousand billion, and Regions such as Campania have accumulated a deficit of 115 thousand billion, or such as Sicily, with a deficit of over 142 thousand billion. On the whole, the Regions in the South ran up a shortfall of over 545 thousand billion, equal to 66% of the national total. The Regions in North Italy accumulated a shortfall of 166,391 billion, or 20% of the national total, with a particularly heavy incidence in Piedmont (–62 thousand billion), Liguria (–56 thousand billion) and Emilia Romagna (–55 thousand billion). The deficit of the Central Regions is about 100 thousand billion, with a «heavy» incidence in Tuscany (–63 thousand billion).

Thus, this slide, too, teaches us that the problem of pensions, above all supplementary benefits, must be placed under control. A long-term plan would be needed to make it plain to all the Regions: you must link your costs to your means; and therefore I'd like to invite nearly everyone in this country to make the data count for more than ideological arguments. For example, within the framework of discussions about welfare reform, there has been much debate on seniority pensions and about their elimination; without entering into the merits of the argument whether this would be the right decision or not, I should like to observe that a proposal of this kind would not have the same effect throughout the country. For example, in Basilicata, where seniority pensions account for only 3.12% of benefits paid, this kind of measure would have no influence, while it would become extremely punitive for the Regions in the North with 75% of the total seniority pensions at the national level; among these, Lombardy alone accounts for 34.22% of the total.

Yet it is necessary — I repeat — to be as cautious as possible, given the magnitude of the problem since, considering the «dual» economic structure of the country, one can certainly not fan the flames of conflict by resorting to drastic measures, as some would wish, such as — for example — the suggestion to give a pension only at the age of 65. Someone who started to work at 15 would be told he had to work for fifty years; it might be right, but he would have to be told. So it's important not to create conflict.

3. - The Aims of the New Welfare

In the light of the foregoing — I'm coming to the last point — the aim must be to go on to a new welfare system that is more equal, more efficient and less costly. Extension of the pro-rata contribution is only the first step towards a greater intergenerational equity — we were saying this earlier — but more courage is needed, the burden of contributions on the cost of labour has to be lightened, to guarantee hope for the youngsters in terms of greater employment.

The new system, which I have summarized in Table 7, should be characterized by a compulsory public-based social security, at a lower rate of funding, such as to guarantee cover of between 40

TABLE 7

OBJECTIVES OF THE WELFARE SYSTEM

---

a) basic welfare
   1) public
   2) compulsory
   3) low financing rate
   4) guaranteeing a minimum standard of life

b) supplementary welfare
   1) private
   2) voluntary
   3) tax breaks
   4) maintaining the standard of life

---

and 50% of the last income; at any rate, in proportion to the contributions paid. For those who (on the basis of paid contributions) do not achieve such levels, assistance must be given, managed at a local level and financed by general taxation. On the other hand, supplementary benefit should be private, voluntary, given tax breaks, allowing pensioners the same standard of living after retirement. Only on the basis of these twin pillars can we think of developing, so that all the social tensions are not vented on the Institute of Social Security, because everyone relies on unemployment benefit, or disability benefit or some small pension, because it is the only source of support.

Unfortunately, our country is very backward with regard to the development of pension funds, the fundamental means for both «economic democracy» and also, above all, participation in social security. Graph 5, shows that — the data are still from 1997 — we bring up the rear. While the pension funds in the United States added up to 12 million, 250 thousand billion lire in 1997, vastly greater than our National Debt of 2.5 million billion, Italy comes after Brazil and after Chile and the pension funds in Italy came to 38 thousand billion, almost wholly relating to the old funds of the banking system.

The same situation is met with (Graph 6) in the ratio between the pension funds and the gross national product; while the Dutch

PENSION FUND ASSETS

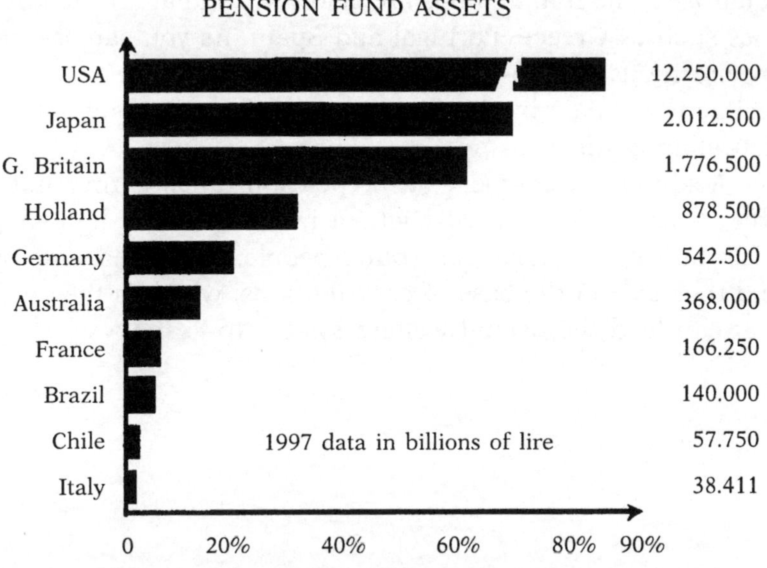

Source: data from OCSE e MERCOSUR, processed by BRAMBILLA A.

PENSION FUND ASSETS

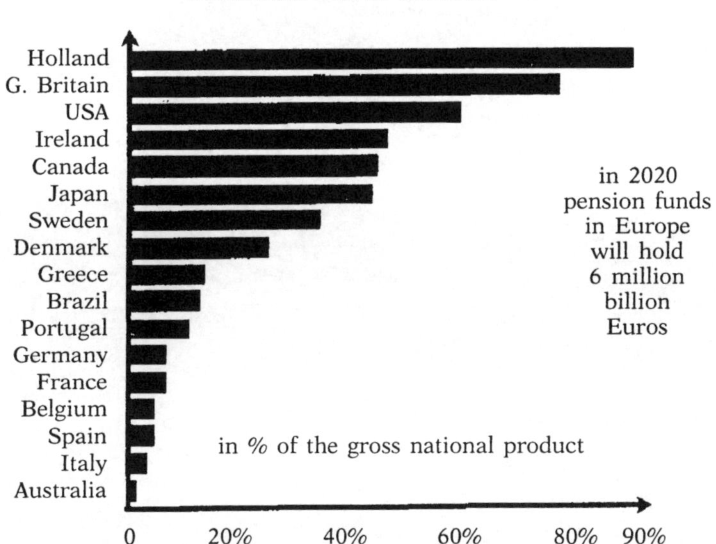

Source: data from OCSE e MERCOSUR, processed by BRAMBILLA A.

pension funds equal 88% of the local GNP, and the English ones
equal 75%, the Italian funds are below 4% and are beaten by countries such as Greece, Portugal and Spain. As you can see, there is
an enormous gap to fill, but nevertheless we cannot foresee any
real actions taken by the government to launch a suitable project
for catching up.

A sound development of the pension funds is thus indispensable — as I said — to strengthen public welfare, lighten labour
costs and create hope for young people, to extend employment
and thus extend the base of contributions, which is the only thing
that can lead the overall welfare system to «safety».

Public and Private Welfare: a Choice

Mario Orio
ANIA, Milano

Introduction

The need for a reorganization of the overall social expenditure in Italy is no longer in doubt.

This implies, first of all, that important measures should be taken as regards the pension system. The effects of these measures would benefit the public financing of the health and long-term care systems: two fields which need, in their turn, to undergo an in-depth reform, in order to be able to face the new, primary needs of an ageing population.

As a matter of fact, the public social expenditure — in spite of the efforts already made in order to make it more effective — can meet only a part of these needs. As a consequence, it becomes necessary to implement, for each of the three areas of social security (pensions, health, long-term care), a mixed model which finds its source in the principle of the so-called selective universalism.

The public sector could therefore continue to meet the welfare needs of the population as a whole, but it could — for certain groups of people and for some particular benefits — rely upon some kind of self-support, both at the collective level (pension funds, health funds, care funds, group policies) and at the individual one (typically: insurance policies).

1. - The Pension System

Several studies have already analysed the ways of changing a PAYG public pension system into at least a mixed one, which would be based on a balance between the PAYG and the capitalization parts of the system.

I am referring to a specific study — whose authors are Prof. Castellino and Prof. Fornero — which suggests a partial transfer of the contributions paid by employees (new employees only) to a capitalization system.

In my opinion, this solution has an important, positive point in its characteristic of graduality. However, it would also be possible to imagine a more direct approach, in order to reach — at the end of the transitional period — a higher "capitalization to PAYG ratio", by taking advantage of the cost reduction allowed by capitalization itself (on condition — of course — that the financial markets yields proved higher than the GDP).

Some calculations — based on similar assumptions — show that indepth reforms are possible, on condition that the final goals can be achieved through a transitional period of a few decades. In this way, the additional deficit which would be generated in the PAYG system during that period could be kept within acceptable limits.

2. - Supplementary Pension Schemes

The above-mentioned reform would lead to a more flexible system, which would allow people to choose both individual and group supplementary pension schemes on the basis of their third- and fourth-age needs and to keep — at the same time — a coverage from the compulsory pension system.

A few ideas come from the reforms recently announced in Britain. The goal of the British Government is to improve the so-called "first pillar" for the poorest part of the population, with a rise in the minimum level of guaranteed income. At the same time, new private basic pension schemes would be activated — the so-called "stakeholder pensions" — especially designed for those medium/low-income citizens who are poorly inclined to save for retirement and, consequently, need the strongest incentives to join a pension scheme. I think that this matter is going to be throroughly analysed tomorrow, when the British way to the new welfare state will be described.

It is known that, in Italy, art. 3 of Law no. 133 dated May 13th, 1999 (Fiscal annex to the *Financial Law* 1999) enables the Italian Government to: 1) reform the fiscal regime of supplementary pension schemes; 2) regulate forms of personal saving for retirement; 3)change the tax regime of life insurance contracts.

In my opinion, it is doubtful that the maximum amount (ItL. 10 million) deductible from personal income for fiscal purposes will prove to be fully adequate. This is particurarly true if we consider that the sharp reduction of widows' pensions (as stated in the Italian Law 335/95) will lead insurers to enrich supplementary pension schemes with clauses allowing the widow to receive higher sums, with a consequent, evident need for higher amounts in order to build an adequate annuity.

As to regulation of personal saving for retirement, the fact that the participation in such schemes (through "open" pension funds and pension insurance contracts) is only "supplementary" to the participation in a pension fund, in accordance with art. 9 of the Legislative Decree 124/93, is likely to influence the decisions of those employees who have access to a closed pension fund, limiting to a mere residual option any free initiatives in the field of pensions.

As to self-employed workers and professionals, it seems reasonable to conclude that the above-mentioned constraint is valid on the sole condition that the worker has already accepted the agreement promoted by trade unions or trade associations, at least at a regional level.

The reform of supplementary pensions will remain incomplete, until defined benefit pension schemes (especially designed by the Italian Law for self-employed workers and professionals) are duly regulated.

The opportunity of setting up these particular plans comes from the awareness that the new (contributive) method used to calculate public pensions will seriously penalize self-employed workers. As a matter of fact, it is absolutely right that all those who completely sustain the burden of self-financing their pension benefits should have the opportunity to choose the supplementary pension scheme which better meets their needs.

The choice can be rightly oriented towards a defined benefit pension scheme. In such a case, the desired supplementary pension amount can be fixed in advance and both financial and demographic risks linked to the pension plan are immediately transferred to the insurer.

The value of this immunization, immediately perceivable in the case of financial risks, is, actually, of the same importance in the case of demographic risks (particularly with reference to the fast-growing risk of longevity).

In a defined contribution pension scheme, the higher the life expectancy at retirement, the lower will be the annuity paid out; on the other hand, defined benefit pension schemes offer protection against the economic consequences of an increasing longevity.

As to the role of private insurance in welfare matters, it's worth mentioning a subject — till now unexplored — recently highlighted by Mr. Desiata, President of ANIA. It regards the opportunity to transfer to private insurers the pension burden relating to some categories of retired workers.

An in-depth analysis of this subject is of course needed, with particular reference to the following aspects: *a)* the starting date and period covered by the private insurance system (either through life annuities or through temporary annuities, if cover is limited to a given period in time); *b)* whether to maintain whole or to divide the burden sustained by the State; *c)* the types of assets (both real estate and securities) which would be transferred by the State to private insurers, because of their taking over the burden of existing pension rights.

I think that the subject deserves our attention.

3. - The Health Care System

In comparison with the draft at first approved by the Government, the final text of the legislative decree n. 229 of 19.6.1999 (the socalled *"Third" Health Care Reform*) is considerably different as regards the question (which is focal) of the basic and universal benefits which should be supplied by the National Health Service.

In fact, these benefits will be identified in the context of the financial resources assigned to the National Healt Service, «in observance of the financial constraints defined for the whole system of public finance in the Economic and Finance Planning Document (DPEF)».

Such a principle will be probably widely debated, not so much regarding what benefits are to be considered basic, as how to identify — taking the financial constraints into consideration — the level of the benefits which can be provided through public financing.

4. - Supplementary Health Care

This subject could be relevant for the activity of supplementary health plans.

As is known, the *"Third" Reform* (art. 9) gives a role — unfortunately only a residual one — to supplementary health funds, whose activity is clearly oriented towards the acquisition of services (specialised treatment, diagnostics, hospitalisation in a private room) supplied within public hospitals by doctors working freelance, while it is well known that public hospitals lack for the moment, apart from a few cases, suitable structures for these kind of services.

Also for health funds, the above-mentioned Law nr. 133/99 (art. 10) enables the Government to issue a decree reforming the fiscal regime of health care benefits, in order to: 1) concede, on the one hand, an overall tax relief to supplementary health funds; 2) pursue, on the other hand, the aim of an equality of tax regimes for funds which are different from the so-called "DOC" funds mentioned above.

This last provision could enable: *a)* first of all, the creation of a transitional regime for an adequate period (five years) for those already enrolled in pre-reform health care funds, during which the present tax relief system would be maintained, so allowing them to continue to enjoy their present benefits, until the new system is set up and effective; *b)* secondly, the opportunity for those who subscribe to supplementary health funds to subscribe also to other funds (less favourable from a fiscal point of view), through which health benefits can be obtained that meet needs identified by the Regional Health Plans and by the other local bodies.

Here is an opportunity to reform the fiscal regime of supplementary health funds; the chance to rationalise and equalise, also from a fiscal point of view, personal health care with particular reference to health insurance, should not be missed.

5. - Long-Term Care Reform

It is known that the Parliament is now examining a unified bill (based on serveral other bills recently promoted), aiming at an in-depth reform of public long-term care expenditure, now amounting to 30.000 billions, 16.000 of which regard disability and accompanying persons allowances.

Briefly, the bill aims at creating, all over the country, basic long-term care levels, with a greater attention to services than to cash benefits.

More than ever, the long-term care system must cope with a lack of financial resources and this should lead to a strengthening of the present timid steps towards greater private financing.

For this reason, it would seem reasonable to make some corrections to the proposed regulation, for example in order to: 1) ensure that when the services network becomes operative, the forms of self-help to be incentivated — with particular regard for home-care for elderly and not self-sufficient people — should also include long-term care, health and legal expenses insurance; concerning long-term care insurance, we can think of medical aid through remote control devices, home nursing services, and so on;

concerning health insurance, we can think of home hospitalisation; and concerning legal expenses insurance, it suffices to think of legal advice for both the sale of the right of property on the home and the correct assessment of the relevant annuity; 2) reform the system, as far as cash benefits are concerned, in order both to better support the weakest groups of the population (for example, decreasing the disability threshold and increasing the amount of the cash benefit) and make available, for the others, basic forms of collective self protection, through closed and open funds, set up by non-profit organizations, mutual societies and insurance companies.

The current formulation of the unified bill merely provides that home care services can be offered within the supplementary health funds (with reference to the "Bindi decree"), so making them appear purely accessory.

In the long-term care area, as in the two other social security areas, personal forms of self-protection will have to be developed — and be encouraged — to create the third long-term care pillar.

To this end there is also the need to redefine some types of private insurance, offered in order to support seriously frail people.

I am referring, particularly, to insurance policies directed at seriously disabled people, intended to offer financial guarantees when they lose the support of their parents.

Conclusions

Summing up, considering the three areas of the welfare system (pensions, health care and long-term care), the choice can only be in the direction of recognising for the private sector a role which, although not alternative or substitutive of the public one, but supplementary to it, must be of increasing importance.

As far as the private sector is concerned, it is needless to say that covering risks, first of all those related to persons (longevity, health, or quality of life) is the business of the insurers, who have

always been operating in the life, health and long-term care areas, with specific qualifications and adequate professionality, under the supervision of the Authority, and are ready to carry out
their role, expecting to have a consistent reward — also in terms
of tax relief — for their contribution to satisfying more completely
the evolving social needs.

Capitalising the Future of the Pension System

Riccardo Illy
Sindaco di Trieste

We agree with D'Antoni on the fact that even if the Social security (INPS) deficit has been and still is at the expense of the State Budget (definitely a serious fact), the Italian pension system should not be seen in a catastrophic light.

There are many other problematic facts which cause this catastrophic situation, such as the stagnant growth of the Italian economy, the loss of competitiveness of the country-Italy system, the insufficient creation of jobs and a serious situation in terms of unemployment which is evergrowing.

There are two principal causes of these facts: on the one hand, the gross domestic product in Italy increases less than the productivity. Therefore, it is clear that jobs cannot be created until the growth of the economy is greater than productivity, and this has not happened for many years now. On the other hand the economy has not grown for two reasons: due to economic trends and structural reasons. The reason connected with economic trends is defined as the drastic treatment that the Italian economy has undergone in order to succeed in respecting the Maastricht parameters. In the last few years Professor Modigliani had suggested how we could have ended up in a virtuous spiral by respecting the parameters, reducing interest rates and reducing the cost to be sustained by the State Budget in order to pay off the public debt, but this seems to have been forgotten.

The structural reasons why our country is incapable of growing in economic terms probably derive from some competitive disadvantages. 1) Despite the fact that the reform has considerably reduced taxation, the tax on the company income is higher in Italy than in other European countries and other industrialised countries such as the United States. 2) There is a severe shortage of infrastructure. We need simply consider the fact that our country does not have a high speed railway network that works properly, like there is in Spain, France and Germany. Moreover most of the gross domestic product is not exposed to competition, in fact Professor Savona stated in Cernobbio that the percentage of GDP not exposed is more than 50%. We still have ineffective and inefficient bureaucracy which gives responses which are slower, less significant and at a higher cost. We have a justice system which works so badly that even in civil cases it takes 20 years to get a final judgement. Our education system is less effective than in other European Union member countries, and maybe also in the United States. Finally, one thing that should particularly worry us is the difference that can be found between the cost of labour and the workers' net income, or rather how much the workers receive in their pay packet. This is the principal reason why it is impossible to make the Italian economy grow.

It is true that the cost of labour in Italy is not among the highest but the problem lies in the difference there is between how much the worker costs the company and how much the worker effectively receives in pay. The problem also affects the companies because if the worker's income is low, he will have less possibility to purchase the products of that same company.

Treasury (MIT) statistics show that in Italy about 40% of the cost of labour goes towards social security — of this, 32% goes to the State for current social security payments and the rest goes under the form of retirement indemnity (TFR).

This appears to be the basic problem, more serious than that regarding the social security (INPS) accounts and more severe than the deficit that can more or less be sustained by the state budget. This all appears most irrelevant when faced with Italian labour costs which impose 40% tax towards social security. This really penalises companies and the Italian economy.

Other elements make the situation worse. For example, many workers receive a higher income when they retire than their salary while employed. The reason for this is that even if the pensions is only a part of the salary, there is no longer a social security tax on this which instead burdens the salary, so the net salary is higher for pensioners and this naturally forces people to retire. The high cost of labour obviously encourages illegal work and the checks carried out by the Labour Office will not succeed in resolving this situation. In Italy help is given to the unemployed, which favours the growth of a new category of "unemployed-for life" citizens; 30-35-years-olds are still supported by their parents, while they exploit their parents' or grandparents' pension, and obviously will ultimately be assisted by the state.

Finally a pension system like the current one makes the citizens less responsabile. They are considered as subjects to be protected, or rather people incapable of deciding for themselves how to use a part of their salary because the cost of labour for the company — apart from the taxes to be paid on that income — should all be income for worker, except for a small percentage to be destined to obligatory social security, so as to allow for a vital minimum at the time of retirement. The management of the remaining income should be entrusted to the workers themselves so that they can spend it immediately, invest it in whatever they want, including pension funds or other private pension schemes.

Of couse the Trade Unions are against to any changes and any sacrifices because their aim is practically to keep the status quo. However, the Italian people have shown that they are willing to make sacrifices in order to reach important targets. We saw an example of this when the Maastricht parameters had to be respected in order to enter the European Monetary Union. SO let's take the example of Spain where, with unemployment at 20%, President Aznar proposed an convinced his citizens that it would be possible to reach total employment by making some sacrifices.

If this objective of reaching full employment is considered feasible in Spain, it should be twice as manageable in Italy where, only a few years ago, unemployment was a little over half that in Spain. Thus the Treasury's proposal of how to reform the pension system can represent one of the means of reaching full employment in Italy. The Treasury's proposal certainly deserves all this attention but we need to ask ourselves whether it also deserves some improvement since sixty years have been foreseen for carrying it out and even if objective seems very attractive, sixty years appear too many.

So, to reduce time we ask ourselves if it would not be better to consider the use of a higher percentage of the retirement idemnity (TFR) accrued, while the government proposes to put the retirement idemnity still being accrued directly into the pay packet. This will evidently be carried out under certain conditions, or rather with the regime style contributory system which, should it require decades, will never be resolved with the abolition of the 35-year seniority pension. This is because under the contributory system a person who decides to retire before this time will benefit from the pension for more years but obviously to a reduced degree. The state should favour a virtuous circuit with the exit from companies of economic resources such as part of the retirement indemnity (TFR) but with the entry in Stock Exchange markets and therefore with the possibility to return these economic resources to the companies in the form of capital. Naturally, if these is a more efficient allocation of financial resources than that carried out by the State today this will therefore also bring a greater democracy to companies or, in a more general sense, to the Italian economy. Even if today the retirement indemnity (TFR) belongs to the workers, practically they do not have any right over it at all. However, some time in the future if their retirement indemnity (TFR) becomes part of the capital they will also to participate in company decisions, which is why the State could fiscally provide incentives for this circuit.

Companies would benefit from the reduction in contributions which would in some way be divided between greater income for the workers and lower labour costs. A greater vision is necessary, however, a global view of the problems. It is necessary to analyse the whole situation of the Italian economy in wide terms where the pensions represent one of the blocks, one of the problems.

However, even the competitive disadvanteges should be faced and this will require further, expensive, difficult reforms in our country.

Social Security:
System Founded on Three Pillars

Cesare Salvi

Ministro del Lavoro e della Previdenza Sociale, Roma

Unemployment and welfare state are two issues that need to be handled together, even with a view to understanding what type of a welfare reform needs to be implemented and formulating in an appropriate manner the question of the relationship between welfare spending and employment.

If we want to implement those "work-fare" policies that are considered a must at a time when jobs are changing and the productive evolution is proceeding at an extremely fast pace, we need to spend. The work-fare policies are not free of charge.

If we need to have access to an efficient employment service that might effectively match labor demand and supply by actually relating a given enterprise with a given worker; if we need to boost training in order to allow workers to be placed back in employment and allow this Country to make a qualitative step forward (rather than using training as fig-leaf concealing contracts that allow the acess to tax concessions in exchange for a worker's training that, in point of fact, is not provided), then some spending is required.

There is, nonetheless, a more fundamental core issue. Indeed, to consider the relation existing between unemployment and welfare state (over and beyond the popular refrain "cut the welfare spending so that we are going to save and this will lead to more employment and we will all save") means also to probe into the causes of the high unemployment witnessed since a few years in Europe and Italy. Are these structural causes? Cyclical factors have nothing to do with them. What is the relation between one and the other datum? Considering the restrictive policies that have been implemented since quite a time, and that in Italy had the intensity we are all aware of as they rightly aimed at our entry into the European Monetary Union, is it possible that they might be a reason, one of the reasons why there is such a high unemployment in Europe and in Italy?

To cope with these issues means to deal with economic, productive and tax-related data, but also with moral questions. It is a moral problem to debate whether the welfare state should be gradually dismantled, being considered a restraint on development. It is a moral problem to debate whether the welfare state should be gradually dismantled, being considered a restraint on development. It is a moral problem to accede to this idea — without considering the ways and means to implement it — that in the face of the major problems of men and women (such as old age, disease, want of jobs) the route to be determinedly followed is to go back to the times when each one managed on his/her own. Or else, whether the great idea that western Europe is going to pass on to the future is the concept that it is right and fair for the entire community to manage it, even with elements of solidarity; an idea that it is still extremely meaningful for the future, modifying what needs to be modified, and this is but obvious, since no one thinks to have recourse to the same mechanisms, the same recipes.

Then, let's say that a Keynes — quite obviously of the year 2000 — and a Beveridge of the year 2000 are no longer useful, only one of them is of service. Which one? This is a fascinating subject and we have to delve into it since, should we merely consider the simplistic refrain that views welfare spending, the welfare state, exclusively as a restraint to development, we run the risk of making a step backwards, not only with respect to the level of social protection but also with respect to the quality of the system.

More and more I have this feeling that there are those who

view in some kind of an Italian welfare dumping the new road towards a competitive devaluation course. In fact, we know that the industrial system in this Country, even in the first half of the Nineties, succeeded in moving ahead thanks to the Country's competitive devaluation, and we do understand why part of the industrial world was not too keen on the decision to join the European Monetary Union, since that meant the end of that possibility. Being there no chance to have recourse to the competitive devaluation, there are but two alternative routes. To recover a high quality of Italy as a global system — and this means, even with respect to the enterprises, to start to reason and move with a view to making a quality leap forward in their proposals, their management, the type of their investments, the type of production they intend to pursue — or else, to follow the competitive devaluation road with respect to social protections and labor rights guarantees. This is not a very well defined alternative, in view of the fact that when we talk about an excess welfare spending in Italy we need to consider the issue in European terms: six points below France and Germany (and I intend to leave aside the bulk of the litigation as to the way the gross, or net retirement allowance should be calculated, etc., which, according to a few, would make this gap even wider).

Then, we certainly need to cope with the problem of an inner rebalance of this expenditure that, after all, todate amounts to the social security spending in Italy. But certainly we do not need to cope with the problem of cutting the Italian welfare spending since, a reduction of the Italian welfare spending — that, for the time being, is already so much lower than the European average figure — would mean to ask this Country to enter the road of the competitive social devaluation of rights with respect to the other European countries. A road that leads nowhere, as I don't believe that our future might witness a competition with Romania or Slovene on the cost of labor, social protections and workers' guarantees. Just as the road to competitive devaluation no longer led us anywhere, as in the end it allowed the Italian industries to innovate rather than renovate and caused additional negative effects and consequences.

To cope with the cyclical part of unemployment and to reform the welfare system in order to meet the requirements of
the new societies are issues that must be dealt with by Europe
since, should each individual Country take a road of its own,
beyond a certain limit, we run the risk of creating problems. Is
is clear that when dealing with such an issue as the interpretation or the likely modification of the stability pact, it is definitely a mistake to deal with it on the front of the derogation
for Italy, since it is the problem that must be tackled by Europe
as a whole. Are such restrictive policies, is such a severe — and,
according to a few, myopic — interpretation of the stability pact
still justified, or is it the time to get to an understanding and
harmonization of the differences? This applies to the problem
of the harmonization of the European social and taxation poli-
ties, particularly in the prospect of the European integration and
extension. Should we fail to initiate a process of harmonization,
do we really believe that we are going to reach the borders of
Russia with negotiations still going on, a single currency, and
levels of social protection and life styles that are so far apart?
The latter question brings with it an issue which the current
President of the Republic has called attention to on a number
of occasions, both in the past and from the high office he is
now holding. This is the fact that we need to build a European
political subject, macroeconomic policies, fiscal and social policies, since it is not possible to have in Europe a single policy
— and decision — making subject that is the European Central
Bank. Therefore, this is today's major topical issue, for Italy and
Europe. Should we fail to cope with it, we enter a vicious circle having a different sign.

The road of this Country may not be — and unquestionably
is not the road taken by this Government — to replace the competitive devaluation of the past with a competitive devaluation in
terms of a reduction of social protection and, *tout court*, a reduction of rights. A reform of both the welfare state and the welfare spending is a must, we need to implement it, but not with a
view to attaining the aforementioned purpose. The reform of the
labor law is a requirement because we need to adjust the labor

law and the guarantees of the past to changing jobs. Our rules are built around the concept of a stable job, a Fordist factory. An array of protections and interrelations was built around this model. Nowadays, this model is increasingly less useful and, therefore, we may build an array of guarantees and relations suitable for a changing labor situation. In any event, we should not think that, since society is changing, we have to see to the progressive dismantlement fo the founding principles of labor law, with special regard to the principle whereby a labor contract is strcturally different from a standard privatistic contract, since it considers two parties that are not exactly in the same starting position. And this is the reason why a labor law has been in force since a couple of centuries.

With reference in particular to the social security spending, Italy is not facing a pension-related catastrophe. All the data available to us, all the elements, all the calculations of the Welfare Spending Valuation Nucleus of my Ministry, as well as the INPS and the Accountant and Comptroller General's Office data are quite evident. The problem is represented by the infamous bulge. This allows us to debate, to reason, to time decisions and verifications with a schedule that has nothing to do with drama and emergency. Were we faced with a catastrophe, were we to cope with an emergency, we would have to take drastic measures at once. Fortunately, we are not facing any such situation.

As for Prof. Modigliani's reform proposal, I must say that I would not define it a Chilean model since, in any event, it provides for a compulsory system with public management. The basic difference between the existing reform and the modification proposal is that while our reform provided for a social security system founded on two pillars — the public pillar based on contributions and the supplementary one based on a capitalization system — proceeding along parallel couses, the modification proposal is said to lead, even though over a period of sixty years, to a progressive replacement of the first pillar with the second one. It is an installation-based difference, which is definitely relevant for political decision-making purposes, since a radical change of course entails an additional cost which is political but also economic. The transition costs that are studied in the civil law economy are also present in the public law systems, meaning that each passage, each change of couse entails in any event a cost, just on account of that change.

The course we are following is the course set within the framework of the horizon and the political decision of this Government. Insofar as the reform is concerned, it entails the preservation of the two-pillar setup. Then, there is a third and fully private pillar that relates to individual choices.

With reference to the first pillar, it may be stated that in Italy the social security reform has already been implemented since the available data show that the infamous bulge is indeed a bulge: it has a beginning and an end. As soon as the bulge ends, the accounts balance once again.

The figures for the first years of implementation are in line with forecasts. We are going to move towards a generalized contribution system, and this means more limited pensions. We need to say things as they are, otherwise we end up beating about the bush. The second pillar is necessary because, on account of the reforms that have already been implemented, under normal operating conditions pensions will be lower than today. This is the reason why the reform was implemented: to reduce the social security spending.

From 1992 till today, Italy — the only Country in the European Union that implemented a social security reform that changes the very mechanism of the system — succeeded in cutting the social security spending by ten points with respect to the Gross Domestic Product. France and Germany have not implemented their reform yet. In France they are trying to talk about something else, even though Chirac said a few days ago that sooner or later they will have to implement it. In Germany, to do something that we have already accomplished, that is to say, to do away with the indexation linked to wages and to link it to inflation, merely for a two year trial period (we are already under normal operating conditions), the Chancellor is risking his office. It is clear that these are extremely difficult issues to be dealt with, as the citizens harbor social security expectations. It is not by chance that everyone appreciates the reforms that concern someone else. In the past weeks the Audit Office resolutely called on us to step in. We read in the papers that the magistrates' pension is being contested as being too high. It is always someone else's pension that requires immediate action. By now, the social security expectation is a proprietary expectation. This is indeed the *new property* theory. The Welfare State benefits are perceived as a property. Not only the entitlement but the expectation, and quite naturally this should be debated. We know that there is no constitutional guarantee. But it is unquestionable that such issues may not be dealt with heedlessly, even on account of the fact that — should we fail to deal with the issue of social consent — no reform may be implemented. There is also this slight detail that, in my opinion, should suggest a certain caution.

Therefore, the issue is that a Country that has already seen to this type of reform with this level of intensity, to-date — and to - date means the period going from now to the year 2001 — this Country faces the problem of verifying whether the timing and means of the passage from the old to the new system were correct or they need to be reviewed in the light of the bulge anticipation.

On the other hand, as far as the supplementary social security is concerned, it is extremely expedient in my opinion to verify the incentives for the supplementary social security. Afterwards, we may reach a conclusion.

I think that there is a political interest in a proposal of this type. It is like saying that it has to be measured against the object — for the time being — of the setting up of a more effective supplementary social security system. There is no doubt that we may not take up again every two years the usual affliction that risks to be all but useful for implementing the relative decisions. It is unquestionable that, at the time when one resolutely moves towards a reform of the welfare state that does not address a reduction of the social spending but indeed aims at its re-qualification in order to allow the transfer of expenses from social security to other sectors (starting from the work-fare sector), the debate, investigation and the formulation of proposals are extremely instrumental for those who are called upon to take political decisions. It is the burden of the responsability that we perceive.